A Breath of Fresh Air

A Breath of Fresh Air

THE STORY OF
BELFAST'S PARKS

◆

ROBERT SCOTT

THE
BLACKSTAFF
PRESS
BELFAST

FRONTISPIECE
Malone House, Barnett Demesne
ROBERT SCOTT

First published in 2000 by
The Blackstaff Press Limited
Blackstaff House, Wildflower Way, Apollo Road
Belfast BT12 6TA, Northern Ireland
for Belfast City Council

Printed in Ireland by Betaprint

A CIP catalogue record for this book
is available from the British Library

ISBN 0-85640-690-2

Contents

PREFACE   VII

1   *Social Gatherings*
The Roots of Parks   1

2   *Elms and Hedges*
Ormeau and Falls Parks up to 1900   11

3   *Princesses and Ponds*
Alexandra, Woodvale and Dunville Parks up to 1900   21

4   *Flower Shows and Fireworks*
The Botanic Garden and the Waterworks up to 1900   28

5   *Burial Powers*
City Cemetery, Dundonald Cemetery, Knock Graveyard   42

6   *Into the Twentieth Century*   48

7   *The War Years and After*   58

8   *Let's Play*
Open Space, Playgrounds and Recreation   67

9   *The Tramways Legacy*
Bellevue, Hazelwood and Belfast Castle   81

10   *During the Blitz*   97

11   *The Lagan Valley Estates*
Barnett Demesne and Sir Thomas and Lady Dixon Park   106

12   *Cemeteries Old and New*   116

13   *A Period of Change*
1950s–early 1980s   125

14   *The Expanding Empire*
New Properties 1970s–1980s   145

15   *The Restoration Period*   160

16   *Green Fingers*   171

17   *A Natural Approach*   183

18   *A New Era*   200

APPENDIX   209

SELECT BIBLIOGRAPHY   210

ACKNOWLEDGEMENTS   211

INDEX   212

Preface

Parks play an important role in the life of any town or city. They are part of the social scene, part of the history, part of the network of sites that makes up the urban environment. To many of us they represent places, images and memories associated with almost every stage of our lives. Where we are pushed in our prams, where we run to the swings, where we play football, where we hang about as teenagers, where we go courting, where we take our children, where we walk as a family, where we sit and watch other park users go by, where we play bowls, where we spend quiet moments as we grow older, and finally, if we avail of the municipal cemeteries, where many of us end up.

Belfast, like any other great city, would be a much poorer place without its green open spaces, parks and public gardens. There are currently more than three thousand acres throughout Belfast looked after by the Parks and Amenities Section of Belfast City Council. That represents over fifty parks and playing fields, more than seventy playgrounds, three working cemeteries, four historical graveyards, a Zoological Garden, Botanic Gardens, and many open spaces and community areas – not to mention several important historic buildings such as the Palm House, Malone House and Belfast Castle.

This legacy is a direct result of the generosity of individual benefactors and the foresight and efforts of city fathers from previous years. Some properties have a varied and well-documented history that includes information on family associations, transfer to municipal ownership, and how the land has been adopted as public open space. In contrast other properties remain something of an enigma; little is known about them. And of course the story is not complete. The way in which we use parks today will automatically become part of tomorrow's history. The current views, ideas and decisions will all be integrated into the continuing narrative of Belfast's parks, gardens and open spaces.

The following is the story so far.

Opposite:
Meadowland at Barnett Demesne
BELFAST CITY COUNCIL

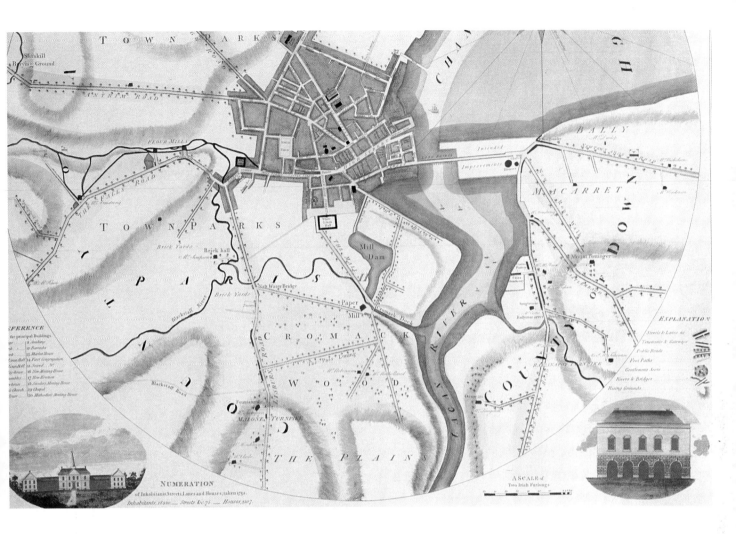

1
Social Gatherings
The Roots of Parks

T he concept of gardens and communal space is as old perhaps as civilisation itself. Certainly the Romans laid out gardens for general public enjoyment and cultivated plant species, including nettles, to grow in them. From pre-medieval times the greens and squares so characteristic of English towns and villages have provided a social focus for local communities. Many Irish towns were also built around a central square, although this seems to have had a utilitarian function rather than a recreational one, being intended principally as a market place.

The idea of public common ground is rooted in English tradition. It consisted of land on which tenants had a right to pasture pigs and cattle, and to collect firewood. Two of the best-known commons around London, Hampstead Heath and Wimbledon Common, were preserved for public enjoyment only after intense

Above:
Map of Belfast, 1791, showing two promenades, 'The Mall' and 'The Bank', running south and east from the town centre. These were used by the 'well-to-do' for Sunday strolls.

LINEN HALL LIBRARY

Opposite:
Cave Hill

BELFAST CITY COUNCIL

battles against landlords and would-be developers. The common ground at Armagh, once used for horse racing, was enclosed around 1800 by a low perimeter wall and laid out with trees to form a public walk or park known as 'The Mall'.

ROYAL HUNTING GROUNDS

It was not until the nineteenth century, however, when many towns were expanding at an unprecedented rate, that land within urban boundaries began to be developed primarily for public open space. By then a number of major cities in the British Isles had public parks, although some of these had arisen by accident rather than design.

The majority of London's parks, for example, were once privately owned by the Crown and became available to the public only many years after their establishment. Henry VIII and Elizabeth I both hunted on land that became Hyde Park, which was opened to the public in the seventeenth century. Regent's Park, another royal hunting ground, was opened in the 1830s. Ordinary citizens, however, were permitted to walk through St James's Park during Charles II's time (1660–85), although this eventually led to the park being designated unsuitable for royal use. One of Europe's largest enclosed parks, Phoenix Park in Dublin (1,760 acres), began life as a seventeenth-century deer park before viceroy Lord Chesterfield had it relandscaped and opened to the public in 1747. It quickly became infamous for robberies and duelling.

Many of the smaller squares in Dublin, such as Merrion and Mountjoy Squares, began life as private greens serving fashionable Georgian residences. They are now managed by Dublin Corporation as public open space. Glasgow's oldest park, Glasgow Green, was acquired in 1662, having been used at times for washing and bleaching linen and for drying salmon nets. Glasgow Green and Dublin College Park (the grounds of Trinity College) are examples of properties that were originally sited outside a town, and which were classed as open space only after significant urban expansion and extension of municipal boundaries.

THE VICTORIAN CONNECTION

By contrast some areas were deliberately set aside and landscaped as public parks or gardens. Sydney Gardens, the oldest park in Bath, was planned and laid out as early as 1795. By the mid-1800s a municipal park at Birkenhead, Liverpool, designed by Joseph Paxton had been opened and no fewer than three purpose-designed parks had been developed in Manchester. By then the practice of developing municipal parks was well established. It became almost synonymous with Victorian times. Queen Victoria, who opened the gardens at Hampton Court to the public for the first time in 1838, had many parks named after her: the Royal Victoria Park in Bath, opened in 1830 when she was still a Princess, the Victoria Embankment Gardens alongside the River Thames, and Victoria Parks in London, Glasgow and, of course, Belfast.

AN 'IRREGULARLY SHAPED ENCLOSURE'

The earliest references to the provision of recreational public open space in Belfast were in the mid-seventeenth century. An 'irregularly shaped enclosure with a circle in the centre, as if marking the spot for some sports or village games' was referred to by George Benn in his *History of the Town of Belfast* (1877), as was a piece of freehold land near the town gate at Mary Street (off Waring Street) that had been set aside for 'some public use'. In 1671 George Macartney, a wealthy merchant and one-time Sovereign of Belfast, returned from Venice inspired by what he had seen, and proposed to create a waterfront scheme of walkways for the town. Sadly this project did not materialise. In the eighteenth century a number of favourite promenades or walks were being used by the 'well-to-do' for Sunday strolls. 'The Mall' ran southwards from the site of the proposed White Linen Hall to Joy's paper mill and the Owen Varra or Blackstaff River, while 'The Bank' stretched from the present Arthur Square towards the River Lagan.

In Belfast the beginnings of public parks can be traced back to three contributory factors: the local custom of gathering for fairs and festivals at sites around the town, such as Cave Hill; the establishment of pleasure gardens and botanical gardens in other parts of the British Isles, and also in Belfast itself; and a growing awareness of the social, moral and health problems directly attributable to rapid urbanisation.

SOCIAL GATHERINGS

The tradition of Belfast people gathering to the north-west of the town on the sloping ground under Cave Hill was already well established when Benn described it in 1823, in an earlier history. There the hedonistic public congregated for 'riotous assemblies' and social festivals, especially at Hallowe'en and Easter. Fairs were held on the grass slopes and tents set up for fortune-tellers, entertainers and vendors, selling everything from mussels to yellow man. Doubtless there was an ample supply of poteen to ensure high spirits among the crowds. A blind harper would often serenade them down off the hill. At Hallowe'en the festivities included bonfires, nut gathering, the telling of haunting tales, and mummers or rhymers, while at Easter children practised the custom of egg 'trilling' or rolling. Eggs were either hardboiled in water containing whin blossom, which dyed them yellow, or handpainted after boiling in plain water. Once they were cool they were rolled down a grassy bank and eaten when the shells had finally broken.

'A SCENE OF THE GREATEST FESTIVITY'

J. Doyle, in his *Tours in Ulster* of 1854, described a typical Easter scene on Cave Hill.

> Upon Easter Monday this mountain presents a scene of the greatest festivity; numerous tents are pitched at the base of the cliff, and are frequented by crowds of people of the middle and lower classes from the town and surrounding country. Happy groups of both sexes are to be seen in every direction, dressed in their holiday attire – some perched upon the dizzy precipices, others reclining in happy circles upon the green sward, on the hillocks, or in the hollows that abound at the foot of the cliff. Games of various kinds amuse the younger portion, and here and there an adventurous youth or gleesome maiden may be seen climbing to visit the caves. Were it not for the occasional intemperance inseparable from such scenes of jollity, it would be exceedingly pleasing to contemplate these seasons of healthy relaxation.

Resting at the first cave after a strenuous climb up Cave Hill.

NATIONAL LIBRARY OF IRELAND

Due to excessive drinking, numerous fatalities, and attempts to hijack the annual Easter fair for political purposes, calls were made to ban the gatherings. In 1841 the Teetotal Society arranged speeches near the caves, calling for sobriety and total abstinence. The celebrations, however, continued, and their popularity began to wane only when alternative venues, such as the pleasure garden at Dargan's Island, became available.

PLEASURE GARDENS

Pleasure gardens were a feature of the eighteenth century in and around London, with the most famous being the Vauxhall Gardens. They consisted of entertainment pavilions for music, dancing, wining and dining, sideshows and other diversions, all set among gardens, meadows and trees. By the time Belfast had its very own pleasure garden, however, changes in attitudes and stricter Victorian moral standards had contributed to a decline in their popularity in England.

Belfast's pleasure garden was at Dargan's Island at the mouth of the River Lagan. Between 1839 and 1841 material excavated from the new cuts at the docks was dumped on the County Down side of the river to form a seventeen-acre island. This work was carried out by one of the leading engineers of the time, William Dargan, who gave his name to the island. In 1843 the Harbour Commissioners began landscaping with pathways and trees and the area soon became more than just an open space. Equestrian events were held in 1844, and occasional band performances by 1849. The island provided an excellent vantage point for spectators wanting to see Queen Victoria on her visit to Belfast in August 1849. The site was renamed Queen's Island in honour of the royal occasion.

Belfast people always enjoyed a good day out, and Queen's Island soon became renowned as a popular resort. A Victoria Fête, the first of its kind, was held there in August 1850. It included magicians, singers, boat races, a balloon ascent and a fireworks display. The success of the venture encouraged the Victoria Fête Committee to stage an even bigger and more exciting extravaganza at Queen's Island the following year.

A CRYSTAL PALACE

By the time this second fête took place a crystal palace had been constructed on the island to provide an indoor facility, an idea prompted no doubt by inclement weather. The committee employed a young Belfast architect, John Boyd, to design the 112-foot-long single-storey structure, which was made from glass, iron and wood. It was based on Joseph Paxton's Crystal Palace, built for the Great Exhibition of 1851 in Hyde Park, London. A central dome was planned for the Belfast palace but was never added. There is a widespread story, still believed by some in Belfast today, that the Queen's Island Crystal Palace was subsequently moved to Botanic

Queen's Island, also known as the People's Park, with its Crystal Palace, can be seen in the foreground of this painting – *Bird's Eye View of Belfast*, *c.* 1843, by J.H. Connop.

Gardens, but this is not the case. The Palm House, in fact, pre-dates the Crystal Palace, although there was no reference made to the botanical conservatory when ideas for a palace were being discussed. Perhaps this was because the two buildings served very different functions.

The palace was officially opened on Thursday, 4 September and festivities began with a two-day bazaar. There were stalls selling needlework, wax flowers, music boxes, dolls, models, live canaries and a host of other items. Exhibitions were staged, including one on the mechanics of the human eye, and a band played inside the Crystal Palace, where a decorative and ornate fountain of Neptune had been installed. This was designed by Giancoma Nannetti, an Italian sculptor working in Belfast at that time. All of this was just a warm-up to the 1851 Victoria Fête, which began in earnest on the Saturday at 2.00 p.m. and attracted some ten thousand people. Over £700 was raised for the General Hospital from sales from the stalls and admission charges, which were levied at 1s for adults and 6d for children.

A third and final Victoria Fête was held in August 1852, but it was a smaller affair and attended by fewer people. Marionettes, balloon and boat races and bands were included in the list of attractions. The finale comprised a fireworks display, followed by a demonstration of electric light.

A CHANGE OF USE

The Crystal Palace was subsequently transformed into a winter garden. By 1859 an aquarium, a small zoo and an aviary had been added. The building was badly damaged by fire in 1864 and never repaired. Nevertheless the island remained a favourite gathering site for some years afterwards, not least at Eastertime. The last organised amusements took place in 1872.

In its heyday Queen's Island benefited many people, including the working classes, who could afford the penny return fare on the ferry. Because of this the island was popularly known as 'The People's Park'. Its finest moments, in terms of enthusiasm from its visitors and commitment from the Harbour Commissioners, were the years between the 1849 visit of Queen Victoria and the 1851 Victoria Fête. Sadly such euphoria was never to be repeated.

During this visit to Belfast, Queen Victoria also went to see the botanical garden, which in 1840, by her command, had been renamed the Royal Belfast Botanic Garden.

BOTANICAL GARDENS

Horticultural and botanical gardens became more numerous in the eighteenth and nineteenth centuries because of increased travel and explorers returning from distant continents with 'vegetable wonders of the world'. Kew Gardens in London was established in 1760, although it did not come under public control until 1841, and by the end of the eighteenth century Dublin (Glasnevin), Glasgow and Edinburgh (from 1820 on the present site) all had botanical gardens. During the early years of the nineteenth century botanical gardens were also established at Trinity College Dublin and the Royal Cork Institution.

John Templeton, the Irish botanist, put forward the idea of a botanical garden in Belfast as early as 1807, suggesting the proposed Academical Institution in College

Square as a possible venue. It was twenty years later, however, and two years after Templeton's death that the Belfast Botanic and Horticultural Society was formed. Under its President, the Marquis of Donegall, the Society resolved to lay out a suitable botanical and horticultural garden in the town of Belfast. In 1827 the Society opened subscription lists, leased an acre of ground at the Malone turnpike and employed a landscape gardener. It was quickly realised that the site was inadequate and so negotiations began to obtain fourteen acres at the junction of the Malone

turnpike and Friar's Bush Road (subsequently called the Stranmillis Road), beside a burial site. The ground referred to was that of Portmore House and farm, owned by a Mr McDowell. It was recommended because of the 'great variety of soil' and the fact that it was already partially planted.

BELFAST'S NEW GARDEN

In January 1828 Dr James L. Drummond, one of the founder members of the Belfast Natural History and Philosophical Society and corresponding secretary of the Belfast Botanic and Horticultural Society, issued a statement in support of forming a garden. He described the chosen ground, which extended from Malone to the River Lagan, as commanding 'on every side, the most rich and beautiful prospects' and said that it would 'prove a desirable place of public recreation'. He dispelled the idea that a botanical garden was 'useful only to persons who have a taste for flowers, or who may wish to pursue botany as a science'. Rather Belfast's new garden would be 'a delightful place of resort, a place for taking occasional air and exercise; for enjoying an agreeable walk, and the pleasures of the summer'.

ADMISSION COSTS

In the early years of its existence the Belfast Botanic Garden was visited only by the rich or moderately rich. A writer in 1865, who described himself simply as an Englishman on a walking tour around Ireland, remarked that it was 'a fashionable resort for the better classes of Belfast, though there seemed no restriction on entering beyond the payment of sixpence and entering your name in a book'. Other sources list the normal

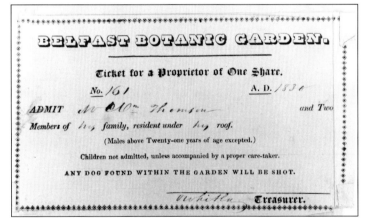

charge for the garden as 1s for adults and 6d for children. Whatever the actual cost Belfast Botanic Garden was expensive when compared to the penny fare to Queen's Island, or indeed the traditional penny entrance fee to Kew Gardens in London. Anyone owning four or more shares was admitted free, as were holders of ivory tickets, a system that was in operation for many years up until 1890. It is uncertain how one became an ivory ticket holder.

There was also the cost of getting to the Botanic Garden. A horse-drawn covered omnibus was run by a Mr Davis from the centre of Belfast to the main gates at

A ticket for a Coronation Fête held in 1838 at Belfast Botanic Garden (top), and one for a shareholder in 1834, which contains the warning – *Any dog found within the garden will be shot.*

MAGNI/ULSTER MUSEUM

Stranmillis from 1840 until 1872. It ran between four and six times a day and the fee for the journey was 3d (a high fare considering the price one hundred years later by tram was only 1d). When this service was discontinued visitors were able to use the General Omnibus horse trams for 2d return. They ran from Castle Place to a terminus at the garden.

Despite these costs the annual visitor figures for the Botanic Garden were high, fifty thousand being recorded during 1841 alone. From 1865, the year after the fire at the Queen's Island Crystal Palace, the working-class public was admitted free on Saturday afternoons. Thereafter crowds of seven to ten thousand on one afternoon were not unusual. A band played on these occasions from 4.00 p.m. to 7.00 p.m. and visitors were not permitted to bring in any 'edible provisions' with them. Food was not the only thing barred: as early as 1834, the following order appeared on tickets for events – *Any dog found within the garden will be shot*. It is not recorded if this threat was ever carried out.

What the Moon saw in Botanic Gardens, BELFAST.

An early postcard depicting the social value of open space.

UNDERWATER EXPLOSIONS

Because of financial constraints the Botanic and Horticultural Society was forced to permit more and more social events to take place. A Coronation Fête was held in June 1838. A Grand Fête, held in 1842, included an underwater explosion in one of the garden ponds. This raised a spout of water forty feet into the air and provided great entertainment for those who had paid for the privilege of watching. In 1860 the Society was replaced by a limited company, a move that issued in a new era of fêtes, shows, fireworks displays, band concerts and balloon ascents (chapter 4).

With Belfast's rapid growth during the mid-nineteenth century, the garden assumed an even greater social importance. What had begun principally as a botanical and horticultural site on the outskirts of Belfast had become a major gathering place for a town that was quickly surrounding the garden and expanding into the countryside beyond.

SOCIAL REFORM

During the first half of the nineteenth century sites such as Queen's Island, the Botanic Garden, the slopes of Cave Hill and other areas of rough ground within the town boundary satisfied the socialising need for everything from a game of football to major festive gatherings. There were no pressing reasons for Belfast to set aside additional open spaces or parks. Within the general population there was no concept of having specific areas freely available for casual enjoyment and little time anyway for such luxury. This situation was set to change, albeit gradually.

Belfast in the 1800s was a thriving town. Thousands of workers, who had previously been living off the land, were attracted into the urban areas by the linen mills. Many others flocked to Belfast during the famine years. Between 1835 and 1850 the town's population virtually doubled to ninety thousand. Most of the people lived in poor-quality, high-density housing beside the mills, which were situated near the streams and hills in the west and towards the centre. There was overcrowding and a dire lack of basic amenities. Epidemics of cholera, typhus and other diseases regularly swept through the town with catastrophic results. Gradually the plight of the working-class areas aroused concern among the middle and upper classes, and calls for social reform began to be heard.

The Victorian Reformist Movement, which originated in England, grew concerned with the lack of open spaces in cities, and believed that public parks would benefit inhabitants in a number of ways: disease would be curtailed by providing space for exercise in the fresh air, and the opportunity of contemplating nature would contribute to moral welfare, reduce social discomfort and discourage drunkenness. It was assumed that workers were being forced into public houses because there was no other place for them to go for recreation. It was also felt that the presence of parks would greatly improve a town's appearance.

A PUBLIC PARK FOR BELFAST

In 1852 James Thomson, brother of the Belfast scientist Lord Kelvin, presented a paper to the Belfast Social Inquiry Society, with the rather cumbersome title of 'On public parks in connection with large towns; with a suggestion for the formation of a park in Belfast'. He alluded to the area between the Linen Hall and Donegall Pass, which was almost free of buildings because of a 'pestiferous influence of a most intolerable nuisance' – he was referring to the Blackstaff River!

Thirteen years later the first municipal reference to public parks in Belfast appeared in the minutes of Belfast Corporation, 9 October 1865. A communication was submitted from the secretary of the Harbour Commissioners requesting that the Mayor and three councillors meet with the Chairman and three members of the Harbour Commissioners to confer on the subject of a People's Park, the term that the popular press had given to Queen's Island. Although the meeting took place a week later and a report was presented to both the Corporation and the Harbour Commissioners, apparently no copy of it exists. Little further progress seems to have been made until 1869 when the Corporation appointed a committee – the Public Parks Committee – to examine the establishment of public parks, on the basis that it was 'most expedient both in a moral and sanitary point of view . . . bearing in mind the present large and increasing population of the Borough'.

LEGISLATION FOR IRELAND

The main problem facing Belfast Corporation was the lack of statutory powers with regard to the provision of parks. A select committee on Parks Walks had been set up in 1833 to consider securing open space in densely populated environments, but this applied only to England. Neither the Public Health Act of 1848, which authorised local authorities to 'provide, maintain, lay out, plant and improve premises for the purpose of being used as public walks or pleasure grounds', nor the Corporation Act of 1860, which allowed for the rating of a district to help finance such schemes, applied to Ireland. The Public Parks Committee therefore recommended that Belfast Corporation should push for appropriate legislation. The outcome of subsequent correspondence with other Irish town councils, including those of Dundalk, Cork and Athlone, was the passing of the Public Parks (Ireland) Act, which became law on 12 July 1869, and gave power for the establishment and maintenance of public parks in towns in Ireland.

Belfast Corporation lost little time in progressing towards a public park. Towards the end of 1869, it entered into negotiation with James Torrens, agent to the Marquis of Donegall, for the purchase of the demesne at Ormeau. At the same time, surplus land at Belfast Cemetery on the Falls Road, then under the jurisdiction of the Corporation's Cemetery Committee, was transferred to the Public Parks Committee for open space provision (the Cemetery Committee was originally separate from the Public Parks Committee: the two later merged into the Cemetery and Public Parks Committee in August 1900).

In November 1869 a resolution was passed that

> the Council hereby determine to establish and maintain two public parks for the use and enjoyment of the persons inhabiting the town of Belfast viz.: One upon the land which formerly constituted the demesne of Ormeau, containing 174 acres or thereabouts, and another upon the land situated on the Falls Road, adjoining the new Borough Cemetery, but without prejudice to the establishment of other parks hereafter.

This resolution was confirmed on New Year's Day 1870. Six months later the Corporation acquired the Donegall lands at Ormeau. Ormeau Park opened the following year to become Belfast's first municipal public park.

2
Elms and Hedges
Ormeau and Falls Parks
up to 1900

Up until the mid-nineteenth century the town of Belfast lay entirely within the Marquis of Donegall's County Antrim estate, which was originally granted to the family (Sir Arthur Chichester) by James I in the early
seventeenth century. The family also owned land in County Down at Ballynafeigh.
While the origins of most of Belfast's parks can ultimately be traced back to land

The view of Belfast, as seen from
Ormeau Demesne in 1805;
drawing by D.C. Thompson.

Ormeau House was built in Tudor Revival style with many chimneys and turrets; drawing by J. Molloy, 1832.

once owned by the Donegalls, those of the first public park, Ormeau, are very directly linked with the family's history.

ORMEAU COTTAGE

The second Marquis of Donegall, George Augustus, returned from England to live in Belfast in 1802, having been forced to leave London because of inherited debts in the region of £250,000. He was the first of the family to live in Belfast for almost one hundred years. He took up residence in a house on the corner of Donegall Square and Linenhall Street (now Donegall Place) and opposite the former Robinson and Cleaver's store. In 1807 he moved to Ormeau Cottage, which was beyond the boundary of the town and could be reached by way of the seventeenth-century Long Bridge (at the end of Ann Street) across the Lagan. At that time foreign names for estates were fashionable. The name Ormeau was derived from the French for elms by the water (*orme* meaning elm, *eau* meaning water). The thatched cottage was enlarged to accommodate the household of the second Marquis, but the extensions proved to be inadequate. The building was replaced between 1823 and 1830 by a larger and grander Ormeau House, built in Tudor Revival style and ordained with many chimneys and turrets. It was three hundred feet in length at one point with over twenty rooms, excluding servants' quarters and kitchens. The house stood near the centre of today's park.

A CRENELLATED BATTERY

During the 1830s and early 1840s Ormeau was a busy and moderately prosperous estate. Local people were employed as domestic staff, grooms, stable boys and estate staff. A nearby farm provided fruit and vegetables for the household. This farm is remembered in the present-day street names of Haypark. The Marquis loved horse racing and shooting. He owned a racecourse just south of the estate and kept pheasants in the grounds. The estate also contained a walled garden (parts of the wall still surround the bowling greens at Park Road), gardens, glasshouses, two sum-mer houses, a porter's lodge at the Ravenhill Road entrance, an ice house and a 'crenellated battery' – a folly with cannons and flags overlooking the river.

INHERITED DEBTS

The second Marquis lived at Ormeau until his death in 1844. When his eldest son inherited the estate he found himself immediately in debt, despite £330,000 hav-ing been raised from the sale of perpetual leases some years earlier. The third Marquis, Lord Donegall, discovered that many of the former creditors had never been paid. It is likely that some of the money had gone into the building of Ormeau House. Lord Donegall never lived at Ormeau; he made the army his career. He allowed his cousin and agent, Thomas Verner, to occupy Ormeau House for ten years. Verner was the last Sovereign of the old Belfast Corporation before it was replaced by an elected Town Council (the first elections took place in 1842).

VICTORIAN TOURISTS

In 1841 the *Irish Penny Journal* informed its readers that access to the Donegall Estate at Ormeau was freely given to 'all respectable strangers'. In the 1850s tourists could get permission to enter the gates and walk through the grounds, although Doyle, in his *Tours in Ulster*, described the demesne in 1854 as presenting 'no object of particu-lar interest, the timber is for the most part young, and the grounds low and unpicturesque'. He commented on the Lagan as having 'the appearance of a noble river, being very broad at this place', but then spoiled the compliment by referring to the 'large and unsightly slobs and a dis-agreeable effluvia' at low tide.

Four years later some of these unsightly slobs were reclaimed, changing the line and breadth of the river. (The river's original line is now marked within the park by a steep grassy bank planted with trees and daffodils.) By then Ormeau House was occupied only by a caretaker. The contents were auctioned in 1857, one wing was damaged by fire in 1861 and never repaired, and in the late 1860s everything remaining of value was taken from the house and the empty shell left to decay.

CITY OF BELFAST.

SURPLUS LANDS AT ORMEAU PARK.

VALUABLE BUILDING SITES.

To be Sold by Auction,

IN THE TOWN HALL, BELFAST,

On Friday, the 3rd day of May, 1895, at One o'clock,

BY MESSRS. CLARKE & SON, AUCTIONEERS,

The Estate and Interest of the Lord Mayor, Aldermen, and Citizens, in Portions of the Surplus Ground of Ormeau Park, held in Fee Farm, subject to Moderate Ground Rents.

For further particulars apply to

SAMUEL BLACK, Town Clerk.

Some of the ground at Ormeau was auctioned for development in 1895. The area became known as Park Road.

BELFAST CITY COUNCIL

SUBURBAN VILLAS

Ormeau Demesne must have looked rather abandoned during those years. The grass areas were no longer grazed and all of the standing trees, many of which had been planted by the Donegalls at the beginning of the century, had been cut down and sold as timber to a merchant called McCavana. Possibly this had already been

done when Doyle wrote his rather unflattering description.

At that time the estate was examined as a potential building site. In January 1865 an English landscape architect called Edward Kemp produced plans to convert the 175 acres into suburban gardens. The estate was to be divided into forty-two lots, each with a substantial villa and garden or terrace. This scheme was abandoned, and in 1869 Belfast Corporation acquired the property, negotiating the rent at £1,752 16s. 3d (just over £10 per acre) with an agreement by Fee Farm Grant (a long-term lease with a fixed annual rent) dated 1 June 1870. The remains of Ormeau House were demolished and much of the usable brick was sold to John Robb for the rebuilding of his warehouse in Castle Place.

The Corporation followed the example of several English authorities by allowing part of the demesne to be used for housing development to help pay for the rent. Of the total 175 acres, 37 were let for grazing and over 40 as building sites. The latter were rented at £20 per acre, and now form North Parade, South Parade and Park Road. Some lots of Park Road were not allocated until 1895 when they were sold by public auction in the Town Hall.

THE OPENING PROCESSION

When the park was opened to the public, the landscaping work was not complete, although paths had been defined and some planting carried out. There were two entrances with gates, one on the Ormeau Road and one at Ballynafeigh. The official opening date was changed from Easter Monday 1871 to the following Saturday, 15 April, to accommodate the attendance of the 'industrial classes'. Despite the morning rain and the muddy conditions, a large crowd turned out to watch the opening procession and ceremony.

At 4.00 p.m. trade and friendly societies gathered with bands at Carlisle Circus. The procession included members of the Belfast Bakers' Society, Bricklayers, Belfast Cabinet Trade, Carpenters and Joiners, Queen's Island Shipbuilders, Belfast Coopers' Society, Friendly Society, Flaxdressers, Ancient Order of Foresters, Operative House Painters, Operative Stonecutters, Independent Order of Rechabites, Good Templars, and Tenters and Dressers. Many wore ribbons and insignia, some carried banners and others were headed by bands. The Agnes Street

Band and Belfast Constitutional Brass Band were both on parade. Spectators lined
the route and flags were displayed from houses along the streets where the colourful and noisy pageant was expected to pass. The parade left Carlisle Circus and
made its way along Donegall Street, Bridge Street, High Street, past the Linen Hall
to Chichester Street, Cromac Street and up the Ormeau Road.

On arriving at Ormeau Park, members of the parade and spectators gathered
around the platform that had been erected for the occasion. Of the estimated thirty thousand people present, many must have failed to hear anything of the speeches. Councillor John Sufferin, Chairman of the Public Parks Committee, referred to
'the higher orders having their suburban residences and their botanical gardens', but
said that with the opening of this park at Ormeau the working classes would be
able to 'enjoy their leisure hours on quiet, natural and healthy recreation in the
valued society of their wives and children'.

The Mayor, Councillor Philip Johnston, replied by noting that, next to education, 'there could be no better way in which to spend money than on healthy recreation for the people'. At 5.00 p.m., after a short speech, he formally declared the
park open. There were several other speeches before the procession formed up
again and returned to Carlisle Circus by a different route (Corporation Street,
Great George's Street and York Street). Those remaining were left to explore the
new park. The *Belfast News-Letter* recorded that 'while the adult portion of the
assemblage was content to explore, the more active youths climbed the trees with
an eagerness reminding one of the boys dismissed from school for the play hour.
The trees thus laden with product not their own formed quite a feature rising
above the perfect sea of faces, on which they appeared like frequent landmarks.'

BYE–LAWS

The Corporation had to draw up bye-laws to regulate the new park. A draft of
these was proposed and passed at the Council meeting in April 1871. The rules stated the opening and closing times and banned public speaking, preaching, lectures,
public discussion, and religious or political meetings. Occasional gatherings of
schoolchildren, however, were permitted at the discretion of the Public Parks
Committee. The bye-laws also prohibited such activities as throwing stones, taking
in a dog without a lead, the shaking and beating of mats, and drying of linen. The
penalty for breaking any bye-law was set at £5. Although the driving of cattle
through the park was not allowed, permission was given to the Agricultural
Association of Ireland to hold its annual cattle show in Ormeau Park in 1872.

The bye-laws were displayed at the entrance along with notices cautioning the
public against trespassing or injuring shrubs in the park. The Corporation minutes
recorded that a member of the Inland Revenue was requested to give a written
apology to the Public Parks Committee for being in the park after closing time.
His apology was accepted, on the basis that he paid 10s for the offence.

STAFFING

The first two park rangers, pensioners and former soldiers Nelson Higginson and
David Collins, were appointed on 18 May 1871 at 10s per week. They were supplied with uniform and lodges. A post of park superintendent was proposed in 1873

and the salary set at £100 per annum. The following year Thomas Dickson was elected by ballot over four other candidates and he was offered the job, which came with a house in the park. A gun licence was issued in his name for the sole purpose of 'keeping down vermin'!

COMPETITION

In 1873 the Corporation announced a public competition to find the most effective design and layout of one hundred acres of the park at Ormeau. Seven entries were received, including a French-sounding scheme entitled 'Champs-Elysées'. The prize of £100 was very nearly not awarded as none of the schemes was initially accepted. After several meetings, however, the Public Parks Committee agreed on the plans of 24-year-old architect Timothy Hevey, who was responsible for designing a number of churches in Belfast and the entrance archway to Milltown Cemetery. The appearance of Ormeau Park today reflects Hevey's winning design, although his work has been modified by the introduction of a golf course on the eastern boundary of the park and the road along the embankment.

In 1877 the *Belfast Directory* praised the park as 'undulating … and portions have been laid out in magnificent parterres, variegated with the choicest flowers and shrubs, and as the Lagan meanders along its northern boundary, the scene in the park could scarcely be surpassed for sylvan beauty'.

ALL MANNER OF GIFTS

From 1877 onwards many items were presented to Belfast Corporation for use in Ormeau Park. That year local businessman Richard Patterson gave twenty-five garden seats and Councillor Ewart donated a drinking fountain. Gifts of animals were not unusual, and included pet deer, Egyptian geese, goldfish, a pair of swans and three Australian emu. The offer in 1887 from a Mr McAuliffe to present an eagle to the park was, however, declined.

DEVELOPMENTS

While some of the features of the former Donegall Estate were retained under Hevey's design – the battery on the river remained and was recorded as having been damaged by a lighter barge in 1875 – others undoubtedly disappeared. An area described as 'the old castle' was filled in and levelled to make way for a croquet ground. Belfast Corporation augmented Hevey's layout with fresh ideas and developments, which included the building of a superintendent's lodge in 1878 at a cost of £645. This replaced an earlier house and was sited in the centre of the park, to the south of where Ormeau House had once stood. An additional entrance to the park was constructed at the south end of Ormeau Bridge in 1879. The following year 'The Ride', a tree-lined walkway, was formally opened by the Mayor, Councillor John Browne, and a gate lodge was constructed at the Lagan Village entrance, near the site of the present bowling pavilion alongside the Ravenhill Road.

Twenty-four years after the park's opening, permanent entrance gates at Ormeau Road were finally installed at a cost of £1,000 by the firm of Thomas Brown and Co. By that time, a sizeable pond had been landscaped in the lower ground towards

the river (now the site of Ormeau Recreation Centre). It was circled by a path and seats were provided. A viewpoint, complete with flagpole, overlooked the Lagan, possibly on the same site as the Donegalls' original battery.

By the end of the century everything from football and cricket to bowls and polo was being played at Ormeau, and park users were allowed to sail model yachts on the pond. Belfast's first public park was proving to be a success.

During the 1880s members of the Northern Cycling Club gathered in front of the superintendent's house in Ormeau Park before setting off for Portrush.

MAGNI/ULSTER MUSEUM

ROYAL VISITORS

After laying the foundation stone of the Albert Bridge on 22 May 1889, HRH the Prince of Wales (who later became King Edward VII) visited Ormeau Park. Men of the Scots Greys, the Gordon Highlanders and the Royal Irish Constabulary kept a square clear of spectators while the Prince, in uniform of the Captain of the 10th Hussars, presented colours to the Black Watch. The ceremony took place in glorious weather in an area of the park known as the recreation ground. The *Belfast News-Letter* recorded that 'every portion of the park from which a view of the ceremony could be obtained was fully availed of, even the trees in the vicinity being utilized for the purposes of a superior view'.

On 8 September 1897 the Duke and Duchess of York (who later became King George V and Queen Mary) drove through the park on their way to visit the Lord Mayor, Alderman W.J. Pirrie, at Strandtown. The royal couple also visited the Botanic Garden on that day (chapter 6).

COATS AND CYCLING

In 1898 one of the rangers working in Ormeau Park asked the Public Parks Committee to arrange for a watchman's box so that he would not get wet when guarding the flower beds. He was politely reminded that he had been already provided with two coats, a waterproof one and an overcoat, and that he should be moving throughout the park in the course of his duties rather than remaining static. The result: no watchman's box!

Cycling was becoming more and more popular as a pastime, and caused problems in Ormeau (and in years to come in other parks) with people and children being knocked down. In an attempt to counteract this, the Corporation constructed a cycle track on the lower ground near the river. The bye-laws, which did not permit cycling, had to be changed to allow cyclists access to this track.

The cycling bye-laws must have been relaxed during the 1880s to accommodate members of the Northern Cycling Club who gathered in front of the superintendent's house in the middle of Ormeau Park before setting off for Portrush. The all-round trip of more than one hundred miles lasted two days – undertaken on penny-farthings!

ORMEAU AS A BURIAL GROUND

Some years before the opening of the park a portion of the land at Ormeau had been considered for a public cemetery. In 1865 Belfast Corporation's Cemetery Committee examined a number of potential areas for burial grounds, including the 'Deer Park' at Cave Hill, Ormeau Park and the estates of Thomas McClure at Ballydollaghan. Ormeau was the preferred area, but an offer of land on the Falls Road for burials (to become Belfast Cemetery, later the City Cemetery – chapter 5) saved Ormeau at the last minute. This was not the only covetous approach on Belfast's new park: a proposal in 1881 to extend the gasworks site into Ormeau Park was turned down. In contrast, the surplus land that had been grazed up until 1892 was given over to Ormeau Golf Club to be transformed into a golf course. The rent was the same as for grazing – £66 per annum. The following year the club was granted permission to erect a pavilion or clubhouse.

NEW LEGISLATION

In January 1870 the Cemetery Committee appointed a two-man subcommittee to investigate if fifty-seven acres of ground at the new Belfast Cemetery on the Falls Road could be utilised as a public park. There was one problem – the land lay outside the borough boundary and therefore the Public Parks (Ireland) Act 1869 did not apply. The Corporation had to wait for an Amendment Act in 1872, which gave power to establish and maintain parks outside the town boundary, and the Provisional Order Confirmation Act of 1873, which authorised the payment of £5,000 towards the reduction of the cemetery debt (which stood at £19,000), before proceeding.

No sooner had the legal authority been gained than it was decided the proposed fifty-seven acres was too generous, and thirteen acres were earmarked for return to the cemetery. In the event, only eleven of these were transferred back, and not until

1880. The discrepancy arose from the fact that the additional two acres lying to the south-east side of the Falls Road had already been sold by auction to the Trustees of St Patrick's Industrial Schools for £1,000. Once the legislation and land transfer had been passed and agreed the Corporation was able to fulfil its good intentions of creating a second public park.

Falls Park opened in 1876. At that time there were several water features including this pond, complete with swans.

HAWKS AND HOUNDS

The area designated for the new park, to be called Falls Park, lay within the townland of Ballymurphy, on land formerly known as the Mountain Bleachgreen. The land was owned by the Sinclair family, who were merchants and linen drapers and whose residence was in Donegall Place. The Sinclairs hunted at Falls with hawks and hounds, and exercised the family's horses on the property. In 1820 at least part of the land was being used as a bleachgreen for bleaching brown linen. The last of the family to have connections with the property was Thomas Sinclair (1812–67), who was Chairman of the Belfast Harbour Board from 1863 to 1867. He sold the land at Falls to Belfast Corporation for use as a cemetery in 1866 (chapter 5).

ROAD OF THE HEDGES

The Public Parks Committee visited the site in April 1875, and subsequently established bye-laws and approved development plans. An advertisement for a park ranger was placed in the newspapers stating that the wages were 12s per week and that a house and uniform came with the job. Twenty-six applications were received, and William Stuart was appointed. The park was formally named on 3 June 1875 – the name Falls comes from the Irish *Tuath-na-bhfál*, meaning district or road of the hedges. George McCann, who was superintendent of the City Cemetery, was given responsibility for the park, and instructed to allow the public in from January 1876. At the time of opening, a beetling mill complete with working machinery stood beside the stream, a former ice house in the grounds was being used as a tool store, and the tramways ran up the Falls Road from Belfast to a depot immediately beside the park. The ice house was pulled down around 1885 and the stones utilised, along with foundations of a dwelling house, to form the base for a new road. Some of the shrubs and trees in the adjacent City Cemetery were thinned out and the surplus planted in both Falls and Ormeau Parks. The superintendent was authorised to engage additional hands, including women, to make hay each year from the grass areas in the upper part of the park, a practice that continued into the early twentieth century.

WATER FEATURES

The principal advocate of Falls Park was Alderman Bernard Hughes, an enterprising businessman and founder of the famous Hughes Bakery, who presented £50 towards the cost of a drinking fountain in 1877. A year later a horizontal bar and round swing were installed, the first mention of children's play equipment in a public park in Belfast, and a ranger's lodge costing £230 was built in 1879. In 1887 the first of three bridges was constructed over the Ballymurphy Stream that ran through the property to join the Blackstaff River. This was not the only water in the park. There were at least three ponds or dams, which were regularly used by local people for ice-skating in wintertime. For safety reasons they were eventually fenced off and their depth reduced to three or four feet. Despite this precaution a twelve-year-old boy drowned in what was known as the spring pond in 1894 while fishing for sticklebacks.

SPORTS

Cricket, football and hurling were played on the upper hay fields, sometimes all at the same time – much to the chagrin of the superintendent, who found it hard to control the use of the open ground. The same area was used for a time by soldiers from an adjacent camp who had been given permission to train daily in the park. A lawn tennis court was constructed by the parks staff in 1892 and a bowling green was opened in 1905, for which bowls could be rented at 2d a pair. As it was considered undesirable to 'have people coming from games passing through funeral parties', the Corporation closed the gate linking Falls Park with the City Cemetery.

SUCCESS IN NUMBERS

Shortly after its opening Falls Park was described as 'nestling in a pocket of great natural scenic beauty under the shadow of the Black Mountain. It has great sylvan charm with a mountain stream running through its romantic glen.'

The foundations of providing public parks within Belfast had been set: Belfast Corporation had begun the process and the people of the city had responded. In July 1876 some 37,000 people were visiting Ormeau Park each week, while the average weekly attendance in Falls Park was recorded as 2,500. It was now inevitable that other parks would follow.

3
Princesses and Ponds
Alexandra, Woodvale and Dunville Parks
up to 1900

I n October 1882 there was a strong movement to acquire a park for the north of Belfast. In response to public advertisement, Belfast Corporation was offered land at Skegoneill, Ashfield, Crumlin Road, Shankill and Oldpark, but after discussion settled on seven acres of ground at Castleton. This land was conveyed to the Corporation from Sir John Preston by deed on 10 July 1885 for the sum of £981 13s 1d. At the same time, a further one-quarter acre, which included part of the Milewater Stream and a pond, was acquired by Fee Farm Grant from two firms, Philip Johnston and Sons Ltd and the York Street Flax Spinning and Weaving Co. Ltd, subject to these companies' water rights. This second area was free of charge except for a yearly rent of 1s if demanded. A further portion of ground was obtained by Fee Farm Grant from the same two companies in 1887.

The park, having been acquired somewhat piecemeal, was scheduled to be named the Princess Park, because the Prince and Princess of Wales visited Belfast during 1885. In October of that year, however, the name was changed to Alexandra Park,

after the Princess's name rather than her title. The park was laid out by J.C. Bretland, the Borough Surveyor. Trees were planted and the grounds landscaped with seats and flower pots. The pond remained a central, distinctive feature. Alexandra Park opened on Saturday, 7 May 1887 but, unlike the opening of Ormeau Park sixteen years earlier, there was no formal ceremony. The *Belfast News-Letter* reported that the gates were 'simply thrown open by the Park Ranger'. Despite this, a large crowd visited the new park during its inaugural weekend. Access at that time was restricted to entrances at Jubilee Avenue (off the Antrim Road) and the Limestone Road.

VANDALISM

Only a matter of days after the opening, the superintendent had to report to the Public Parks Committee that 'serious destruction had been caused to the Council's property in Alexandra Park by the public'. As a result several police constables were detailed to assist 'servants of the Council' in the protection of the property. The park was closed for a fortnight from 19 May to allow for repairs and necessary security arrangements. The railings were extended along the Limestone Road, and a rail fixed under the road bridge to prevent youths from getting into the pond. The property was reopened to the public on 2 June.

William Smith was appointed foreman gardener in November of 1887 at a salary of 18s per week with a house included. The gate lodge at the Jubilee Avenue entrance was completed a few months later. This two-storey gabled and dormered lodge was built in Gothic Revival style and was a larger version of the Falls Park lodge constructed eight years earlier. Both houses were probably designed by Bretland himself. The small conservatory or greenhouse at the rear of the lodge at Alexandra Park was not part of the original design, but was added in 1899 at a cost of £82. In 1891 the temporary gates at the Limestone Road entrance were replaced with wrought-iron gates. The park was later extended, once again piece-meal fashion (chapter 6).

WOODVALE PARK. BELFAST. 2527.W.L.

A FOURTH PARK FOR BELFAST

Before Alexandra Park had even opened, negotiations for a park on the Shankill Road were already well under way and had been reported in the press. The Corporation had again invited offers of land, this time in the north-west of the borough. In November 1886, after 'careful investigation', it was decided to establish a public park on twenty-four acres of land at Woodvale. This ground, at the junction of the Woodvale, Shankill and Ballygomartin Roads, was purchased by Fee Farm Grant dated 20 August 1887 at a yearly rent of £217 13s 2d (the equivalent of £9 per acre). It had been owned by the Reverend Octavius Glover who lived in a house called Woodville. The house stood, with its small garden, towards the south of the park near Woodvale Avenue, and was joined by a driveway to gates on the site of the present main entrance. There was a lodge positioned just to the north side of the gate. The estate had been planted with trees around the perimeter with occasional central copses and specimen plants, but otherwise seems to have been fairly featureless. To add interest a pond costing nearly £200 was constructed in the north-east corner, and facilities for cricket and football were provided. The park was enclosed by railings at a cost of £295, which included stone gate piers.

A MAYORLESS OPENING!

As with Alexandra Park, the new park had a change of name before opening. The original name of Shankill Park was changed at a committee meeting in September 1887 to Woodvale Park.

The official opening date was fixed for Saturday, 18 August 1888 at 3.00 p.m. The day turned out very warm and a large crowd congregated outside the park gates

Woodvale Park opened in 1888. This pathway leads down to the pond near the entrance at Woodvale Road.

NATIONAL LIBRARY OF IRELAND

Dunville Park was presented to the city by Robert Dunville, and was opened in 1891. Behind the shelter can be seen the balustrade of the Ionic temple-style gate lodge.

for the ceremony. The Mayor and Chairman of the Public Parks Committee were scheduled to formally open the park, but by 3.35 p.m. they had not turned up. The officials present decided that Councillor Forsythe should open the gates instead. He duly took the key from the ranger and made a short impromptu speech in which he referred to the opening and closure of Alexandra Park the previous year due to the vandalism. He said that he hoped there would be no repetition of this at Woodvale Park. The crowds were then admitted into the new park.

The same day Mr Firth of the Whiterock Bleaching Company presented a swan for the pond. More birds were donated later, one of which apparently did not appreciate the facilities provided for it: four boys were rewarded with 1s each for retrieving one swan from the Blackstaff River.

THE PARK TOO SMALL

When Woodvale Park opened, the landscaping was incomplete: there were out-standing plans for flower beds, tree planting and a porter's lodge. The staffing had not been finalised either. James Patton was appointed foreman gardener one month after the opening. The Belfast Street Directory for 1888 commented that Woodvale Park was too small for the number of people who used it. The property was enlarged twelve years later, through an exchange of land at Ballygomartin between a Mrs Corry and Belfast Corporation, but the deal increased the area by only a quarter-acre – hardly sufficient to cope with the demands of the users. Male and female toilets were built – the first time that public toilet facilities were provided for ladies – and a greenhouse was added in 1899, the same year as the lodge con-servatory in Alexandra Park.

DANGEROUS SPORTS

Unofficial skating during the winter months on the ponds at Woodvale and Alexandra Parks gave cause for concern as the ice was normally very thin. The foreman at Woodvale was authorised in 1892 to engage an extra man to 'keep the ice in order'. There were potential hazards on the field as well. In 1894, when cricket was warily first permitted in Woodvale, the foreman was instructed to report to the Committee immediately if he noticed any risk of injury or danger to other users of the park.

All recreational and public facilities were monitored very closely. A number of children's penny slot machines had been allowed in each of the parks, and when the Corporation received complaints in 1896 that they were not working properly, the firm was ordered to remove them immediately.

FIRST GIFT TO THE CITY

The first park to be presented to Belfast (a city since 1888, by virtue of the Royal Charter granted by Queen Victoria) was Dunville Park. At a special meeting of the Public Parks Committee on 31 July 1889, the Town Clerk read a letter from Robert G. Dunville offering a piece of ground of about five acres at the junction of the Falls Road and Grosvenor Road. Needless to say the Committee accepted the offer with 'the warmest thanks'.

The Dunville family was both wealthy and prominent in Belfast life. In 1825 John Dunville began a wholesale tea and wine business. As the latter flourished he built a distillery in Divis Street to make Dunville Irish Whiskey. On the profits, he was able to build a large house known as Richmond Lodge on the Holywood Road. The site of this house is now part of Knocknagoney Linear Park (chapter 14). John Dunville served as an alderman for many years and sat on the Managing Committee of the Belfast Academical Institution. The eldest of his four children, William, carried on the family business and inherited the home at Richmond Lodge.

THE SORELLA TRUST

In 1872 William Dunville, who had no children of his own, endowed a trust fund for educational purposes in memory of his sister, Sarah, who had died nine years earlier. This Sorella Trust (*sorella* being Italian for sister) consisted of £8,000 vested in the names of trustees and about six acres of land. From the trust came funds of £140 per annum for the highly prized Dunville Studentships at Queen's College, first awarded in 1874, the year of William Dunville's death. The trust fund also provided £100 per annum to the Government School of Art in Belfast.

On the death of William Dunville, the business passed to his nephew Robert Grimshaw Dunville who lived at Redburn, a large house in the Holywood Hills. He also inherited the new distillery at the back of the Grosvenor Road, which was built in 1869 and had a fermenting capacity of over half a million gallons. Robert Dunville acquired from the trust about five acres of land that had been waste ground and the scene of many riots. He invested £7,750 in Belfast Corporation stock and from the interest he discharged the rent of £264 per year owing to the

The grand terracotta fountain (left) was the principal feature of Dunville Park.
POSTCARD

Sorella Trust for the ground. Through this generosity he was able to present the ground to Belfast Corporation for development as a public park, while at the same time increasing the income of the Sorella fund trustees by over £250 per annum.

Robert Dunville also gave £5,000 towards the laying out of the park. Over £1,000 was paid to Mr Musgrave for the provision of railings in 1890 and £665 to Messrs Doulton and Co. of Lambeth for the erection of a fountain. This was designed by A.E. Pearce and is similar to the French Renaissance-style Victoria fountain in Glasgow. It was constructed of buff terracotta with panels depicting aquatic life in relief near the base. It bore the inscription 'The park, formed and completed, was presented as a free gift to the City by Robert G. Dunville, of Redburn, 1891'. A further £1,150 was spent on the building of a gate lodge in 1892, which stood at the Grosvenor Road entrance. Built for the superintendent of the park, this lodge resembled a scaled-down version of an ancient temple. The park also contained a number of shelters, and swings for children.

TO DIMINISH SECTARIAN STRIFE

Dunville Park was officially opened in 1892 by the Marquis of Dufferin and Ava, who said on the day that 'the provision of such a park in an industrial area was symbolic of a new era when employers would think not only of the housing and sanitation of their workers but of their recreation as well'. Sadly, after his generous efforts, Robert Dunville was not able to be present at the opening ceremony due to the recent death of his wife. His son John attended on his behalf and replied to Lord Dufferin's speech by pointing out that his father had thought of building a model school on the land but had changed his mind, thinking that a park would be 'more useful in the overcrowded and industrial area'. He said that he hoped 'the park, by providing a place where people of all creeds would meet, would help to diminish sectarian strife in the area'.

Because the park was sited across the road from the County Lunatic Asylum (now part of the Royal Victoria Hospital) it was nicknamed the 'Looney Park' or 'Looney Fields'. Through its proper title, the Dunville family name has been perpetuated in Belfast. A sizeable mausoleum in the older section of Clifton Street Graveyard, now appropriately owned by Belfast City Council (chapter 12), holds the family's burial place.

THE GROWING LIST

As the century raced to a close, Belfast had five public parks: Ormeau, Falls, Alexandra, Woodvale and Dunville. Before the twentieth century was heralded in, however, another public park had been added to the list: one that encapsulated the very essence of the Victorian Age – the Royal Belfast Botanic Garden.

4

Flower Shows and Fireworks
The Botanic Garden and the Waterworks
up to 1900

The Belfast Botanic and Horticultural Society established the Belfast
Botanic Garden on the present site in 1828. It was one of the first botanic gardens in the United Kingdom to be set up entirely from public subscriptions. Over the years this was to prove as much of a disadvantage as an
advantage, for money was always in short supply. The Society, formed in 1827,
began what was to be a never-ending financial battle by issuing five hundred shares
at seven guineas each and forming a committee of twenty-one shareholders to
manage the garden.

PROFESSIONAL BOTANISTS

The first professional botanist to be engaged was Thomas Drummond, who was in post at Belfast by August 1828. He remained for two years before leaving on a plant-hunting expedition to North America. His successor was David Bishop, who left after a short stay to set up a nursery at Malone. The next curator was John Campbell, the son of the head gardener at Pollock Gardens, Glasgow. He too stayed at Belfast for only a short period, with relationships between himself and the Society strained at times. Certainly the shareholders' committee did not look favourably on Campbell's forthcoming marriage. Concerning this he wrote in 1834 that it was best 'not to oppose the will or wishes of the Committee until I be a little more permanently fixed in my situation'. Campbell recorded that in March of 1834 the committee was making plans to raise money for a range of glass at Belfast, but before much progress had been made Campbell left his post. He was replaced by Daniel Ferguson in 1836. Campbell subsequently died from typhus in January 1838 on board the ship *Minerva*, bound for Sydney, Australia.

A CONSERVATORY

To have considered the possibility of a conservatory so early in the life of the garden underlines the pioneering enthusiasm of some of the Society's founder members. They engaged one of the top architects of the day, Sir Charles Lanyon (responsible for many fine Belfast buildings including Queen's University and the Crumlin Road Courthouse), who produced an initial design for a Palm House that bears little resemblance to today's building. He envisaged a low central square dome with smaller terminal domes at the end of each wing, but exchanged these for a single, higher, elliptical dome, adopting the system of curved glass and curved iron-ribs developed by John Claudius Loudon in 1816.

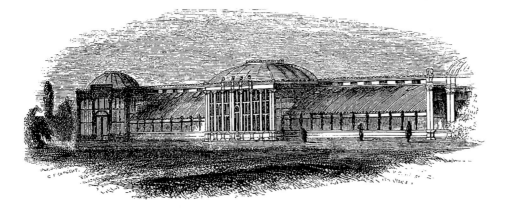

The committee appointed Richard Turner of Hammersmith Works, Dublin, to oversee the practical design details of the conservatory and to construct the two wings. The Marquis of Donegall laid the foundation stone in 1839 and the ceremony was followed by a day of festivities for the public. The two wings of the Palm House, each sixty-four feet long, were completed the following year at a cost of £1,400. The west wing was opened as a cool house, the east wing as a tropical house.

The original design for the Palm House, as drawn by architect Charles Lanyon, *c.* 1830.

LINEN HALL LIBRARY

Botanic Gardens, Belfast JV 16/91

Writing in 1847, the secretary of the Society (by now the Royal Belfast Botanic and Horticultural Society), Thomas Sinclair, said that 'the great range of glasshouses built by Mr Turner of Dublin for this Society has reached near completion state and is a wonder in glass and iron, and has met with the approbation of all whom it concerns and the general public'. The 37½-foot-high dome was not completed until 1852, at a further cost to the Society of £1,000, a fifth of which had been raised from a fête held at the Corn Exchange in Belfast in February of that year. In all the Society raised £850 towards the dome, but was compelled to add the outstanding amount to its growing debts. By that time Richard Turner had gone on to build the Great Palm House at Kew Gardens (finished in 1848), and so the firm Young of Edinburgh was engaged to construct the dome at Belfast.

SOCIETY TO COMPANY

In 1860 the Royal Belfast Botanic and Horticultural Society was superseded by the Royal Belfast Botanic and Horticultural Company (Limited) with a board of fifteen directors. It inherited from the Society a main conservatory, glasshouses and other houses valued by Charles Lanyon at nearly £5,000, plants and shrubs of an estimated value of £1,500, and debts of £2,500. After the transfer, Daniel Ferguson was kept on in his post as curator. One of his first recommendations to his new bosses was to replace the brick flue heating system in the Palm House with a hot water system. Unlike previous botanists, who had stayed only a relatively short time, Ferguson remained at Belfast for twenty-eight years until his death in 1864. The growing reputation of the Belfast garden for horticultural excellence was due in no small measure to his enthusiasm and work. He was responsible for publishing a comprehensive guide to the garden in 1851, a book that sold for 6d, in which he described the plant collections in great detail. In the same year, he visited London and returned with seeds of the giant water lily (*Victoria amazonica*). He had a house specially constructed for this spectacular plant, which has floating leaves of up to six feet in diameter. Ferguson was one of the first in Ireland to persuade his giant water lily to flower.

The curator's efforts were remarked on in C.R. McComb's *Guide to Belfast,* published in 1861, in which he described Belfast Botanic Garden as follows:

> The surface is gently undulating and is most agreeably diversified with wood and water, shady vistas, floral parterres and tracts of smooth shaven greensward. The conservatories are magnificent, extensive and richly stocked; and in them are many of the rarest specimens to be found in any similar collection in the United Kingdom. The laying out and keeping of the grounds, and the arrangement of the greenhouses, etc., reflect the highest credit upon the taste and judgement of the curator, Ferguson, who has a handsome residence in the gardens.

Daniel Ferguson was succeeded by his son, William Hooker Ferguson, who stayed just four years before being asked to resign following a financial scandal. In 1868 Joseph Forsyth Johnston, of the Manchester Botanic Gardens, and formerly from the Duke of Devonshire's seat at Chatsworth, was appointed curator.

FINANCIAL CONCERNS

The Company directors had financial responsibility for the garden. In 1871 the secretary expressed concerns that due to many subscribers to the garden having withdrawn and despite the efforts in obtaining fresh subscriptions, the year had realised a net loss of over £70. Contributions from the mill owners and other employers, paid to secure free access to the garden for their workforce on Saturday afternoons, had decreased by £81, and the rent of £15 from an archery club using the garden had also ceased. The secretary concluded that had it not been for the Easter Fête realising the sum of £160 the Company would have had to report a heavy deficit in its funds for that year. Because of administration problems the free admission fund for employees was discontinued and instead employers were invited to buy books of tickets to distribute to workers. By the mid-1870s, by which time Ormeau Park was open free of charge (chapter 2), even this option had become less popular.

CONSTANT STRUGGLE

There were also expenses related to vandalism, although this was not a major problem. Incidents ranged from names and initials being scratched on to plant leaves to fences being broken and tomatoes being stolen from the conservatory. In 1863 Ferguson complained that the 'young visitors are more destructive than twenty-five years ago'. Twelve years later Forsyth Johnston was reporting that the rockery had to be replanted each year because of damage caused by children. In the same report he commented that the conifers were covered with grime from pollution. There was a constant struggle to keep plant labels up to date and in the right places. In his last year of office, Ferguson had a man stand guard to catch whoever was destroying the labels. He apprehended a boy, a Master Cupples, who had been shooting at them with his catapult. The boy's father was ordered by the Company to pay the 18s wages to the watcher. By 1889 it seems that the Company had abandoned the cause: by then all the outside labels had gone.

Not all younger visitors to the garden were bent on destruction, however. In 1865 an Englishman on tour described the recreational scene he encountered. 'A party were playing croquet, and I observed that this game possesses the singular advantage of placing all on a perfect equality. A little girl was playing with some boys, and though at many other games she might have been snubbed, she was here treated with as much deference when it came to her turn as if she had been a grown-up person.' All this was happening among 'greenhouses containing beautiful flowers' and near 'a small sheet of water'.

FEATURES OF THE GARDEN

Relationships between Belfast and other botanical gardens were good and numerous specimens were exchanged and donated. Daniel Ferguson's guide of 1851 gave a full account of the plants and horticultural features of the Botanic Garden. These included a pinetum (a collection of conifers, many new to the country), which had been established within ten years of the garden being opened. Beside it was a collection of deciduous and evergreen oaks (in front of the present Ulster Museum), while an *Acer* or maple collection was planted beyond the Palm House. There were two further plant collections near the site of the present Tropical Ravine, one laid out in arrangement according to the botanist Linnaeus, the other in what was termed 'natural order'. There was also mention early on of a grass collection so that agriculture would be 'materially served'.

The layout at that time included an upper pond (presumably the 'sheet of water' referred to by the Englishman on tour) and two lower ponds which supported a range of aquatic plant species, swans and other waterfowl. The area around the lower ponds was laid out as a rockery and grotto, where, in 1886, a small tower or gazebo with a winding staircase was erected to give views of the garden and the Black Mountain. A tree-lined promenade stretched from the main area of the garden to the River Lagan. There were several buildings within the garden during its history, including an orchid house and propagating house, erected in 1842, a curator's house (1844), a back gate lodge (1865) and a front gate lodge (date unknown).

A plan of the Botanic Garden, from Daniel Ferguson's guide of 1851. Features include the Palm House (without the dome)(1), the pinetum (2), botanical collections (3), main lawn (4), ponds (5), the river promenade (6), the orchid house (7) and the curator's house (8).

LINEN HALL LIBRARY

This last building, at the main Stranmillis Road entrance, was replaced in 1878 by a new lodge designed by William Batt in Venetian Gothic style. It contained a public room, a ladies' cloakroom and a lavatory. Two years later a clock tower was added with money from public subscriptions. The back gate lodge was also replaced around that time.

THE NEW FERNERY

The second major building to be erected in the garden was the Tropical Ravine House. It was the brainchild of Charles McKimm, head gardener of the garden from 1877 when Forsyth Johnston resigned. McKimm had come to Belfast in 1874 and after only three years was promoted from foreman to head gardener at a salary of £70 per year. There seems to have been some debate whether the work and circumstances warranted a curator or merely a head gardener. On at least one occasion McKimm, who referred to himself as head gardener, was permitted to assume the style of curator, so that he was not at a disadvantage when dealing with curators from other botanic gardens. One of his duties was to present an annual report to the Company, giving details of progress on any major developments, the state of the garden and a list of plants donated and their sources. He oversaw many changes at Belfast Botanic Garden. New nursery houses were erected in 1877, the paths in the greenhouse were widened, a large fountain was installed and extensive repairs

The Tropical Ravine, a fine example of Victoriana, featured grottoes lit by candles, fountains and this waterfall – as well as tropical plants.

carried out to the Palm House, including the installation of gas lighting and the laying of encaustic tiles at the front entrance. Nevertheless he is best remembered for the Tropical Ravine.

The new fernery, or Tropical Glen as it was first called, was built on the site of the former orchid and propagating houses. Work began in 1887 and was largely carried out by McKimm himself and his team of gardeners. The original building was 97 feet long by 35½ feet wide, and consisted of a sunken glen viewed from a high-level, railed balcony. The first visitors, who included the Marquis and Marchioness of Dufferin, were admitted in the summer of 1889. Some of the tree ferns and orchids were transplanted from the orchid house into the new Tropical Ravine. In true Victorian style several grottoes were landscaped into the walls. These were illuminated with candles – as many as seven hundred on occasions – and fitted with mirrors to create intriguing lighting effects. Above the pool was a waterfall, where the flow of water could be started by means of a chain and pulley system, a mechanism often likened to flushing a lavatory.

NON-BOTANICAL BOTANICAL GARDEN

The Royal Belfast Botanic and Horticultural Company, like the Society before it, faced an ever-present financial burden. As a result, events of both a botanical and non-botanical nature were held in the garden with the prime reason of raising extra funds. Very often the income received from such occasions barely covered the expenses occurred in preparing the ground, or the purchase or hire of equipment such as tents. This was certainly the case for the flower show held in September 1871 and the Great International Fruit and Flower Show of August 1874. This latter event contained more than nine hundred exhibits, including fruit from Queen Victoria's hothouses and a bunch of grapes weighing twenty-two pounds entered on behalf of the Earl of Durham. The secretary regretfully had to report that the show, 'far from being of any advantage to the Gardens in a pecuniary point of view, did not add one penny to our funds but, on the contrary, left us to bear the extra cost incurred for some months previously in bringing the grounds into the most favourable condition'.

And so Belfast Botanic Garden came to be associated with band concerts, military tournaments, fireworks displays, Punch and Judy shows, dog shows, fancy dress parades, torchlight processions, funfairs, performing Zulus, gymnastic performances, choral fêtes, dances and other events. On 16 August 1861 Mr Blondin, the first man to walk across the Niagara Falls on a tightrope, performed his famous act in front of a large crowd in the garden. A Grand Tournament on Easter Monday 1887 by the 5th Dragoon Guards included items of 'Lemon Cutting', 'Cleaving the Turk's Head' and 'Tilting at the Rings'. The highlight of the day was a representation of 'A Night Attack on a Russian Outpost'. A gala on the same holiday two years later featured Captain Whelan's parachute descent, Herr Holtum the Cannon King who could reputedly catch a fifteen-pound cannon ball fired towards him from a distance of sixty-five feet, and a 'Grand Military Assault at Arms'. Admittance for this was 1s with first- or second-class grandstand seats 2s and 1s extra respectively.

On 6 October 1883 a crowd of thirty thousand packed the Botanic Garden for the Great Conservative and Orange meeting.

ENGRAVING FROM *THE GRAPHIC*, 13 OCTOBER 1883

MEETINGS GALORE

As religious and secular groups were prohibited from holding meetings in the new public parks under the bye-laws, they regularly met in the Botanic Garden. The Belfast Total Abstinence Society, the Temperance Association, the Band of Hope and students from Queen's College all held rallies or meetings. On 6 October 1883 a crowd of thirty thousand packed the garden for the Great Conservative and Orange meeting. This followed the opening of the constitutional club in Belfast and had as its guest of honour Sir Stafford Northcote. The day, although 'conducted on the whole with admirable order' according to *The Graphic*, was not without incident. On the train journey to Barnscourt afterwards a stone was hurled at a carriage, injuring one of the party, Lady Crichton.

Sometimes the Company asked for a deposit (£50 was demanded from a Protestant meeting in 1862) and an assurance that damage would be paid for. With some of the larger gatherings damage was inevitable. After the Ulster Unionist Convention on 17 June 1892, the *Northern Whig* reported that the 'excellent herbaceous development must have suffered badly!' This convention was attended by twelve thousand delegates and a crowd estimated at three hundred thousand, all determined to illustrate their disagreement with the recurring threat of Home Rule. A special hall was constructed (where Rugby Road is today), covering an acre of ground. Three platforms were erected for speakers in the Botanic Garden: one on the main lawn, one by the 'rosary' and one near the oak collections. It was quite probably the largest attendance ever recorded in the garden.

Poster for the 1889 Easter festivities in the Royal Botanic Gardens, Belfast

BELFAST CENTRAL LIBRARY

A DANCING SALOON

On a more permanent but smaller scale, a timber framework was fixed in position on the site of a former pond from about 1870. This frame could be covered with canvas to provide shelter during events. In the early 1880s an exhibition hall was put up adjoining the rear of the Palm House, the roof of which came from a gunboat shed used by Harland and Wolff to build small warships for the Admiralty. The hall could accommodate fifteen hundred people and although it was intended for flower shows it was probably never used for that purpose. Instead, after a suitable floor for dancing had been laid, it catered for social functions, causing one shareholder to refer distastefully to it as 'a dancing saloon'. A small collection of birds was also housed there.

THE BALLOON GOES UP

Perhaps the most popular and renowned of all events in the Botanic Garden were the balloon ascents, so much so that a permanent gas pipeline was installed into the main lawn to facilitate these occasions. One ascent in July 1864 saw eleven people carried aloft in Mr Coswell's 100-foot-high balloon called *Britannia* – the largest in the world at that time.

In 1867 a grand ascent by William Hodsman (the first man to cross the Irish Sea by air) was advertised for 5.00 p.m., Monday, 17 June. A crowd of fifteen thousand filled the garden and hundreds more spilled on to the adjoining streets. Inflation of the 42-foot-diameter balloon began at 1.00 p.m., but four hours later the great brown silk bag was still flopping about on the ground. By 7.30 p.m. the crowd was restless and began to clamour for action. The people pressed forward, looking to turn the balloon into 'silk for new shirts'. The developing riot was controlled by the police and by the diversion of a fireworks display. Gradually everyone was appeased with a chit and the promise of alternative entertainment in the Ulster Hall the following evening.

Over the years these non-botanical uses provoked considerable disagreement and acrimony among the shareholders, some of whom felt that horticulture was coming a poor second to public entertainment. But in the end it was the lack of money that was the telling factor.

SELLING OUT

The idea of selling the property was raised (not for the first time) at a shareholders' meeting in June 1892. The following year a vote was passed for the Company to go into liquidation and for a new company to be formed, but this decision was subsequently rescinded. Negotiations opened with Belfast Corporation regarding purchase of the Botanic Garden. The Company refused the Corporation's initial offer of £8,000 but finally accepted £10,500. The Corporation retained the services of the eight members of staff and raised their wages to match those of the Parks Department staff – at that time an outside foreman was earning 20s per week. The Royal Belfast Botanic Garden was renamed the Belfast Botanic Gardens Park and opened free to the public from New Year's Day 1895. An opening ceremony took place on 6 March of that year at which the Lord Mayor officiated, and afterwards guests were treated to a cake and wine luncheon in the exhibition hall.

And so, after sixty-eight years of private ownership, many shareholders' meetings, much debate about finance, and a plethora of public entertainment events, the Botanic Gardens (referred to in the plural from then on) became Belfast's sixth public park.

A PROBLEM OF WATER

The events held regularly in the Botanic Garden were almost surpassed in spectacle and popularity by aquatic galas staged in the 1880s and 1890s on the water reservoirs on the Antrim Road – known to generations as the Waterworks and created as a response to growing demands for water.

With the passing of the Belfast Water Act of 1840, a newly formed body called the Belfast Water Commissioners took over responsibility for the provision of water supplies from the Belfast Charitable Society. The new board inherited the system that brought water from Lester's Dam (now within the property known as Lagan Meadows – chapter 17) into the town. It was clear then that this supply was insufficient to meet the demands of the town's growing population or indeed the industrial thirst for water. Steam engines, spinning mills, foundries and other factories all used large quantities and domestic needs were also increasing. The young Lord Belfast, then living at Ormeau, placed more pressure on the system when he addressed a meeting of artisans in May Street and urged for better homes and working conditions. He suggested that a day would come when even the smallest house would have a bath of its own.

CAVE HILL. BELFAST R.W. ST.

The lower area of the Waterworks, showing the Antrim Road gate lodge in the foreground, and the conical roof of the ice house behind it.

MAGNI/ULSTER MUSEUM

The new Commissioners took steps to solve this water requirement. Two ponds were constructed on the Antrim Road: the middle or town basin and the upper clearwater basin. They were fed by the Milewater Stream (also known as Carr's Glen Stream) from a reservoir at Carr's Glen.

William Dargan, the engineer who constructed Queen's Island (chapter 1), submitted an estimate for the construction work of £8,250. This was accepted by the Water Board on 19 October 1840. The minutes noted the sympathy of the Commissioners with the two gentlemen who had been unsuccessful in tendering. This condolence took on a more practical nature than mere words. The second candidate, William Sykes, was awarded £50 for the satisfactory way in which he furnished his estimate and Daniel Collins £15 for submitting the third place estimate.

Several mill owners held water rights to the Carr's Glen Stream and because of the conflict of interests between themselves and the Water Commissioners many lawsuits followed the building of the Waterworks. One particular trial in 1851 of the *Water Commissioners v. Robert Howie* lasted six days. It involved Lord Belfast and other notables such as the architect Sir Charles Lanyon and engineer William Ward, who had carried out much of the construction work at the Carr's Glen site. Ward had used a home-made level during the work, a tool that became the object of

much amusement. Consequently the legal case attracted much more public interest than was usual. The jury eventually awarded the plaintiffs a farthing damages and a farthing costs.

The upper pond, or clearwater basin, at the Waterworks; this was used for boating, swimming and diving.

WATER SHORTAGE AND THIN ICE

It was lawsuits such as this, along with disputes over rights of way, that held up further progress in water provision and contributed to a water famine in 1865, when it was reported that there was insufficient water in the town to 'boil an egg'. Conflict over public access to the Antrim Road site came to a head when the Water Board erected a barrier to prevent local people from using the property as a short cut through to Oldpark. Watchmen stationed at this barrier had to be given police protection. Such back-up was not always available and so they were provided with 'twopenny horns' to blow loudly when they were attacked or the property was 'being molested'. Angry crowds broke the gates and locks on many occasions despite the forlorn blowing of the watchman's horn. Eventually the Water Commissioners were obliged to compromise and allow entrance to the grounds to anyone who was willing to sign their name and address in a book at the gate, and who would undertake to obey the rules for visitors posted up in the hall of the porter's lodge.

This entrance lodge was not built until 1850 and was not in Dargan's original estimate for the site work. His tender did, however, include the erection of a small conical ice house. The walls of this tower were specially thickened for insulation and the floor was twenty-seven feet below ground level. The Water Board intended to collect and store the ice from the basins in the winter and sell it during the summer. In practice the ice proved to be too thin and brittle to fetch even the poorest price and after a few winters the scheme was abandoned. In 1860 a number of local fishmongers rented the ice house from the Commissioners to store ice imported from Norway.

FUTURE USE

Despite having the honour of being the source of the first water to be piped under pressure to houses in Belfast, the Antrim Road basins served the town for only twenty years or so and were superseded by the reservoirs at Woodburn, above Carrickfergus. Even then, they continued to attract debate, this time over their future use. An Act of Parliament had decreed that the reservoirs were for supplying water, and lawyers argued long and hard as to whether or not they could be used for purposes such as public entertainment and recreation. With or without legal permission the Water Board decided to take an example from the Royal Belfast Botanic Garden and stage a Grand Promenade at the Waterworks.

A SPLENDID GIRANDOLE

According to advertisements the evening's entertainment included a grand display of fireworks by Mr Hodsman (of balloon ascent fame), an illumination of the middle reservoir by coloured lights, an aquatic fire ship, 'brilliant emerald' and 'splendid crimson' illuminations to represent a sunset glow, and fêtes of aquatic monsters and mermaids. A military band with full drum corps began playing at 6.30 p.m. followed at 8.00 p.m. by what was billed as the most magnificent pyrotechnic display ever seen in the North of Ireland. The finale was a grand sea battle in which two ships fired hundreds of red-hot balls at each other, causing one of the ships to catch fire and explode in a spectacular way, representing the igniting magazine. At this point the whole atmosphere was filled with two hundred rockets forming 'a splendid girandole'. The cost of admission to this extravaganza was 2d, with no change given!

OUT WITH THE BAND

This novel type of performance was so well received that the Waterworks soon became a popular place for outdoor entertainment. During the 1870s and early 1880s many fireworks displays were staged there and regular band performances were held on Monday evenings. These performances ended abruptly following a rather bizarre incident. The Commanding Officer of the military then stationed at Belfast, Colonel G.B. Stokes, permitted his spaniel dog to enter the Carr's Glen reservoir. An official of the Water Board objected strongly to this and an argument developed. Both reported the incident to the secretary of the Board. As a result the Commissioners issued a summons against Colonel Stokes, who was subsequently fined 1s, with 12s 6d legal costs. The next day the Water Commissioners received a note from Colonel Stokes stating that the band of the 2nd Battalion Royal Inniskilling Fusiliers would no longer play at the Waterworks. And so the musical evenings at the Antrim Road site were discontinued from August 1885.

It was not, however, the end of all public entertainment. In March 1896 three members of the Belfast Natural History and Philosophical Society asked for permission to hold an exhibition in the Waterworks grounds. This took place some weeks later when John Shaw Brown, a pioneer of motoring in Ulster, exhibited a horseless carriage before a large audience. Each person had paid 6d for the experience of seeing what looked like a large perambulator parading around the embankment at speeds of up to six miles an hour.

At a public meeting in 1897 a deputation was appointed to interview the Commissioners and recommend that the grounds should be set aside entirely for amusement and recreation of an aquatic nature. It was only with the passing of an Act two years later that the Water Board was fully empowered to do so. It is interesting to note that a suggestion at this time to sell the property to the Belfast Corporation (perhaps inspired by the recent sale of the Botanic Garden) did not meet with the approval of the Commissioners. This followed an earlier unsuccessful attempt by the Corporation to obtain a portion of the Waterworks for a public park in 1883.

The Water Board agreed to provide pleasure boats, on the understanding that no more than £500 a year should be spent on upkeep. Tom Boyce, a boating contractor who ran a ferry across the Lagan to Ormeau Park, was consulted regarding craft. As a result twelve second-hand rowing boats, repainted and renamed, were launched on to the middle basin in June 1900. These boats were featured on several early photographs and postcards of the property. A diving board was also positioned towards the Cliftonville end of the upper pond to encourage swimming and diving.

And so the Waterworks entered the twentieth century, not as public reservoirs, but as recreation grounds providing pleasure and entertainment for the countless visitors to the site.

WATERWORKS.

GRAND PROMENADE.

The most magnificent pyrotechnic display ever seen in the North of Ireland.

GRAND DISPLAY OF FIREWORKS
by Mr. T. Hodsman, of Dublin.

ILLUMINATION OF THE MIDDLE RESERVOIR
by coloured lights which will give a fairy-like appearance to the water.

FLOATING FIREWORK MECHANISM!   AQUATIC FIRE SHIP!
with hundreds of fiery monsters creating great amusement.

BRILLIANT EMERALD ILLUMINATION.

SPLENDID CRIMSON ILLUMINATION
representing a sunset glow.

FETE OF AQUATIC MONSTERS

FETE OF THE MERMAIDS.

GRAND SEA FIGHT
between two ships.

HUNDREDS OF RED HOT BALLS
will be fired at each other and the fight continued until one of the Ships takes fire, and suddenly the Magazine ignites, when will be represented

A GRAND EXPLOSION
when the whole atmosphere will be filled by

200 ROCKETS FORMING A SPLENDID GIRANDOLE.

BY KIND PERMISSION THE BAND OF THE 16th REGIMENT (P.W.O.) WITH FULL CORPS OF DRUMS WILL ATTEND.

Band at 6.30.   Fireworks at 8.

ADMISSION TWOPENCE.   NO CHANGE GIVEN.

Advertisement for a pyrotechnic display and other festivities at the Waterworks, c. 1890.

5

Burial Powers

City Cemetery, Dundonald Cemetery,
Knock Graveyard

The cast-iron fountain in the
City Cemetery installed by
George Smith and Co. of Sun
Foundry, Glasgow, in 1880.

The old Belfast Corporation owned a churchyard at High Street, where St
George's Church stands today. The ground was overcrowded and prone to
flooding at high tide, and so it was closed towards the end of the eighteenth century. Up to the middle of the nineteenth century burial grounds in
Belfast were controlled by religious denominations or societies. Because the Belfast
Corporation Act of 1845 prohibited the making or opening of any new cemetery,
there was no municipal graveyard in the town.

The situation changed following an amendment to the law in 1856 allowing
Belfast Corporation to begin the process of establishing a municipal cemetery. In

1865 it was reported that the Town Improvement Committee had been searching for two years for a suitable site, and had considered several proposals, including some of the ground within Ormeau Park. The Corporation, under the auspices of its newly formed Cemetery Committee, eventually obtained possession of ground at Falls Road from the Sinclair family in 1866, after the Belfast Burial Ground Act of that year provided the necessary legislative power. This land cost the Corporation £12,000.

THE BELFAST CEMETERY

Mr Gay of Bradford was appointed to supervise the laying out of the new cemetery – at first referred to as Belfast Cemetery, and later as the City Cemetery. This involved construction of boundary walls and the provision of drainage, roadways and wrought-iron gates. The ground for burials was divided as follows: ten acres as a public Catholic ground with a separate entrance, five acres for a Catholic chapel and Catholic graves, seventeen and a half acres for Protestant graves and thirteen and a half acres as public ground for other religious denominations. A Jewish section was allocated in 1871 and extended in 1916.

GROUND ALLOCATIONS

The fifteen acres that had been allocated for Catholic burials were divided from the rest of the cemetery by a sunken wall at the behest of the Catholic Church. It seems that the intention was to keep Catholics and Protestants apart even after death! In the event this area was never used by the Catholic Church. The Bishop of Down and Connor could not consecrate the area because he felt, even with the sunken barrier in place, that he did not have proper control over the ground. The Privy Council met in Dublin Castle to hear the case and agreed to withhold its warrant for the closing of Friar's Bush Graveyard, the only other Catholic burial ground in the vicinity of Belfast at that time, until the matter was sorted out. In the meantime the Catholic Church purchased fifteen acres from James Ross on the eastern side of the Falls Road at a cost of £4,200. Eight acres of this were to be used for burials, in what became known as Milltown Cemetery, while the remainder went to St Patrick's Industrial School. An audience of twenty thousand, there to witness the opening ceremony and consecration of Milltown Cemetery in 1870, heard an address by Dr Grimley, Bishop of the Cape of Good Hope, South Africa.

To allow the Catholic allocation at the City Cemetery to be used instead for Protestant burials, the Corporation paid £4,000 compensation to the Catholic community to offset the cost of Milltown. This was confirmed by the Belfast Corporation Act of 1884.

BURIALS IN THE CITY

In 1869 a Mr Calcutt was appointed the first registrar of the City Cemetery at a salary of £100 per year plus a £20 allowance for a house until accommodation was provided on site. The cemetery opened on 1 August that year, and as a result portions of the graveyards at Shankill (chapter 12) and Friar's Bush were closed. Initial charges for the new cemetery ranged from £1 for a grave by the public ground to £9 for a wall grave. There was an incremental scale between the two extremes

The mortuary chapel at the City Cemetery built in 1874 by contractor Samuel Carson at a cost of £1,040.

depending on the exact position of the plot and the number of rows out from the wall. Burials normally took place from Monday to Saturday, but Sunday burials were permitted if there was need for haste: for example, on the production of a medical certificate stating that the deceased had died from an infectious disease.

Some of the ground within the cemetery proved to be very hard rock-sand. As all the graves were then dug by hand, the gravediggers were unable to break through these areas. The Cemetery Committee authorised the purchase and use of blasting powder to overcome this problem.

SUPERINTENDENTS

The first superintendent of the new cemetery was J. W. Moran, who remained only a very short time before Thomas Leeburn was appointed in a temporary capacity. In January 1871 the post was given to James McLachlan who remained until his death in 1876. George McCann succeeded him and continued in post until his retirement in 1917, when his namesake, D. McCann, took over.

In 1872 plans for a superintendent's house and offices were submitted by John Lanyon, of the architect firm Lanyon, Lynn and Lanyon. Mr Lowry was awarded the contract and carried out the work at a cost of £750 the following year. A second lodge was built on the Whiterock Road soon afterwards.

MONUMENTS AND MORTUARY CHAPEL

The first memorial in the cemetery was erected for John Hopkinson of

Ramsbottom, England, on New Year's Day 1870. Very quickly the City Cemetery became a place of extravagant monuments and monoliths, some of which were architectural pieces in their own right: the Herdman Memorial, for example, has Egyptian Revival elements. Despite the growing number of monuments and headstones throughout the cemetery, there was an initial ruling that no gravestones were to be erected in the Jewish section. This decision was repealed in 1929 after a campaign by Rabbi Shachter.

In 1874 a mortuary chapel was built by contractor Samuel Carson at an estimated price of £1,040. Cast-iron fountains made by George Smith and Co. of Sun Foundry, Glasgow, were installed in 1880. A bell, which was rung to mark the closing of the gates, was transferred from the old Linen Hall tower and erected in the cemetery.

PROMINENT GRAVES

Many prominent people associated with the social, political and economic life of Belfast were buried in the City Cemetery: for example, Sir William Whitla, Sir Robert Anderson (of Anderson & McAuley), Sir Edward Harland, Sir Robert Baird (once proprietor of the *Belfast Telegraph*) and Thomas Gallaher (the cigarette manufacturer). Some of those interred had connections with Belfast Corporation and the city's parks: Sir Daniel Dixon (father of Sir Thomas Dixon and Lord Mayor of Belfast 1892–3), Viscount Pirrie (Lord Mayor in 1896–7 and instrumental in the establishment of the Royal Victoria Hospital), Daniel Joseph Jaffé (the fountain named after him is now located in Botanic Gardens), the Cunninghams of Glencairn and Fernhill (chapter 13) and W.H. Lynn (architect of many buildings including the Chapel of the Resurrection at Belfast Castle – chapter 9).

FURTHER BURIAL GROUNDS

The Cemetery Committee realised as early as 1895 that the City Cemetery was being used up for burials so quickly that additional burial ground for Belfast would soon be needed. Two years later the Committee decided to acquire forty-five acres of land at Ballymiscaw, Dundonald. This ground, then referred to as Donall's Fortress because of a nearby motte, was being offered at £5,600. The Belfast Corporation Act 1899 authorised the purchase, which was agreed on 23 March of that year, by which time the price had increased by £430. The Corporation made provision for a £20,000 loan to cover the purchase and subsequent laying out of the grounds. After a visit by a subcommittee to graveyards in London, Manchester, Liverpool, Edinburgh, Glasgow and Dublin, several recommendations were made with regard to the laying out of the new cemetery at Dundonald. Grave sizes were reduced from 9 x $4^{1}/_{2}$ feet to 7 x $3^{1}/_{2}$ feet to increase the number of possible interments, bricked graves and vaults were restricted to one section, and only light traffic was to be allowed on the main avenues to reduce the possibility of damage to the grounds.

In 1904 the allocation of plots was initiated with a quarter of the ground designated for Catholics. The following year this was revised after a Local Government Board Inquiry into how this allocation had been reached. The allocation was later revised again under the 1943 Belfast Corporation Act, which allowed ground initially reserved for Catholic burials to be used for Protestant burials. The first burial in Dundonald Cemetery took place on 19 September 1905. George McCann, already in charge of the City Cemetery, was given responsibility over Dundonald. One of his first tasks was to ensure that the grass growing on areas not then designated for burials was cut for hay at the end of each summer.

GLENALINA AND KNOCK ACQUIRED

In 1910, after lengthy negotiation, the Corporation applied for parliamentary powers to acquire 'by consent or compulsorily' fifty-three acres of the Glenalina estate for an extension to the City Cemetery. The ground was owned by Henry Patterson who had a linen beetling mill on the premises, served by the stream that flowed through Falls Park. In 1912 the price of £5,250 was agreed upon, with Lord

The former country churchyard at Knock overlooks the city of Belfast. The oldest legible gravestone is dated 1644.

ROBERT SCOTT

Shaftesbury receiving £500 for his mineral rights on the estate. The purchase must have pleased McCann, for he had complained to his Committee on a number of occasions about workers using Falls Park as a short cut for transporting linen by cart on their way to the Glenalina beetling mill. Two years later the mill was demolished and the stones used in road making. Early in 1915 what was described as 'other old buildings' on the site were used by the Military Remount Department. The first interment in the Glenalina Section took place on 1 November 1915. The addition of Glenalina, along with minor changes when the boundary with Falls Park was straightened the previous year, brought the size of the City Cemetery up to almost one hundred acres.

The extension of the city boundary in 1896 brought the old burial ground at Knock under the jurisdiction of Belfast Corporation. The name Knock comes from the Gaelic word *cnoc*, which means 'a hill' – this former country graveyard indeed stands on a hilltop overlooking Belfast. The guardians continued to control it until 1900 when the Corporation formally took it over. At that time all of the ground was allocated and only the reopening of some graves was permitted. In 1905 a caretaker was employed to look after the property.

The graveyard contains a number of eighteenth-century graves of local farming people from Knock and Tullycarnet, and its oldest legible gravestone is dated 1644. The site, however, is much more ancient. A church at Knock passed from the Anglo-Normans in the thirteenth century into the hands of the Clandeboye O'Neills. A sixteenth-century traveller referred to a church dedicated to St Columba (sometimes called Knock Columkille) in the area. By 1622 this building had been transformed for Anglican worship and was used until 1737 when it was abandoned in favour of a new parish church at Knockbreda in the townland of Breda. An engraving in the *Dublin Penny Journal* of 1834 showed two ruined gable walls within the cemetery walls, but there are no remains of any church at Knock Graveyard today.

BURIAL RESPONSIBILITY

By 1922 some 126,199 burials had taken place in the City Cemetery and 13,211 in Dundonald Cemetery. With two working cemeteries and the historical site at Knock under public ownership, the responsibility for municipal cemeteries and public burials was well and truly established as a Belfast Corporation function.

6

Into the Twentieth Century

Victoria Park in 1922, with the
shipyard in the background.
A football match is in progress on
the far side of the lake.
MAGNI/ULSTER MUSEUM

During the heyday of Dargan's Island, when it might have seemed super-fluous to have had another pleasure or recreational area so close by, the Belfast Harbour Commissioners were considering a public park beside the Connswater River. By virtue of the Belfast Dock Act 1854 the Commissioners were authorised 'to set aside for the purpose of a public park to be called "Victoria Park" a portion of such land not less than 50 acres in one place and the land so set apart shall not afterwards be used for any other purpose without the authority of Parliament'. The land was referred to again in the Belfast Harbour Act 1870, but nothing seems to have been done regarding the setting up of the park during this time. Even by 1883, when a further Harbour Act allowed the exchange of the original fifty acres on the Belfast side of the Connswater with a similar-sized area on the other side of the river, little or no progress had been made. The Commissioners authorised the spending of £2,000 on the formation of an approach or approaches to Victoria Park, although at that time the ground hardly seemed worth approaching! In a painting of the area by J.H. Connop in 1864, a path is shown along the perimeter beside Belfast Lough, accessed across the railway line by a gate opposite Victoria Road. Subsequent surveyors' comments would suggest that perhaps a degree of artistic licence had been taken by the artist.

SURVEYOR'S REPORT

The first mention in the Belfast Corporation minutes of Victoria Park was in 1876 when the Public Parks Committee seemed eager to take up the offer of land that the Harbour Commissioners were authorised to set apart. The Corporation sent a letter of application to the Commissioners and called for a surveyor's report in 1881. The surveyor commented that the land was so isolated that he could not see how any 'practicable carriageway' could be made to it that would 'serve the inhabitants of Belfast'. He was unable to advise the Corporation 'to undertake the very serious works and great changes which would be absolutely necessary to convert this marsh into a suitable park'. Instead, he suggested that the area would be suitable for 'athletic exercise, skating, boat houses and such purposes'. The Public Parks Committee asked the Harbour Commissioners to consider providing access, entrances and extra land to make the proposal feasible.

A later report, in 1886, described how water accumulating on the site (now sixty-three acres) could be drained at low tide by means of a valve system, and how in wet weather this was inadequate to cope with the water flow, which meant that the ground flooded readily. In short, 'little better than a swamp'. The report recommended that the general level of the park be raised by excavating a shallow skating lake and that the excavated material be used to build up the central ground.

The estimated costs for excavation, draining, fencing and roadways was £8,343. Because the park was bounded on three sides by tidal estuaries, the only fencing required was along the boundary adjacent to the Belfast and County Down railway line. A neat timber fence was suggested here. The surveyor also commented that 'the Park would likely become a popular place for the prosecution of athletic sports' and that he thought it 'useless to attempt forming an ornamental park of the usual type here'.

The Corporation entered into discussions with the Harbour Commissioners and the Belfast and County Down Railway Company over funding and access to the proposed park. The Harbour Commissioners offered to contribute their sum of £2,000, still unused from 1883, towards the formation of an approach road. Negotiations were prolonged but in July 1890 agreement was reached concerning a bridge and approach at Dee Street. The expense of this construction was to be kept down by using infill for the road from the Scavenging Department. The bridge was built by Bright Brothers in 1890 and at last, the following year, Victoria Park was transferred to the Belfast Corporation.

Some four years later excavation work was still being carried out, but advances were made in the early years of the new century. The Cemetery and Public Parks

DONEGAL SQUARE, BELFAST. 2411. W.L.

Belfast's new City Hall was completed in 1906. The grounds were landscaped by Charles McKimm, General Superintendent of Parks.

NATIONAL LIBRARY OF IRELAND

Committee (the separate Public Parks and Cemetery Committees having merged in 1900) agreed to sanction a loan of £5,000 towards the development of its new property. In 1903 the Belfast and County Down Railway Company offered to construct a subway entrance under the line near the Connswater River. The Corporation paid £500 for the provision of this approach. In 1904 the lake was enlarged to accommodate boating and, not for the first time, the idea of an outdoor swimming pool was raised.

OPENED EVENTUALLY

Victoria Park was officially opened on 15 September 1906 with Alderman John McCormick officiating – some fifty-two years after the first proposals for a public park in that area of Belfast had been made. The outdoor swimming pool was not completed until after 1908. Up until then, anyone wanting a dip would have had to use the public bathing stations at the battery (Ormeau Park), one of the ponds at Botanic Gardens or the water race at Alexandra Park. The pool at Victoria was intended for boys only. It was four feet deep and filled with salt water by means of a tidal valve. On a good summer's day as many as fifteen hundred boys bathed there. This pond was later replaced with a larger swimming pool (chapter 8). Victoria Park, as had been foretold by the surveyor in 1886, did become the venue for sporting activities with boating, swimming, football, cricket and bowling facilities all being present by 1922: by then unofficial football games had been taking place for over twenty-five years! Bands were playing in the park from 1906.

GENERAL SUPERINTENDENT OF PARKS

The landscaping of Victoria Park was the responsibility of Charles McKimm who, in November 1903, was promoted to General Superintendent of Parks. This new post was created when the superintendent at Ormeau, Thomas Dickson, resigned. It excluded responsibility for Falls and Dunville Parks, which remained under the supervision of George McCann, the superintendent of the City Cemetery.

Charles McKimm continued to live in the curator's house in Botanic Gardens. Through him, the Cemetery and Public Parks Committee spent the early years of the twentieth century consolidating its parks, erecting shelters and public toilets, planting shrubs, installing features such as drinking fountains and bells to be rung at closing times, and adding railings where necessary. The railings from around the old Linen Hall were offered to the Committee and were used in parks and some of the shrubs were removed and replanted in Botanic Gardens. McKimm then drew up plans for the grounds around the new City Hall.

STREET TREES

In 1900 street tree planting was taken over by the Cemetery and Public Parks Committee from the Improvements Committee. Charles McKimm was 'charged with the duties of planting trees in the streets of the city'. In 1909 £250 was set aside for planting, a sum that allowed for tree guards as well as the trees themselves. Many trees were planted before and immediately after the First World War. Species such as lime and London plane were selected for their ability to withstand the atmospheric pollution so rife in the early years of the twentieth century. Years later, car owners were to rue the choice of lime trees, as they became infested with aphids and dropped sticky sap on to vehicles parked underneath.

CHANGES TO BOTANIC GARDENS

McKimm was able to spend considerable money on the property closest to his heart, Botanic Gardens. This expenditure covered restocking, replanting and reno-vation work to some of the buildings. During 1895, the year the site was opened, the Corporation spent £2,600 on the garden, an amount that the former Royal Belfast Botanic and Horticultural Company could only have dreamed of spending. The repainting of the Palm House alone cost £300.

In 1900 the Tropical Ravine was extended to provide a second section, to be kept warmer than the original and used for tropical plants rather than temperate species. This work cost £1,000 and was carried out without altering the essential charac-ter of the house. Observant visitors today might make out the bricked-up outline of one of the original doorways on what is now the dividing wall, and the remains of the original hollowed-out steps among the lush vegetation. In 1902 £340 was spent on a further extension to allow a heated pond to be installed in which to grow the giant water lily, some fifty years after curator Daniel Ferguson first suc-ceeded in getting the plant to flower in Belfast (chapter 4). These alterations added seventy-six feet to the length of the Tropical Ravine.

Inspired perhaps by the typical Victorian engravings that showed young children sitting happily on top of the open leaves of the giant water lily, Charles McKimm

The Tropical Ravine was extended in 1902 to accommodate a pond for growing the giant water lily from South America.

BILL KIRK

allowed his baby grandson, Bert, to be placed on one such leaf in the new pond for a family photograph. Recalling the incident in later life, Bert McKimm tells of how the 'leaf promptly sank and I was fished out of the pond'. Charles McKimm's wife pronounced in a matter-of-fact way that at least the baby must have been well nourished!

The Cemetery and Public Parks Committee spent a considerable portion of its annual budget of just over £9,000 on the Tropical Ravine and other work in the gardens, including extending the pinetum and repairing the bandstand. In 1901, when all parks, with the exception of Dunville, had their own greenhouses, a new range of wooden-framed glasshouses was constructed at Botanic Gardens behind the 'bothy' (the horticultural term for gardeners' quarters) at the rear of the Palm House. These propagating houses served as a nursery for the Parks Department for many years. In 1902 the tank holding a crocodile donated to the park was to be enclosed, for obvious safety reasons!

The Corporation's finances were not inexhaustible, however. When the Belfast Naturalists' Field Club made a deputation to the Botanic Gardens' new owners for the outdoor botanical collections to be revived and an aquarium to be added, the ideas were not taken up. In an attempt to generate income the Corporation rented out the exhibition hall to various groups. The building was renovated frequently, and had a new floor on rubber springs installed to improve its dancing characteristics. It was also used for social events and activities such as roller skating.

Perhaps the most significant change to the Botanic Gardens after the takeover by the Corporation was that ladies were first allowed to use the public toilets in 1896 – it had been a long wait until then!

ROYAL PROCESSION

It was Charles McKimm who was responsible for the preparation and decoration of Botanic Gardens for the royal visit of the Duke and Duchess of York (later King George V and Queen Mary) on 8 September 1897. The royal party passed through Botanic Gardens and Ormeau Park at a gallop on its way from the York Street Spinning and Weaving Co. Ltd to Ormiston House, beyond Strandtown, the residence of the Lord Mayor, Alderman W. J. Pirrie. The Botanic Gardens were closed to the public during the visit; one thousand entrance tickets had been printed and twenty-five given to each councillor.

The gardens were elaborately decorated for the occasion. Three floral arches stood at the main entrance with the Irish welcome *Céad Míle Fáilte* worked with holly leaves in Irish characters and decorated with fairy lights. Trophies and bannerettes adorned the main avenue, streamers flew from the trees around the lawn and Japanese lanterns in chains were suspended from the Palm House. Members of the Boys' Brigade and Church Lads' Brigade lined the route. Bands played the national anthem while large crowds watched from every vantage point. The party paused opposite the flower beds where the Parks Committee Chairman, Councillor Masterton, was stationed, and a bouquet of orchids, roses and ferns was presented to the Duchess.

The procession left the gardens through an archway of flowers at the rear entrance and headed for Ormeau Park by way of Botanic Avenue, University Street and Ormeau Road. They were greeted in Ormeau by large numbers of people who had purchased admission tickets. Among those present were the pupils and staff of the Ulster Institution for the Deaf, Dumb and Blind. The Duke of York Flute Band performed from the bandstand and played the national anthem as the cavalcade drove by.

THE MAN WITH GREEN FINGERS

Charles McKimm was famous for the bananas and varieties of pom–pom chrysanthemums that he grew in his hothouses. His family claimed that he truly had green fingers and that if 'he planted an empty flower pot he could raise a prize bloom from it'. He was born in Donaghadee in County Down in 1848 and apprenticed as a gardener on the estate of Lord Farnham in County Cavan. He served Belfast well during his time with Belfast Corporation.

By all accounts he was something of a character, loved and respected by all ages. On one occasion he encountered a gang of boys raiding some currant bushes in the garden. In the rush to escape one of the youths was left behind, hanging by the seat of his pants from the spikes of the iron fence. McKimm lifted the culprit down, examined the damage, and pronounced judgment. 'The Lord has castigated you on the place provided – but next time He'll probably leave the job to me.' He gave the crying child an apple and sent him on his way.

McKimm would often remove his greatcoat and play cricket with the local boys. He was known to distract youths with games when he did not want them on a soft piece of ground or when they tried to steal birds' eggs. He was not behind in keeping councillors waiting while he whittled a catapult stick for a small child. One day he caught a pickpocket red-handed during a balloon ascent, when everyone else was 'looking skyward'. He was sadly missed when he died in 1907 at the age of fifty-nine.

James Davies, the foreman at Ormeau Park, was appointed his successor in January 1908. He was given the title Superintendent of Parks and occupancy of the curator's house in Botanic Gardens.

ADDITIONS AND SUBTRACTIONS

The exact size and shape of some parks changed quite frequently. For example, over the years ground was both taken away from and added to Botanic Gardens. In 1904 the park was extended by two acres, while during the years up to 1910 several approaches were made by Queen's University for small pieces of ground. In 1911 the Corporation purchased land adjacent to Agincourt Avenue and a further six acres from a Mr Crawford. The following year the idea of an art gallery and museum within the gardens was put forward. This was approved in 1912 and resulted in the loss of over an acre of ground. In 1913 there was a further addition – not land, but a statue of Lord Kelvin, the famous Belfast-born scientist. Designed by Albert Bruce-Joy it was erected just inside the main entrance. The following year the first shelter was built in the park.

AN OLD FOGEY

Changes within parks did not take place without the public voicing its opinions. Such feelings were often summed up by a writer in the *Northern Whig*, who went under the pseudonym 'An Old Fogey'. The column featured regular criticism of Belfast Corporation in its dealings with Botanic Gardens and other parks, although the writer did give credit where credit was due. He described the lawn at Botanic Gardens in 1912 as being 'singularly free of the daisies and plantains that spoil the beauty of the lawns in the Dublin and London parks'. This was despite the fact that parts of the grass were dug up each time a fireworks display took place to enable the largest pyrotechnic pieces to be positioned.

A LOWER GLEN

New areas of ground were also being acquired by the Corporation in the north of the city, transforming the character and size of Alexandra Park. When it first opened in 1887, this park was already an amalgamation of three separately acquired pieces of land. Between 1904 and 1908 four further sections between Mountcollyer Street and Alexandra Park Avenue were added. The first of these was a four-acre site, acquired by Fee Farm Grant from a Mrs Deacon. This land bounded the north bank of the Milewater Stream. Three years later the Corporation leased two acres on the south bank from John Thompson, and the following year two more pieces of ground were leased from Philip Johnston and Sons Ltd and the York Street Flax Spinning and Weaving Co. Ltd to complete the south bank and the boundary of the park at Deacon Street.

The Milewater Stream ran from the pond, over a series of waterfalls and through

a lower glen formed by these new acquisitions. Two rustic bridges were constructed in 1912, providing a scene more reminiscent of the Mourne Mountains than a
city park. The area was certainly very different in character from the upper parkland, which by then featured formal flower beds, tennis courts and a bowling green.

The lower glen at Alexandra Park
had a very rural appearance when
it first opened. Two rustic bridges
over the Milewater Stream were
built in 1912.

MAGNI/ULSTER MUSEUM

MUSIC IN THE PARKS

In the days before gramophones, radios or recording, the only musical performances that anyone heard were live ones. It was natural, therefore, that parks would
become outdoor arenas for those prepared to give such performances. A minute
was passed by the Public Parks Committee in April 1875 permitting Paddy
Murney, a blind harpist, to play in Ormeau Park, thus beginning a long tradition
of music in public parks. Of course, bands had provided popular entertainment on
Queen's Island, in the Royal Botanic Garden and at the Waterworks site before
then.

The band of the regiment stationed in Belfast was appointed to play on Saturdays
in Ormeau Park, while the Belfast National Band played at Falls Park in 1876.
By 1880 local and military bands were playing regularly in both parks. Each

performance had to be ratified by the Public Parks Committee prior to the date. The Belfast Corporation Act of 1899 permitted the Corporation to contribute funds not exceeding £250 per annum towards the provision and maintenance of a band for giving performances in parks. In response to public advertisement five bands applied to participate in this scheme: Ballymacarrett Brass and Reed, Sirocco Lodge Brass, Willowfield Brass, Belfast City Brass and Reed and Belfast Temperance Brass. Performances were held in the bandstands at Ormeau, Falls, Alexandra and Woodvale Parks, and Botanic Gardens, over a twelve-week period starting 1 June 1900. The bands played in rotation in different venues on Tuesday to Saturday evenings with the week's programme advertised each Monday in the *Belfast Evening Telegraph*. The bands were paid £2 10s for a performance, with the proviso that the programme of music was supplied beforehand for approval. This was the first organised programme of band performances to be held in the parks.

BANDSTANDS

From the budget of £250, £30 was set aside for Mr Crowe's Orchestral Band to play in Botanic Gardens. The bandstand there was enlarged by one-third to allow for the orchestral players, particularly the violinists, who needed extra space for bowing. Bandstands at that time were temporary wooden structures: the one at Falls Park was to cost no more than £30 to build in 1875. They were often badly sited on a hill with the audience below the musicians instead of the other way round whereby the music could 'float up to the listeners'. These temporary structures were later replaced with more substantial iron stands with timber roofs, and had seating arranged in horseshoe-shaped areas in front of them.

   Members of the Craig family set up 'The Craig Band Fund' in 1902 in memory of James Craig, father of the Right Honourable Sir James Craig, Bart., MP. The money was to be used for payment of military bands to play in parks and open spaces, although in the interest of economy a band of a 'non-military' type was permitted. The Belfast Police Band was later included. The conditions specified that performances should be as near as possible to 'thickly-populated portions of the city', and should take place after working hours on weekdays, on Saturday afternoon or evening, and 'on Sundays when public opinion in the City will permit thereof'. In 1907 a law was passed permitting the sectioning off of an area for bands and the levying of an admission charge.

VANDALISM

From an early stage the public parks were open to abuse. Alexandra Park suffered badly shortly after its opening (chapter 3) and in the later years of the nineteenth century the Public Parks Committee received regular reports of trouble and wrecking. In 1897 the flower beds in Dunville Park were badly damaged, and crowds of youths – smoking, spitting and using bad language – were reported to be 'hanging around' the entrance to Botanic Gardens. The shelters in Ormeau and Botanic Gardens were also gathering places and the local constabulary had to be called in on numerous occasions. Complaints were lodged in 1907 about frequent card playing in public and warning notices were displayed after several birds' nests were destroyed.

HEALTH EXPERIMENT

A rather unusual medical experiment was suggested in 1903. Shelters were constructed in the walled garden at Ormeau Park for the sole use of those suffering
from pulmonary restrictions and consumption. The Public Health Department
believed that such facilities would alleviate symptoms – presumably by providing
copious amounts of fresh air – but no records are available to show if or for how
long they were used, or if indeed they had any beneficial effect.

THE EDWARDIAN DREAM

From music to bowls, from health experiments to pom-pom chrysanthemums,
Belfast's parks were providing entertainment and diversions of a wide-ranging
nature in the early years of the twentieth century. Public open space was still a nov-
elty; private gardens were as yet only for the privileged few. The idea of playing
sports such as cricket and tennis in public places, of walking leisurely through a
manicured park and enjoying ostentatious displays of flowers and plants, somehow
suited the Edwardian optimism, in an era when everything seemed perfect and
opportunities golden. Unfortunately times were set to change.

A fancy dress cycle parade
in Alexandra Park in the
early 1900s.

POSTCARD

7
The War Years and After

The wartime allotments by the River Lagan (on what is now part of Botanic Gardens).

MAGNI/ULSTER MUSEUM

The 'war to end all wars' reached out and affected the lives of everyone, including those who worked in the parks and those who visited them. It also changed the very appearance of some parks. The most visible transformation was brought about by the establishment of allotments. As part of the war effort, areas of both Ormeau and Falls Park were rented to the Garden Plots Association in 1916. Four acres at Ormeau were then sub-let by the Association to tenants for the cultivation of vegetables. In all, 256 allotments were in operation at Ormeau and 145 at Falls, most of which were let to local residents. These plots, which 'produced luxuriant crops of vegetables and flowers', remained in use until well after the war was over, only being finally abandoned in March 1921. There were also extensive allotments beside the River Lagan in 1917 on ground that was later to become incorporated into Botanic Gardens (chapter 8). Much of this low-lying ground was swampy and prone to flooding; nevertheless, vegetables were successfully raised.

Many park employees rushed to the recruitment queues to join up. Their jobs were kept open for them, but one member of the City Cemetery staff on his return to work in 1919 was informed, rather bizarrely, that he had missed the issue of clothing for that year and would have to wait until the tenders were prepared for the following season.

The more tragic side of war was reflected in the cemeteries. In 1916 a section of the City Cemetery was set aside for the burial of sailors and soldiers killed in action. On 6 November 1918, only days before the end of the war, a further section was designated for the burial of American soldiers from the transport ship *Otranto*. The vessel had been wrecked off the coast of Islay the previous month. Two years after the war the Commissioners from the office of the Lord High Admiral purchased graves in Glenalina for the burial of members of the Navy and their relatives.

TEMPORARY HOSPITAL

As the need for hospital space grew in 1914, the Headquarters Council of the Ulster Volunteer Force (UVF) made an offer to the War Office to provide a fully equipped hospital for the wounded. With the permission of the Cemetery and Public Parks Committee the exhibition hall (chapter 4) at Botanic Gardens was chosen. The hall was adapted to take eighty-four beds, and was opened as a hospital on 8 January 1915. Before long it became known as 'The Carson Ward'. The need for space became so dire that the hospital spread outwards until it virtually surrounded Queen's University. By then it provided accommodation for 350 patients. The exhibition hall was eventually vacated by the Ulster Volunteers on 1 November 1921. In a letter informing Belfast Corporation of the vacation of the premises, the superintendent of the UVF Hospital Board referred to the many thousands of Ulster men who had received treatment during the six years of its existence. Afterwards the hall was used as an auxiliary barracks for the Royal Ulster Constabulary, before finally being demolished in 1927.

ON PARADE

There was a rally held for members of the Ulster Volunteer Force on the land beside Shaw's Bridge in 1913. On 6 June of the following year there was a review of the volunteers in the fields in front of Fernhill House, on ground that now forms part of Glencairn Park (chapter 13). On this occasion there was a considerable number of volunteers on parade and a large crowd of spectators, but only part of the force was able to sport uniforms. Two years later the North Belfast Ulster Volunteers paraded in the grounds of the Belfast Castle Estate, then in ownership of Lord Shaftesbury (chapter 9), prior to joining the (36th Ulster) Division at the Somme.

To raise funds for the Red Cross and St John Ambulance Brigade a grand fête was held in Botanic Gardens in June 1918. The guest of honour was Lord French,

the Lord Lieutenant, representative of the King. There were hobby horses, swing-boats, stalls, music by the Dixie Minstrels, and a waxworks show. The Palm House was converted into a strawberry and ice cream garden. The event raised just over £5,000. The following year the Comrades of the Great War held an autumn fair in Botanic Gardens with a similar aim – to supplement depleted funds.

DECLARATION OF PEACE

Ormeau Park was closed to the public on Saturday, 9 August 1919 so that children could be entertained in 'celebration of the Declaration of Peace' after the end of the war. The peace celebrations lasted all weekend. There were festivities at Botanic Gardens on the Friday evening, and special trees were planted in Falls and Woodvale Parks to mark the occasion.

While the war had a dramatic effect on many people, and changed the way in which they looked upon life, some aspects of domestic and municipal life continued throughout the war largely unchallenged and unaffected. For example, in the years preceding, during and succeeding the war, a number of developments took place at Ormeau Park.

MUNICIPAL GOLF COURSE

The agreements drawn up between Belfast Corporation and Ormeau Golf Club concerning the thirty-seven-acre golf course were amended in 1909 and in 1911. According to the new proposal, the entire area was to be considered as a municipal golf course within the park. This was partly because the Corporation had been publicly criticised for sanctioning restricted access to an area of a park. As a result a condition was laid down that the trustees of the golf club should 'permit any member of the public to play golf and to have free access to the pavilion erected on the golf links and have free use of the same at a charge of one shilling per day'. By the end of the war the fees had been increased to 1s 6d per day, with Saturdays more expensive at 2s 6d, and the golf club's annual rent to the Corporation was £100. In 1929 the lease was renewed on a short-term basis and the rent increased to £200.

PLAYGROUNDS AND PONDS

In 1912 a children's playground was established in Ormeau Park with equipment that included swings, see-saws and a maypole, all purchased by Councillor Frank Workman. The playground was fenced off with iron hurdles and floored with tarmac and sand. It was formally opened in May of the following year, and a games organiser was put in charge of the facility. The pond in the park was enlarged in 1922 under a scheme 60 per cent financed by the Ministry of Labour to provide work for the unemployed. In March of the following year the *Belfast Telegraph* reported that work was proceeding on what it referred to as the 'new children's open air swimming pool at Ormeau'.

MISCELLANEOUS MOMENTS

Over the years Ormeau was the setting for some rather unusual scenes and incidents. In June 1900 a ceremony was held in the park to present the Freedom of the City to General Sir George White of Broughshane, defender of Ladysmith during the Boer War. In 1903 a pair of lion cubs was given to the city and kept (presumably in cages) in the park. They were named after two worthy members of the Corporation. One cub disappeared the following year, while the other ended up on display some years later at the Donegall Road Branch Library – as a taxidermy specimen. In 1904 the park received a gift of a pair of ostriches from the Duke of Abercorn. There is no record of these birds being named; perhaps no one wanted them to disappear like the lion cubs, or perhaps they simply did not look like anyone in the Corporation!

During the dockers' strike of 1907 the Middlesex, Berkshire and Essex Regiments were stationed in Ormeau Park. The men were billeted in tents around the pond and flat region of the park opposite the gasworks site. Early photographs reveal the rather primitive outdoor kitchens used by the military. Local residents doubtless had to put up with considerable disturbance at that time but may have felt unwilling to complain. This was not the case some years later when those living on the Ravenhill Road lodged complaints about being kept awake at night by the bleating of the sheep that were allowed to graze in the park.

Permission was granted in 1916 for pet dogs to be exercised in a restricted area, and in 1923 for the Special Constabulary to parade through the grounds. The advance of the motor car during the 1920s brought about amendments to the park bye-laws and major changes to the shape of Ormeau Park. A speed limit of 10 m.p.h. was placed on vehicles in the park (complaints about cars in the park had begun in 1903), while an embankment road from Ormeau Bridge to the Ravenhill Road was constructed. The river frontage of Ormeau, which architect Timothy Hevey had initiated some fifty years earlier (chapter 2) and so many visitors had enjoyed, finally disappeared. Strange as it may seem, the alterations made to the bye-laws to restrict the speed of cars came six years before further changes allowing bicycles to be ridden and perambulators to be pushed into parks (although prams had appeared in numerous photographs of parks taken well before 1928).

MARBLES AND EGGS

The game of marbles was extremely popular during the 1920s. Ormeau Park
became the Mecca for the top marble players, who met on Thursday evenings for
tournaments. Their skill was such that some could 'drop one marble right on top
of another'. The marbles men reputedly played better when a band was performing – the music urged them on to greater heights. Ormeau was also the site for egg
rolling at Eastertime. Eggs that had been prepared in the time-honoured fashion
(chapter 1) were taken to the park and 'trilled' (or rolled) at Dummy's Hill. The
exact position of this hill is uncertain, but may coincide with the hillock near the
Ravenhill Road bowling green, sometimes referred to as the 'Fairy Hill'. Some of
those who came bearing eggs for rolling may have crossed the river by means of
the ferry which ran from Balfour Avenue, off the Ormeau Road, to Ormeau Park.
The price of this crossing was one halfpenny. It was run by contractor Tom Boyce,
who also supplied boats for the Waterworks (chapter 4).

GRAVE PROBLEMS WITH HORSES

The cemeteries too had their fair share of incidents. In 1919 a lady was arrested for
stealing two bunches of cut flowers from a grave at the City Cemetery. She subsequently appeared before the authorities. In the same year two of the horses used at
the cemetery were 'off work' for a time. One developed mange while the other, a

bay, was reported to have gone lame. In the event neither horse returned to work at the cemetery. An 'equine vandal' was observed one day at Dundonald Cemetery. The animal was pulling a coach, presumably containing relatives visiting a grave, when it was startled by a passing train. It bolted and damaged three tomb railings in the cemetery before being brought under control.

The high standards of horticulture at Botanic Gardens continued into the twentieth century, as illustrated by this planting near the Tropical Ravine (background) and the curator's house (right), 1913.

FLOWER SHOWS AND GARDEN PARTIES

The tradition of holding events in Botanic Gardens, begun in the early years of the nineteenth century, continued into the twentieth century. On 25 July 1913 the Irish Rose and Floral Society organised a flower show. A similar event for the following year was planned but had to be cancelled at the last minute. After the First World War garden parties were organised frequently. In 1921 parties were held by the Presbyterian General Assembly and by Lord and Lady Londonderry. One such garden party with six thousand guests was described in 1923 by the *Belfast News-Letter* as a 'pretty and animated scene'.

NEW PARKS

From the opening of Victoria Park in 1906 until 1920 there were no new parks formed in Belfast. Then, in the space of a few years, several new properties were opened, including Bellevue Pleasure Gardens off the Antrim Road (chapter 9),

Musgrave Park and Drumglass Playcentre on the Lisburn Road, and Glenbank Park off the Crumlin Road.

MUSGRAVE PARK

At the end of the Council meeting on 20 February 1920 the Lord Mayor announced that before coming into the chamber he had received a 'most important and interesting communication from Mr Henry Musgrave, DL, that veteran gentleman who always had the interest of the City and the citizens at heart'. The Town Clerk then read out a letter in which Henry Musgrave offered lands known as the Model Farm to the Corporation. The following is an excerpt:

> Believing that it is desirable that a public park should be provided for that end of the City, I have pleasure in offering, through you, to hand over to the Municipality the entire Model Farm premises as held by one under the Rt. Hon Sir W. G. Ellison McCartney, KCMG, the lands to be used at the discretion of the Corporation either for a public park or for educational purposes.

The reading of the letter was greeted with spontaneous applause. The offer included the Balmoral Industrial School and immediate grounds, a total area of 111 acres. The Corporation announced that 60 acres were to be set aside for a park while a strip of land adjacent to Stockman's Lane was to be reserved and possibly let for building purposes.

The Cemetery and Public Parks Committee was given permission to begin work on the park before the conveyance was finalised. This meant that labour could be carried out under the scheme for relief of unemployment, managed by the Lord St David's Unemployment Grants Committee (with the establishment of the Government of Northern Ireland in 1921, schemes for the relief of unemployment were administered by the Ministry of Labour – as in the case of Ormeau Park). Plans for the layout of the first section of Musgrave Park were drawn up by the Superintendent of Parks, James Davies, and work began on 18 October 1921. Landscaping work in the 1920s was labour-intensive: this first stage employed 100 men for fifteen weeks. It then took 150 men a further six months to lay out the second, third and fourth sections at a total cost of £12,694.

Musgrave Park was officially opened in 1924 by Lady Edith Dixon of Wilmont. The farmlands given so generously by Henry Musgrave had been successfully transformed into a recreational public park with shrubberies, a rock garden on the brow of a hill and an ornamental lake and islands.

THE GREEN RIDGE

Henry Musgrave lived at Drumglass House, not far from where Musgrave Park was being developed. He had been elected and admitted as an Honorary Burgess of the City of Belfast in 1917, illustrating the high esteem in which he was held by his fellow citizens. Sadly he died on 2 January 1922 before Musgrave Park was finished.

In his will Henry Musgrave bequeathed six acres of his Drumglass property, between his stables and the Lisburn Road, to be used and maintained as a public park or children's playground. A wall was built from the stables to Cranmore Park to delimit the area. The name Drumglass means the 'green ridge' or 'green hill', an

Glenbank House and gardens: the house was demolished in the mid-1920s when the gardens were laid out as Glenbank Park.

appropriate definition for a park. Henry Musgrave's house and remaining ground became part of Victoria College Girls' School. Drumglass House dates from before 1860, when it ranked among the most prestigious houses in the Malone area and was valued at £200. The gate lodge on the Lisburn Road (now in the park) was the original lodge for the estate. It was built in Queen Anne Revival style around 1882, and replaced an earlier villa erected in 1854. The Musgrave monogram appears above one of the doorways and on the sandstone tops to the gate pillars: a small reminder of previous times.

The park was titled Drumglass Playcentre (although it is often locally referred to as Cranmore Park or Marlborough Park), and was officially opened by the Lady Mayoress of Belfast, Lady Turner, on 9 September 1924.

GLENBANK PARK

The first mention of Glenbank as a park occurs in the minutes of the Cemetery and Public Parks Committee dated 29 May 1920 when, only three months after the letter from Henry Musgrave, another correspondence was read out. This time the benefactor was G. Herbert Ewart, then Director of William Ewart and Son Ltd. The firm offered the Corporation the 'house and grounds of about $7^1/_2$ acres known as Glenbank House ... for use as a public park'. The deal included free rent, subject to the company's water rights, and was on a long-term lease of 967 years running from 1883. The offer was gratefully accepted and ratified by the Corporation the following month. The statutory resolution to establish a park 'of inestimable benefit to the residents in the Ligoniel district' was passed on January 1921. That year the firm added a further three-quarters of an acre to square off the shape of the park.

As with Musgrave, James Davies supervised the work of laying out Glenbank Park, once again using labour under the scheme for the relief of unemployment. Fifty-three men were employed for four months at a cost of £3,000. The Ewart family contributed funds to set up a children's corner with playground equipment. The Improvement Committee, on request, was granted permission to widen the road beside the park, an exercise that involved 'stealing' a narrow strip of land from the perimeter.

THE EWART FAMILY HOME

Towards the end of the eighteenth century Glenbank had been owned by the Sinclairs, who also owned the bleachgreen at what is now the City Cemetery (chapter 5). By 1823, however, a Mr Grogan was recorded as residing at Glenbank. By the middle of the nineteenth century the Ewart family had acquired the estate. The Ewarts were linen manufacturers, with a large mill sited on the Crumlin Road and a bleachgreen beside Glenbank. Glenbank House was home to three generations of the family. William Ewart was Mayor of Belfast in 1859–60 and, in subsequent years, other members of the family took an active part in municipal affairs. The last of the family to reside at Glenbank was Lavens Matthew Ewart, JP, one of the founder members of the *Ulster Journal of Archaeology*. He died in December 1898 and was buried in the family grave at Clifton Street Graveyard.

Mrs Herbert Ewart officially handed over the property on 18 August 1923 and the new park was declared open by the Lady Mayoress. A proposal to demolish Glenbank House was passed a month later. The building had been vacant for some years and was in need of structural repair. It had been suggested that the building could be used as a branch library, but the expense involved and the unsuitability of the interior design resulted in the idea being abandoned. The ground where the house stood was levelled and terraced with flower beds. Some of the underground cellars remained intact, as parks' staff discovered in the 1980s when a flower bed and gardener sank into them through a hole that suddenly appeared in the ground.

The seven-acre park may be small and relatively unknown outside of the locality, but it has provided pleasure over the years to many, not least because of its attractive setting and views over Belfast. By the time Glenbank and Musgrave Parks were opened, memories of the First World War were receding, and there was time to enjoy outdoor recreation and facilities in parks – the recession of the 1930s was still beyond the horizon.

8
Let's Play
Open Space, Playgrounds
and Recreation

s early as 1896 Belfast Corporation received complaints from the Moravian Church about unruly gatherings on rough ground beside its church building at the junction of the Lisburn Road and Malone Road. This land, which formed a tunnel over the railway, had been transferred to the Corporation from the Great Northern Railway Company in 1891. As such it could be considered to be Belfast's very first municipal open space, in contrast to the enclosed public parks. For such a small site it was to have a turbulent history.

The complaints of 1896 were only the beginning. Further incidents occurred, including one in which some of the site chairs were damaged. In an attempt to upgrade the area the Corporation planted it out with grass and shrubs to form a garden, which was looked after by the superintendent of Botanic Gardens. Further unrest forced the Corporation to enclose the garden with railings, raising the question whether the site was still an open space or the smallest enclosed park in Belfast. At any rate the railings enabled the site to be closed to the public on Monday and Wednesday evenings during services in the Moravian Church, thus preventing

King William Park: established in 1891 but only officially named in 1964, this is probably the smallest enclosed park in Belfast.

BELFAST CITY COUNCIL

disturbance to worshippers. Some years later the church used the garden to hold outdoor meetings. In 1927 an advertising company applied to have an 'Empire' advertising hoarding erected on site. The garden was first referred to as King William Park in 1947, but it was not officially given this title until much later, in January 1964. Tradition has it that King William of Orange stopped nearby on his way south in 1690.

PUBLIC OPEN SPACE

The idea of small open spaces grew in popularity at the start of the twentieth century. In 1903 a suggestion was made to try St Anne's Market as an experimental public space, but no record was made regarding the success or failure of this. The Open Spaces Act of 1906 enabled local authorities to create open spaces with free public access, and gave power to 'lay out, plant, improve and maintain lands for the purpose of being used as public walks or pleasure grounds'. This function notwithstanding, the Act was primarily aimed at facilitating the transfer of disused burial grounds into public ownership. Hence the Board of Guardians offered a portion of its paupers' burial ground on the Donegall Road to the Corporation. The ground was no longer needed for burials and was proposed as a suitable open space. It was accepted by the Corporation and later developed into a children's playground (chapter 12).

By the 1920s there was public open ground at Eastland Street, Matchett Street, Abbey Street, Lilliput Street, Shore Road, Peter's Hill, Scotch Row (Ballymacarrett), Little York Street, Henry Street and Westland Street. A site at Peter's Hill had a particularly brief lifespan as an open space. It was asphalted and equipped with garden seats as a 'resting place for aged-people', but was soon closed due to vandalism and trouble in the area. It later vanished altogether under the extension to the Peter's Hill Baths.

The Cemetery and Public Parks Committee set up an Open Spaces Subcommittee to manage these public sites. This meant considering proposals that were not always practical or financially viable. Not surprisingly, the suggestion to build an outdoor swimming pool in the open space at Little York Street and Henry Street was not followed up. It also meant having to deal with problems of maintenance: for example, very little seems to have been done with the area at Eastland Street other than enclosing it with railings in 1904. These were vandalised and the area became little more than a neglected piece of tarmac. Complaints soon flowed in. It was described in 1922 by the Town Clerk as a 'nuisance and a menace to the neighbourhood'. The ground at Matchett Street fared little better. It was left to 'take care of itself' at first, before being levelled and asphalted so that the local children would 'have no facility for damaging houses by throwing stones, as there will be none to throw'. Because of the railings and enclosed nature of the site it was nicknamed a 'closed space' instead of an open one.

All in all it was not a very auspicious start to the provision of public open spaces.

PLAYGROUNDS

The Open Spaces Subcommittee was also detailed to examine children's play equipment as early as 1911, with the ultimate aim of turning some of these open spaces into playgrounds. The group visited Dungannon to view play equipment, a trip that may well have provided inspiration as two years later the playground in Ormeau Park was operational.

A further nine years passed before a deputation of the Cemetery and Public Parks Committee visited sites in Manchester, Birmingham and Liverpool to research the playgrounds there. The members were impressed by what they found: these three cities had about 1,500 acres of parkland each, compared with 420 acres in Belfast. The deputation was particularly interested in the sand gardens provided for children in Manchester. These were fenced-off areas where no children were admitted unless they were 'reasonably clean'. The Manchester Corporation supplied the spades and flags for playing in the sand, and a female supervisor to watch the children. Seeing this encouraged Belfast councillors to provide similar sand gardens in Belfast, such as those at Hemsworth Street, Drumglass Playcentre and Bellevue (chapter 9).

By the end of the 1920s there were playgrounds in Ormeau, Falls, Alexandra, Glenbank and Victoria Parks and additional playgrounds (referred to as playcentres) at Drumglass, Eastland Street, Donegall Road, Scotch Row, Henry Street, Clara Street, Boundary Street and Hemsworth Street. The last site was also known as 'The Hammer', because local children used to play tig with hammers on the waste ground. In 1929 one acre of ground at North Queen Street became available due to road widening. McLaughlin and Harvey Ltd, engaged to carry out the construction work, agreed to enclose and lay out the surplus ground as a playground free of charge. The firm also installed the play equipment as a memorial to the late William Henry McLaughlin, the former head of the firm, who had worked for the greater part of his career in the area. The Corporation gratefully accepted the generous offer. The site, which had an estimated value of £2,500, became known as Castleton Playground.

CHANGE OF TITLE

In October 1924 the name of the main committee was changed from the Cemetery and Public Parks Committee to the Public Parks and Playgrounds Committee, reflecting the increase in popularity of the playgrounds. Cemetery affairs were dealt with by a Cemetery Subcommittee. It was felt to be something of an anomaly to have the supervision of Falls and Dunville Parks under the cemetery superintendent, and the rest of the parks and the City Hall grounds under the Superintendent of Parks. Consequently the responsibility for Falls and Dunville was transferred to James Davies, then Superintendent of Parks.

One of the first roles of the new Public Parks and Playgrounds Committee was to establish and enforce bye-laws covering the use of playground facilities. Separate sections and equipment were to be provided for boys and girls, and for very young children, with 'ample accommodation for their parents and friends to sit and look on'. Drumglass Playcentre was to be set up as a role model for children's playgrounds. Women were appointed to several sites to organise suitable playtime and games, and to supervise the children. Music was provided once a month in the larger centres by the band of the Balmoral Boys' School. It was recommended that shelters, toilets and drinking fountains should be provided, and the

Corporation noted that 'when the grounds are opened, and for some little time, it may be necessary to employ a man to supervise; but this should be a matter of careful consideration'. Men were, in fact, subsequently employed in a number of playcentres.

During the 1930s offers of land for playgrounds and open space came thick and fast to the Committee. Additional playgrounds were established at Willowbank (on ground purchased from Celtic Football Club), Roden Street, Springfield Road, Mersey Street, Woodstock Road, Frederick Street, Hay Market, York Street (on ground offered by Gallahers Tobacco Firm), Severn Street (on land obtained from Belfast and County Down Railway and extended with ground given by Gallahers at Connswater) and Boundary Street.

In 1930 a loan was raised to landscape and furnish a small area, to be named Queen Mary's Gardens, at the junction of the Cave Hill Road and Antrim Road, beside the Waterworks. A rest area, tennis courts, playground, drinking fountain and flagpole had been installed by the time the site was officially opened by the Lady Mayoress on 8 July 1931, although the month of June is engraved into the iron-work above the gate.

STREET PLAY

Under the Belfast Corporation Act (NI) 1930, certain streets were closed to traffic between set times to allow children under fifteen to play in them. Coates Street, Balaclava Street and Howard Street South were included under this scheme, but there were immediate complaints from residents and from the police authority about traffic disruption. Despite these concerns the scheme continued into the 1950s, by which time the selected streets were being closed from 10.00 a.m. to 11.00 p.m.

RECREATIONAL FACILITIES

The first bowling green to be opened was the Park Road green in Ormeau Park, which saw its first ends played in 1892. Such was the attraction of the sport that a companion green had to be laid, using turf brought from Castlerock, County Londonderry, in 1911. The green at Musgrave Park was opened in 1926 with an official ceremony; on the same day the putting green was opened 'without ceremony'!

By the end of the 1920s the range of recreational facilities in parks was increasing rapidly. The number of pitches, courts, greens and creases indicated the rise in popularity of using parks for sport. In all there were forty-five tennis courts for public use, six putting greens, eight bowling greens (then in all parks except Dunville), twenty-three cricket creases – both grass and matting – four hockey pitches and thirty-four football pitches. From time to time permission was given for informal games such as rounders and bicycle polo to be played.

Along with the pitches came the plethora of associated buildings – bowling pavilions, changing rooms and ticket kiosks – although often players had to wait a considerable time before these facilities were added, making do in the meantime with temporary structures or none at all. The tennis pavilion in Falls Park, for example, was erected in 1933 to serve courts that had been laid out before the turn of the century.

The question of a municipal golf course was raised on several occasions. Plans for a miniature golf course at Hazelwood (chapter 13) were in progress and the course at Ormeau was being well used, but some felt the need to provide a true municipal golf course somewhere in Belfast. Cliftonville and Fortwilliam were inspected as possible venues but due to financial restraints the proposals were not followed through.

The parks were used for more casual recreation as well as formal organised sport. By the 1930s the band of the Royal Ulster Constabulary was performing on average fifty times per season. The Corporation paid the salary of the conductor and provided his uniform, the musical instruments and music, as well as a room for rehearsals. For those who simply came to the park for a walk or to sit in the open, there were shelters, which generally were simple wooden structures such as those erected in Botanic Gardens and Drumglass in 1933. Around that time photographer John Hoy was given a licence to take what he called 'While You Wait' photographs in a number of parks. These early Polaroids were developed using a tin plate rather than a negative. It was not unusual for a photographer to bring with him a van that served as a portable darkroom.

DUFF'S SHOP

At Victoria Park, William Duff, a former chief engineer on the SS *Magnetic*, built a wooden shed to use as a shop where he sold sweets, drinks, windmills, buckets and spades, balls and kites. When Duff died the thriving business was taken over by 'Granda' Robinson, who kept a grey parrot in a cage hanging from the ceiling of the shop, no doubt to the great delight of local children.

WATER SPORTS

The boating lake at Victoria Park continued to be popular, and the sailing of model boats was commonplace on the ponds at Victoria, Ormeau, Falls, Woodvale and Alexandra Parks and Botanic Gardens. Many a wooden sailing ship was manoeuvred around the ponds by proud owners using long bamboo poles wit rubber-covered hooks on the end. When the ponds froze over in winter young, and not so young, ice-skaters took to them, regardless of any danger. But the water features were not always looked upon so favourably. After complaints about the stagnant and foul-smelling water, the last pond in Botanic Gardens was filled in during the 1920s. The ponds in Ormeau, Musgrave and Woodvale Parks survived a little longer, but were filled in after the end of the Second World War (chapter 10).

Outdoor swimming pools were constructed at Victoria Park and at Falls Park. In 1923 it was proposed to section off a portion of the Victoria lake at the back of the island as an outdoor swimming pool. This was to be 100 feet wide and 400 feet long, with six dressing boxes and a springboard. The dimensions were quickly reduced to 30 feet by 150 feet and the position changed to the far corner of the park. The original boys' swimming pool at Victoria (chapter 6) was relegated to being the children's pool once the new pond was opened. The inlet on the northwest side of the park became known as the 'sucking bottle' because of its resemblance to a baby's feeding bottle.

Many swimming galas, diving competitions and water polo matches were held over the years at the outdoor swimming pool at Falls Park, which was known locally as 'The Cooler'; *c.* 1960.

BELFAST CITY COUNCIL

The open-air pool at Falls Park was known locally as 'The Cooler' – a reference perhaps to the temperature! It was officially opened on 13 August 1924 by the Lord Mayor, Alderman Sir William Turner. He was invited to take the first plunge, but Councillor McAlevey came to his rescue and dived from the springboard (with an 'emphatic splash') to open the pool. The Clonard Swimming Club followed this with a programme of swimming exhibitions, races, diving competitions and water polo matches.

The pool cost £3,000 to construct. The second-largest outdoor swimming pool in the United Kingdom, it measured 200 feet by 160 feet and held 650,000 gallons of cold water. The water reached a depth of six feet at the deep end, where there was a diving board. The pool was fed by the mountain stream in Falls Park and took several days to fill up each season after being drained over the winter. The normal charge for swimming was 2d for adults and 1d for children. Sadly, only a week after the opening, there was a tragic drowning accident.

Bathing was also permitted at the Waterworks, which at that time was not in Belfast Corporation's ownership. The former reservoirs were ideal for large-scale swimming galas, and for diving demonstrations such as those performed by the Brown sisters from Bangor in 1930. They were part of a team that did stunts and high diving at outdoor pools around the country. Speedboat racing, hydroplane racing and water polo were introduced to the upper pond about that time, and model yacht sailing, which had been popular many years earlier, was revived. For the benefit of would-be anglers, the middle basin was stocked with trout from the

Water Commissioners' hatchery at Oldpark. Fishing was also allowed at Alexandra Park.

FIRST PLAYING FIELD SITES

Until the 1930s, despite the provision of recreational and sporting facilities, parks were mainly used for passive recreation: fresh air, relaxing, walking and enjoyment of flowers. It could be argued that they had been used as a mechanism of enforcing social reform. The bye-laws and their prohibitions exemplify this – for example, the banning of drinking and bad language in public. From the 1930s onwards there was much more emphasis placed on active recreation and sport. The National Playing Field Association set ideal standards whereby there should be six acres of space for active recreation per one thousand people, as opposed to only one acre for passive recreation. The consequence of this was the growing separation of active and passive recreation and the establishment of playing field sites principally set aside for sporting activities, although several properties initiated at that time did not come into full public use until twenty or thirty years later.

THE HOUSE AT GROVE

Many of the sites that were destined to become playing fields had, in common with parks, their origins in the private estates of Belfast. A typical example was Grove Playing Fields on the Shore Road, which was acquired by the Corporation in 1931 and became the first playing fields site to be established. The former estate was known as 'The Grove', and was occupied by James Carson up until 1810. It was purchased by William Simms whose grandson, also called William, sold the estate to John Sinclair. He pulled down the old house and built a new one. When he died the grounds were sold to Francis Ritchie. In the 1880s the house was quite extensive, with a small conservatory on the south side. Servants' quarters, estate buildings, two courtyards

Diving displays by the Brown sisters, seen here, and others were a common feature in the 1920s and 1930s at the Waterworks.

BELFAST TELEGRAPH

and glasshouses adjoined the rear of the house. The main entrance faced east and was reached by a sweeping driveway leading from York Road. The wooded grounds contained tennis courts, a summer house, rockeries, formal gardens and two gate lodges. By the 1920s the house had fallen into disrepair and there was an abandoned air to the grounds.

The Corporation raised a loan of £16,000 to purchase the Grove and commissioned photographer Andrew Hogg to take pictures of the site before any development occurred. It took several years for the work and layout of the site to be completed, although some football was played there from 1932. The property was officially opened to the public on 20 May 1936. Two years later a bowling

green, a pitch and putt course and a lengthy cinder cycle track were all part of the facilities on offer.

At that time the seeds of other playing field sites were being sown. Land at Orangefield, Grand Parade, Silverstream, Avoniel and Connswater was inspected and became, in time, Orangefield Playing Fields, Dixon Playing Fields, Ballysillan Playing Fields, Avoniel Playing Fields and playground (and subsequently leisure centre) and King George V Playing Fields respectively.

ORANGEFIELD

John Holmes Houston was one of four partners in the Belfast Banking Company established in 1808. He was at that time living at the estate of Orangefield in east Belfast with his cousin Eliza, to whom he was married. Their daughter Mary Isabella, born in 1793, married Richard Bayly Blakiston. The family joined names leaving J. Blakiston-Houston in charge of Orangefield from 1857. Orangefield House was sited at the end of what is now Houston Park, and the original estate once extended to almost three hundred acres. In 1934 Belfast Corporation was offered a portion of the land by the Blakiston-Houston Estate Company to develop as a public park. The Corporation, although keen to acquire the land, felt that the price was too high.

ARBITRATION

The Estate Company then decided to use the land for housing instead. In February 1937 Belfast Corporation ratified a decision of the Improvement Committee refusing the Estate Company permission to develop the land under Article 8 of the Belfast County Borough Interim Development Order (1934). Instead the Corporation reserved the ground for public recreation using its powers provided by the Housing and Town Planning Act. This decision was appealed by the Estate Company and a Ministry of Home Affairs inquiry was held in October of that year. As a result the Corporation agreed to pay a price set by arbitration to compensate the Estate Company for the land. The agreed price was £20,000, and was paid in 1938. The City Surveyor, speaking on the Corporation's behalf at the inquiry, stated that the site 'with its natural amenities, including trees and streams, lends itself very well to being allocated as a public park'. He went on to say that it 'would be nothing short of a calamity' if the land were not preserved.

The proposed park was to be over one hundred acres, made up from four pieces of land including forty-six acres acquired from the Boyd and Cleland Estate, and the disputed forty-five acres from the Blakiston-Houston Estate. In the event the ground from the Boyd and Cleland Estate was subsequently developed, reducing the area of the park to about fifty acres.

The Second World War put a hold on any development, and plans were not drawn up for the site until 1947. The specification included pitches for football, hockey and cricket, a pitch for bicycle polo (by then an officially recognised sport it seems), a bowling green, cycle track, pitch and putt course, tennis courts and a quoits and marbles pitch — as well as pavilions and store buildings. A row of pre-fabricated bungalows stood for nearly twenty years (despite originally having a ten-year lifespan) parallel to Manna Grove: they were demolished in the late 1960s to increase the park area for public use.

FIRST DIXON GIFT

Sir Thomas Dixon (of Sir Thomas and Lady Dixon Park fame) generously offered seven acres near Orangefield for use as playing fields. This was accepted in 1937 and combined with land along the Knock River donated by the Blakiston-Houston Estate to form one site. The extension of Grand Parade across the Dixon ground subsequently reduced the area of parkland. The playing fields were eventually opened on 29 June 1966 and initially entitled the Dixon Park after two members of the family, Sir Thomas Dixon and the Right Honourable Herbert Dixon. The name then evolved into Dixon Playing Fields, although it was known locally for a time as Grand Parade Playing Fields.

BALLYSILLAN PLAYING FIELDS

In reply to an advertisement in 1937 for land in the Shankill and Woodvale district, ground at Silverstream, Ballysillan, was examined and found suitable for sports use. Although the site became known as Ballysillan Playing Fields, the ground was outside the original Ballysillan estate. Ballysillan House, occupied by the Robb family, was positioned to the west of the present playing fields, across the Crumlin

Football was regularly played on the lower ground of Ormeau Park, across the river from the gasworks, 1937.

BELFAST TELEGRAPH

Road and near Mercy Primary School. The Corporation purchased twenty-five acres of land from a Miss Price and eleven from a Miss Dunbar. A loan of £10,150 to cover the cost of purchase and expenses was sanctioned by the Ministry of Home Affairs. A further sixteen acres from the Lyons Estate and two from the Victoria Estate were added to the total land – and an additional £5,000 to the total price. Some of the ground was given over to plots to be rented at £2 per acre (the same arrangement had been used at Orangefield) and the remainder (about forty-six acres) had to await the end of the war before development.

Plans were ambitious, incorporating facilities for soccer, Gaelic football, hockey, bicycle polo and cricket, along with a bowling green, cycle track, paddling pool, two playgrounds, six tennis courts, pavilions, shelters and a rest garden. On reflection the Public Parks and Playgrounds Committee decided that the costs were too high and the cycle track was taken out of the scheme.

KING GEORGE'S FIELD

In 1937 the King George National Memorial Fund announced a grant scheme for the purchase of grounds for playing fields and public recreational use. Any site purchased under the scheme was to be called King George's Field. In response the Committee looked at the Old Asylum property and ground at Avoniel, the estate lands of Avoniel House. In 1939 the Corporation raised a loan of just over £2,000 to add to a grant of £6,000 from the fund to buy this land from a range of owners including the Belfast Ropeworks Company and the Dixon Estate. Eleven acres were also acquired from the Distillers' Company for a nominal £5 and payment of annual rents. The area was occupied during the war by the military (chapter 10), halting any possible development. Because of the delay in derequisitioning the property at the end of the war, the title of King George's Fields was transferred to other land at Connswater and the grant spent on developing this. The property now known as King George V Playing Fields was finally opened on 28 April 1960, while the land at Avoniel eventually became Avoniel Playing Fields and later the site of one of Belfast's leisure centres (chapter 13).

A SWAMP FOR FOOTBALL

In 1930 twelve acres alongside the River Lagan were added to Botanic Gardens. This area was formerly a dumping ground and swamp, allotments during the First World War (chapter 7), and part of a dairy farm (in 1920 several farm cottages were still standing where the Queen's University PE Centre is today). Following the trend towards recreation facilities within parks, the Corporation laid out this lower ground with football pitches. Three years later the unusual Jaffé Memorial Fountain was moved from Victoria Square to a position in front of the gates near the King's Bridge (see photograph, p. 105). The monument, with its cast-iron octagonal canopy, had originally been erected in 1874 in memory of the linen merchant Daniel Joseph Jaffé, whose son, Sir Otto Jaffé, later became Lord Mayor of Belfast.

WHAT MIGHT HAVE BEEN

Not all proposals and ideas resulted in new properties. Between the two World Wars other areas were considered as possible public parks but for several reasons the suggestions were not followed up. In 1924 there was talk of a park being formed between the Crumlin Road and Oldpark Road. The site was investigated, but because of the high cost of laying out and equipping the area the idea was abandoned. In 1932 the Corporation declined options to purchase Pirrie Park, near the Ravenhill Road, and land at Beechmount, on the Falls Road. Two years later, the offer of forty-seven acres between the railway line and Knock River at Bloomfield was turned down, despite talk of the lack of public space in that area. A garden at Madrid Street and Albertbridge Road was mentioned briefly, while land offered at Strandtown Lodge and at Panton Street (near the Lower Falls Road) was considered unsuitable for public space.

The largest areas of land considered were four hundred acres at Bog Meadows, five hundred acres at Cave Hill (to come into public ownership much later – chapter 17) and over two hundred acres at Carrowreagh, Dundonald, planned as an extension to the cemetery. It is easy, with hindsight, to suggest that such offers should have been taken up and that opportunities were missed, but it is important to remember that the financial and social situations facing the Corporation when making decisions then were very different from today. Belfast Corporation, through its Public Parks and Playgrounds Committee, did create a good network of open spaces within Belfast that provided for a wide range of uses and interests. In the fifty years between 1871 (the first park opening) and 1921 the total area of open space and parkland had risen from one hundred acres (about one acre per seventeen hundred people) to over four hundred acres (about one acre per thousand people).

FLORAL DISPLAYS

Although playing fields had been laid out in the newer, lower portion of Botanic Gardens, the upper region continued to be run primarily for horticulture. By 1920 a new rockery consisting of limestone planted around with shrubs and alpines had replaced a small rockery scheme laid down by Charles McKimm some years earlier. The long borders had also been planted out with over one thousand dahlias, which attracted favourable comment in the press. The plant collections in the Palm House and Tropical Ravine were kept consistently to a high standard, despite setbacks such as the boilers bursting in the winter of 1928–9. In 1930 a major display of over four hundred chrysanthemums was set up at the entrance and cool wing of the Palm House, and two years later a rose garden was planted beyond the main lawn. This was laid out in an oval pattern bisected by a stone and timber pergola. Bedding displays were still continued in front of the Palm House, with the circular centre bed landscaped in the form of a raised crown bed.

Four budgerigars of different colours were presented to Botanic Gardens by Councillor Crawford McCullagh in 1931. The practice of giving exotic birds such as canaries, love birds and pheasants to the park continued for many years. They were housed in a small aviary on the east walk, near the rockery, called the Crawford McCullagh House. The aviary was later moved to Bellevue Zoo.

STAFF

By the time these birds were being handed over, James Davies had retired as Superintendent of Parks. George Horscroft, former curator at Glasgow Botanic Gardens, was appointed his successor in 1928 on a starting salary of £450 per year. He took up residence in the curator's house in Botanic Gardens. In the same year Horscroft was elected to the Association of Superintendents of Parks and Botanic Gardens. Under his supervision the Parks Department staff moved offices from the City Hall to the front gate lodge at Botanic Gardens in 1933. This accommodation was rather cramped, and ten years later Horscroft was investigating the possibility of a further move to Oakleigh House (on the Ravenhill Road beside Ormeau Park), which was owned by the Gas Committee and used as the home of the Gasworks Manager. These plans were shelved and the Department stayed put until the 1950s.

Throughout the city each park had a foreman responsible for the manual staff based there. The foremen reported to the Superintendent of Parks. Because of an increasing workload the post of Assistant Superintendent was established in 1933. By 1939 there were five members of office staff in the Parks Department – Superintendent, Assistant Superintendent, two junior clerks and a typist – and five in the Cemeteries Department. The two departments became one in 1942, and the committee was retitled yet again, this time the Parks and Cemeteries Committee. At the same time the two Superintendents' posts were amalgamated, a move facilitated by the retirement of D. McCann after fifty-two years' service, twenty-five of

Outdoor boxing tournaments
attracted large crowds in
Woodvale Park during the
1940s and 1950s.

BELFAST CITY COUNCIL

them as Superintendent of Cemeteries.

A pony and trap was purchased for the Superintendent of Parks and Cemeteries to make supervisory visits to properties, and a youth was employed to drive it. This mode of transport was replaced in 1946 by a departmental car (chapter 13). The pony, and some of the horses used within the parks, were housed in stables in Ormeau Park yard. The Corporation's livestock also included for a time a one-eyed donkey called 'Nellie'.

Notwithstanding the fact that only £39 10s 3d was set aside for purchasing plants in 1929, the horticultural reputation of the Parks Department blossomed during the 1930s. In 1932 alone, some 2,500,000 bedding plants, 81,000 wallflowers and 167,000 bulbs were planted in the parks. The nursery at Ormeau was recorded as containing 500,000 shrubs. The Parks staff regularly provided floral decorations for the interior of the City Hall, particularly for special events such as the visit by HRH the Prince of Wales in 1932 and the Royal Jubilee year of 1935. Plants ended up in a variety of places: the Superintendent was authorised to send flowers to local hospitals from time to time, and in 1929 the Police Committee requested that 'shrubs in tubs' be put into the underground toilets at Donegall Square North and in other 'public sanitary conveniences' in the city.

The Parks Department was involved in the plans for celebrating the coronation of Edward VIII on 12 May 1937. These included planting an oak tree in each park, erecting flags and flagpoles in playcentres, and organising band performances and a daylight fireworks display. In the event these plans were carried out – but for a

different king, George VI. The oak tree in Falls disappeared two weeks after planting, the one in Dunville a month later, and the one in Musgrave by October of that
year. Unfortunately the problem of vandalism, which had troubled the privately
owned Botanic Garden even before the onset of public parks, continued to plague
the Parks Department's work throughout successive generations.

BELLEVUE, BELFAST

9

The Tramways Legacy
Bellevue, Hazelwood and
Belfast Castle

Right up until the 1960s, Belfast Corporation's Tramways Committee (Transport Committee from 1938) owned and maintained three major parkland areas, Bellevue, Hazelwood and Belfast Castle Estate, all looked after by the same foreman. Over the years the Cemetery and Parks Committee, and later the Public Parks and Playgrounds Committee, kept a careful eye on these properties, expressing interest and concern about them on numerous occasions. Any debate about which committee should be in charge of them always came down on the side of the Tramways Committee, at least until 1962 when the Parks Department finally gained responsibility for them (chapter 13).

But let's start at the beginning.

TRAMS IN THE BAD LAND

The area known as Drumnadrough, meaning 'ridge of the bad land', which adjoined Whitewell Village on the Antrim Road, was the main depot of the

Hazelwood and Bellevue were popular destinations during the 1930s: attractions included the zoo (via the bus in the foreground), the café at Hazelwood (to the left in the trees), the Floral Hall and the pitch and putt course beyond.

POSTCARD

THE STEPS, BELLEVUE, BELFAST.   R. 502.

The grand staircase at Bellevue was decorated each year with flowers and fairy lights. A weighing machine stands to the right of the entrance area, *c.* 1935.

POSTCARD

Cavehill and Whitewell Tramway Company from 1882. This independent transport company ran a system of steam and horse traction tram cars between Whitewell and Chichester Park at the northern outskirts of Belfast.

Following the extension of the Belfast boundary line and the consequent need to extend the city tram system, Belfast Corporation acquired the line from the Company in 1911. The tram line, and a thirty-two-acre site that came with it, cost the Corporation a total of £64,500. It included depot buildings, which stood on level ground, and a former quarry area, comprising rough landslip and quarry refuse.

The General Manager of Belfast City Tramways was Andrew Nance, who was faced with the challenge of encouraging people to use the newly acquired line. He was something of a character and an entrepreneur. As the tramways manager he travelled free when he rode on the trams, and sat on the upper deck, puffing his cigar, while his wife paid her fare and sat downstairs. He had a dream of a tram system extending throughout the entire city, including a line from the junction of the Antrim Road and Cavehill Road to – wait for it – McArt's Fort on the very top of Cave Hill. He wanted the 'feeblest and oldest citizens' to be able to have access to the fort. Noble sentiments, but expensive – and somewhat impractical in engineering terms. The Corporation flatly turned down the idea.

THE NEW PLEASURE GARDENS

Andrew Nance came up with the proposal of transforming the depot area into gardens and playgrounds of a unique character. From June 1911 tickets issued by the Belfast Corporation read: 'The Glengormley Tramway is now worked by the Corporation. The trams run from Castle Junction and there is no change of car. Cheap fare, beautiful scenery. Tea houses and other attractions at the end of the line.

Look out for the opening of the new Bellevue Gardens.' The name Bellevue seems to have come into use from the time the Corporation took over the transport depot, and was probably transferred from an earlier amusement ground sited at Glengormley.

Despite the promise on the tickets, patrons had to wait nine years before the pleasure gardens were open. In 1913 a firm of landscape gardeners, Messrs Cheal & Sons Ltd of Crawley, began work that involved grading the rugged slopes, putting in a system of zigzag pathways, planting trees and shrubs, levelling and tarmacking the upper plateau, building a castellated wall around the perimeter of the plateau, and – the *pièce de résistance* – constructing a grand floral staircase. This stone stairway was divided into several flights and adorned with pillars and floral vases. It connected the Antrim Road to the upper plateau.

By any standards, the work was not easy: it involved an enormous amount of earth-moving, most of which was done by manual labour. It was also dogged by setbacks. Serious subsidence and slippage occurred, causing the boundary wall to bulge outwards and the staircase to fracture. Work ceased altogether just prior to the First World War, by which time some £29,000 had been spent. A new wooden tea house was almost complete when it was maliciously burned down in April 1914. The suffragette movement was blamed but its involvement never proved. At any rate the incident brought calls to abandon the entire scheme at Bellevue.

Eventually the Tramways Committee revived interest in the site after the war and authorised reconstruction and repair work to begin early in 1920. Finally, on 10 July of that year, the gardens were officially opened to the public by the Lord Mayor, Councillor Sir W.F. Coates. A plaque (now at the entrance to the zoological gardens) stated simply that it was 'Erected to the memory of Andrew Nance Esq., General Manager, Belfast City Tramways 1904–1916, in recognition of his great services and vision in developing this property as pleasure grounds'.

BANDSTANDS AND PLATFORMS

A programme of bands was arranged for the opening weeks, each band being paid £10 for a performance. Anything of a 'cheap and questionable nature' was not tolerated. All performers were required to 'maintain a high standard of excellence with regard to moral values'. If they did not, they were not invited back. The following season several famous bands were brought over from England to play at Bellevue. Because these performances were always attended by large crowds and the band had to play in a temporary wooden bandstand with no roof, the Corporation commissioned a new stand. W. MacFarlane & Company of Glasgow built an octagonal, cast-iron bandstand with a revolving glass screen for Bellevue plateau at a cost of £1,080. There was seating for about five hundred people around it. (The stand was later moved down the hill towards the Antrim Road and used for a time, without the glass screen, to house racoons in the zoo.) In 1923 a large open-air dancing platform was laid out at the foot of the cliffs. Music for the outdoor dancing was provided by a Stentorphone – a large acoustic gramophone housed in a wooden hut beside the platform. Admission to the floor was 3d. This facility remained until 1934.

The entrance to Hazelwood on the Antrim Road, with a queue waiting for the bus up to Bellevue Zoo. The tramlines are visible in the foreground.

BELFAST CITY COUNCIL

BELFAST'S HANGING GARDENS

In the 1920s Bellevue became a popular destination for day excursions, particularly at Easter, partly replacing the traditional migration to the Cave Hill at that time of year. As well as band performances and open-air dancing, there were concert parties, amusements and fireworks displays. A children's week in 1931 included entertainers the Olva Trio and their performing horse 'Beauty', a juggler, a flying trapeze artist, acrobats and equilibrists. Donkey rides were provided for children throughout the season. The floral staircase was decorated during the summer months from top to bottom with flowers.

Belfast had never seen anything quite like Bellevue Pleasure Gardens. They made such an impression on visitors that they were described as a 'unique possession amongst the municipal corporations of the British Isles'. Sir Robert Meyer, Town Clerk in 1922, was equally profuse in his description: 'Besides its scenery and ozone-laden air, Bellevue has a variety of charms which make it a never-ending source of enjoyment from its historical, antiquarian, geological and botanical association.' The gardens were also compared favourably with the famous Hanging Gardens of Babylon (possibly by someone who was not well travelled!) at a time when they were not even complete. A visiting Guards bandmaster termed the place 'God's own Cathedral', because of the spectacular cliff faces behind the plateau. At that time there was an allegation that Sunday band performances at Bellevue were drawing people away from evening worship: perhaps they were simply exchanging their own churches for this outside 'cathedral'.

THE WOODS OF HAZEL

In 1922 the Corporation seized the opportunity of extending its holding in north Belfast by acquiring the estate of Hazelwood, separated from neighbouring Bellevue only by a mountain stream. The Tramways Committee purchased the property for £7,000. The acquisition included forty-six acres of mountain slopes, a fort at Ballygolan, and Hazelwood House, which had been home to Ebenezer Reid for five or six years and to the Grant family before that. The Reids kept a collection of animals that included goats, ducks, a pony, a donkey, peafowl and rabbits: perhaps a forerunner of the menageries to come. There was a tennis court to the front of the house, and a winding switchback driveway from the Antrim Road. The family regularly entertained bandsmen in the house whenever they played at Bellevue.

The Superintendent of Parks, James Davies, together with the superintendent of Bellevue, T.D. Murray, inspected the site and reported back to the Tramways Committee with plans and costings. Their report included costs of forming a lake at Ballygolan, which was tantamount to re-forming the one that had once surrounded the ancient crannog or lake-centred dwelling (chapter 17). Under the Ministry of Labour's relief scheme, one hundred labourers were to be employed for one year at a cost of £12,000 – an average of £120 per annum each. The Cemetery and Public Parks Committee authorised James Davies to assist with the landscaping, which was finished by June 1924.

CAFÉ HAZELWOOD

The main dwelling of the estate, Hazelwood House, was converted into a restaurant by knocking down dividing walls to provide more spacious dining

Looking across to Bellevue from Hazelwood café (formerly Hazelwood House). The amusement park is sited at the north end of the plateau.

MAGNI/ULSTER MUSEUM

rooms. It became known as Café Hazelwood and was featured in many early photographs and postcards – the conservatory to the rear of the house was instantly
recognisable. Children's playground equipment was installed during the 1920s. But
a new development was to transform the pleasure gardens and give the public a
totally different image with which to associate the name Bellevue.

A ZOOLOGICAL COLLECTION – AT WHAT PRICE?

An offer of exotic waterfowl and a zoological collection in and around the pond
in Musgrave Park was dismissed in 1924 as unworkable. Nine years later a similar
suggestion was made with regard to the gardens at Bellevue. There was much private and public debate, with many letters both for and against the idea appearing
in the press. One reader of the *Belfast News-Letter* thought it more 'merciful to shoot
a lion or a tiger than to give it life-long imprisonment in a cage'. That comment
was signed 'A Friend of Animals'. The opposite view was presented by 'A Lover of
Animals' who claimed the eagle that was chained up 'would otherwise have been
tearing poor little birds to pieces with his horrible beak and claws'.

The Tramways Committee received a deputation of objectors. The group included some ladies who were wearing 'every skin you could mention, with the exception of bear skin'. The 'cruelty to animals' that their fur coats represented was
pointed out to them in no uncertain terms. It somewhat weakened their case. On
the other side councillors put forward the argument that the zoo would provide 'an
education and an entertainment', keep people 'out of the public houses' and
encourage them to 'learn from the jungle'.

Finally Belfast Corporation decided to proceed with the idea of an animal collection on the basis that it would lead to greater use of the trams and more profit
for the Tramways Committee, and gave assurances that the project would not add
anything to the city's rates. G.B. Chapman Ltd of London, one of the largest deal-
ers and importers of animals and birds in the world at that time, offered a collection of animals to be exhibited during the summer months for two or three
seasons. Between June and September 1933 over 200,000 people paid admission to
view the cages which were arranged in a circle on the plateau area. The admission
was 4d for adults, 2d for children, and 15 per cent of the takings was paid to
Chapman's.

Encouraged by this success, and prompted by an offer of financial contribution
from Chapman's, the Tramways Committee decided to establish a proper
Zoological Garden. Further protests about the plans resulted in a public inquiry
being held. It was conducted by Rear Admiral Archdale CBE in the City Hall in
November 1933 and upheld the Corporation's decision to apply for a loan of
£8,000 to develop a zoo.

Twelve acres on both sides of the grand staircase were laid out with cages and a
rock garden, at a cost of £10,000. The rockery was planted out with alpines,
heathers and dwarf shrubs. Some of the enclosures along the lower ground adjacent to the Antrim Road were not completed until after 1935. Nevertheless, on 28
March 1934, the new Bellevue Zoo was officially opened by the Lord Mayor, Sir
Crawford McCullagh. He was presented with a gold key by Mr Woods on behalf
of Chapman's, whose contribution amounted to £2,000 along with further

animals. In 1934 Belfast Zoo entertained 284,713 visitors. The entrance charge was slightly more than to the initial animal collection: 6d for adults and 3d for children.

A MODERN ZOO

Many of the visitors travelled to Bellevue by tram. The General Electric Company erected neon signs at Castle Junction, advertising both Bellevue and Hazelwood as exciting destinations. The Tramways Committee annual report commented that 'the achievement of negotiating, planning and completing the greater scheme, in presenting to the public one of the most modern and up-to-date zoological gardens in the kingdom was all accomplished within the year'.

There is little doubt that the attraction of the zoo did increase the use of the trams. The fare from the city centre to Bellevue on a tramcar was 2d for adults, half price for children. The buses were slightly dearer at 3d for adults. During July and August children on holiday from school were able to travel on the tramcars for a concessionary fare of $1/_2$d. Once inside the zoo visitors could purchase an official guidebook for 2d. This illustrated guide included a map of the layout of the zoo and natural history notes on the animals written by Richard (Dicky) Hunter, the zoological adviser to the zoo, who was a lecturer at Queen's University and ringmaster at the Christmas stage circuses performed at the Hippodrome in Belfast.

To lift passengers from the Antrim Road to the upper plateau three Dennis 'toast-rack' buses provided transport through the Hazelwood property along the former driveway to Hazelwood House. The fittest, and those who could not afford the bus,

The steeply sloping site at Bellevue Zoo meant that visitors had to be almost as agile as the monkeys in this early enclosure.

climbed to the top by means of a steep flight of steps alongside the stream. Visitors could then meander down the system of zigzag paths which had been laid out as part of the pleasure gardens. The grand staircase, which bisected the zoo without actually being included in it, could be crossed by means of either a narrow tunnel near the top or an elevated wooden walkway near the monkey house.

Many events were staged at Bellevue to encourage even bigger crowds. In 1937 there was a 'Zoo Baby Week' when young lions, goats, tigers, ponies, wolves, black bears and deer were put on show. The most popular animals were given names: the baby elephant that arrived in the first years of the zoo was christened 'Sheila'.

All aboard the 'toast-rack' tram to ride up to Bellevue Zoo.
BELFAST CITY COUNCIL

A MINIATURE RAILWAY

A miniature railway ran along the inner edge of the Bellevue plateau between 1934 and 1941. It had a gauge of fifteen inches, a track length of one-quarter of a mile and two stations. The one to the southern end was called Bell Hazel Station (a combination of Bellevue and Hazelwood) and the other simply Bellevue Park. A steam engine pulled three carriages with up to seventy-two excited children at one time. The engine, called the 'Bug', was constructed by the German firm Krauss for an exhibition in Munich in 1926. It worked the Romney, Hythe and Dymchurch line (for the rhd Railway Company) in England for several years before being bought by an amusement park operator in Blackpool. From there it was transferred to Belfast.

On the day of the opening of the zoo, the engine was renamed 'Sir Crawford', after the Lord Mayor, who actually drove it on its inaugural run, but no nameplates with the Lord Mayor's name were ever added. After an appropriate length of time the engine was again renamed, this time 'Jean'. One incident of vandalism is recorded when the rails were packed with stones one night, causing Jean to be derailed. Repairs to the track and rolling stock took several days. The engine, stored for a time by Belfast Corporation after the line closed, was later

The steam engine 'Jean', formerly named the 'Bug', worked the miniature railway at Bellevue for over thirty years.
WILLIAM ROBB

discovered in a scrapyard about 1969 and bought by a Mr McAlpine who sold it back to the RHD Railway. It was later used at the Liverpool Garden Festival in 1985.

In the mid-1930s the entire plateau area was occupied with the miniature railway, the bandstand and seating, a children's playground and an amusement park provided by Harry Kamiya of Blackpool. The amusement park had water dodgem boats, auto-scooter cars, a fairy wheel and roundabouts, as well as smaller attractions

such as a shooting range, a House of Thrills and a Brownie coaster. Kamiya, who was also responsible for running the miniature railway and who had originally brought the Bug to Belfast, had a seven-year lease for the park, which ran until 1940. The lease was renewed under altered terms because of a reduction in business due to the war and by 1943 had been transferred to a Mr Gordon. He ran the amusements until 1949, by which time many of the rides were not working and the area had fallen into disrepair.

The Floral Hall, opened in 1936, became renowned as a dance venue on Friday and Saturday nights, and as a place to sit and relax on a Sunday afternoon by Ballygolan Lake.

MAGNI/ULSTER MUSEUM

A DANCE HALL

In 1933 a proposal was made to build a dance hall on either the Bellevue or Hazelwood site, possibly beside the dance floor at Bellevue. The firm, Stewart & Partners, put together plans and an estimate of £21,900. Although the Ministry of Home Affairs had promised a grant of £15,000, the Corporation felt that to raise a loan for the remainder would seriously hinder the development of the zoological gardens. The proposal was therefore abandoned. A year later, however, the idea was back on the agenda and tenders were invited for the construction of what was being termed a floral hall on a site just inside the Hazelwood boundary. The firm of J. & R.W. Taggart won the contract and built a hall at a cost of just £9,520 to a design by D.W. Boyd. Interior furnishings cost a further £5,000.

The Floral Hall, a fine example of Art Deco-style architecture, was opened by Sir

Crawford McCullagh on 4 May 1936. The ballroom had a diameter of eighty-five feet and could seat one thousand people. There was a stage opposite the main entrance, a small balcony that overlooked the main auditorium, and a terrace café at one side. The original interior colour scheme was blue and gold, and the entrance hall was painted tangerine.

The Floral Hall opened with a week of live shows, although dancing very quickly became the most popular activity. Admission to an evening's dancing was 2s double and 1s 6d single. For 6d one could view the dancing from the balcony. Music was originally provided by a small orchestra. Down the years the Floral Hall attracted countless people – 130,000 in 1947 alone – providing fun and entertainment, and creating memories along the way. Many romances began in the dance hall; doubtless a few ended on the steps outside as well.

CORONATION TREATS

To mark the coronation of George VI on 12 May 1937, all of the children attending school in County Antrim were given free tickets for Bellevue. These allowed each child one ride on the railway, one 'go' on the amusements, entrance to a Punch and Judy show beside the Floral Hall and a free bottle of lemonade. Children attending County Down schools were taken to Donaghadee instead.

On the evening on 26 July 1939 there was a major fireworks display on Bellevue plateau, provided by Mr Brock of Crystal Palace. This was preceded by music from several bands, a variety concert and community singing. Admission was 6d for adults, 3d for children (this seems to have been the standard price for everything) and parking for motor cars was 1s. For those who could afford extra it was possible to book a table at the Floral Hall restaurant to view the fireworks, or to go to the special fireworks dance which ran from 8.00 p.m. until 11.00 p.m. that evening.

HIGH–CLASS CATERING

To coincide with the opening of the Floral Hall, Café Hazelwood was refurbished and reopened in May 1936. The *Northern Whig and Belfast Post* spoke highly of the café with respect to every detail: 'The china has been carefully selected and the silverware is of the same type as that supplied to the Queen Mary.' The café and the Floral Hall together could seat about 650 people, and by 1939 the catering for both venues was under the supervision of a single firm – Tuckshops Ltd. The firm advertised boldly that they would 'pay you a guinea to make a suggestion which will assist us to give you the best possible service in our catering arrangements for the public at Bellevue'.

Despite the extensive landscaping and floral decoration, and despite or perhaps because of the zoo, many people did not regard Bellevue and Hazelwood as true public parks. This may have been because they were owned and maintained by the Tramways Committee rather than the Cemetery and Parks Committee, although most residents of Belfast were probably unaware of this. Regardless of how they were viewed, the two properties did bring many people who lived in other parts of the city across to Glengormley and the north of Belfast. Travelling up the Antrim Road on the tram they would have passed the entrance to Belfast Castle Estate at Strathmore, another property to come into the hands of the Tramways Committee.

BELFAST CASTLE Co. ANTRIM. 2375.W.L.

THE HOUSE IN THE DEERPARK

The story of Belfast Castle and its estate lands begins with the Donegalls of Ormeau. The third Marquis of Donegall, who owned Ormeau House but was an absentee landlord living in England (chapter 2), remarried in 1862. He decided to come and live in Belfast. By then most of the leases had been sold off and Ormeau House had fallen into disrepair. The house was disliked by the Marquis anyway – he described it as an 'ill-constructed residence'. He therefore turned to the Deerpark, to the north of Belfast, and selected it as the site for his new residence. The architect W.H. Lynn, of the Belfast firm Lanyon, Lynn and Lanyon, had already designed a house in Tipperary for the Marquis's sister-in-law. Presumably he had acquitted himself with distinction, for the firm was engaged to design this new residence, which was to be called Belfast Castle. It was not the first building to stand under that name.

The front entrance to Belfast Castle, which was built for the third Marquis of Donegall. The gatepost of the family's former residence at Ormeau House stands on the far right.

EARLIER BELFAST CASTLES

The first Belfast Castle had been built by the Normans who invaded eastern Ulster in the late twelfth century. It was probably on the same site as the later stone and timber castle of 1611, which was surrounded by spacious gardens extending to Cromac Woods and close to Stranmillis. This was the home of Sir Arthur

Chichester (the family later received the title of Earl, and then Marquis of Donegall). The building was destroyed by fire in 1708 when three sisters of the fourth Earl of Donegall were tragically burned to death. Today only street names such as Castle Place and Castle Lane mark the site of the former Donegall residence. For some 160 years Belfast was without a castle.

THE NEW BELFAST CASTLE

The proposal to build a new Belfast Castle was announced in 1865, but progress was delayed because of protracted financial arrangements and an ensuing legal battle caused by Lord Donegall wanting to site the castle only yards away from his neighbour's land. Finally the architect John Lanyon was commissioned to draw up plans, for which he followed the Scottish Baronial style made popular by the reconstruction of Balmoral Castle in 1853.

In the 1870s, Belfast Castle enjoyed a rural setting.
MAGNI/ULSTER FOLK AND TRANSPORT MUSEUM

The cost of the project was estimated by the Donegall trustees at £11,000, but by the time the building was complete in 1870 the price had far exceeded this. The Donegall fortune had dwindled so drastically that the Marquis was unable to

underwrite these additional costs. The castle was in danger of being left unfinished when Lord Ashley, son-in-law to the third Marquis, stepped in and paid for its completion. Set on the slopes beneath the familiar landmark of the Cave Hill, the new Belfast Castle had extensive views over the city, and of Belfast Lough, north Down and the Mourne Mountains.

TWO FAMILIES

The third Marquis of Donegall lived at Belfast Castle for fourteen years until his death in 1884. His Irish estates passed to his daughter Harriet, Lady Ashley, and the title to his brother Lord Edward Chichester. When the seventh Earl of Shaftesbury died the following year Lord Ashley and Harriet became the eighth Earl and Countess of Shaftesbury. Within the space of one year they had inherited the Donegall home at Belfast Castle and the Shaftesbury title. The names of the two families are perpetuated in many Belfast street names: Chichester Street, Arthur Street, Donegall Park Avenue, Donegall Square, Donegall Place, Shaftesbury Square.

The crests of both families appear on the exterior of Belfast Castle. The Donegall coat of arms is carved over the front door and on the north wall. The Donegall family motto – *Invitum Sequitur Honor* (which loosely translates as 'Honour shall follow the invincible'), in one of the panelled reception rooms – is engraved on the ceremonial fireplace, though this is called the Shaftesbury Room today. The Shaftesbury crest adorns the left balustrade of the exterior staircase, which was not included in the original design, but added in 1894 by the ninth Earl of Shaftesbury as a present for his mother, the Dowager Countess. This Italian baroque serpentine stairway connects the main reception rooms to the garden terraces, which were once decorated with cannons that pointed out rather menacingly over the estate.

Two of these cannons, with the Donegall name inscribed, were found in the 1970s at Belfast Zoo. They were cleaned up, remounted on wooden carriages, and set at the entrance to Fernhill House, the headquarters of the Parks Department between 1975 and 1990. They were then moved back to 'guard' Belfast Castle once again.

ESTATE LANDS

The Donegalls enclosed the Deerpark with stone boundary walls when the castle was being built. They brought two gateposts, each comprising three iron creatures on top of a stone column, from the Ormeau Demesne and had them placed in the grounds of their new home as a reminder of the past. The remains of the walls and the restored gateposts can still be seen today. When the new castle emerged from the scaffolding, there were few trees on the surrounding hillsides and much of the lower ground was farmed. Carrots and potatoes were tended along with apple and plum orchards, and livestock grazed on some of the slopes. During the Shaftesburys' ownership there were considerable changes made to the estate. An extensive tree-planting programme began in the 1880s, transforming the area from open farmland to woodland. This mixture of broadleaf and conifer trees was planted according to a carefully drawn-up plan: elms to the south, mixed broadleaved species in the central areas, and larches and pines on the upper slopes. The new trees helped to conceal the large water reservoir dug into the hillside. It gathered rainwater and fed it down to Belfast Castle, as there was no piped water supply to the building at that time.

The estate originally extended right down to the Antrim Road. The driveway continued from the present gate, along part of Strathmore Park North to a gate lodge. This lodge, of the same style and age as the castle itself, still stands at the corner of Strathmore Park and is now privately owned. The gateway, with its octagonal pillars, was on the south side of the lodge. On the top of each pillar was a stone Donegall wolf holding an armorial shield.

BELFAST CASTLE CHAPEL

Within the grounds stood the Chapel of the Resurrection, where the Shaftesburys held regular services. Known initially as Belfast Castle Chapel and designed by W. H. Lynn, this decorated Gothic-style building was put up by the third Marquis of Donegall in memory of his son Frederick Richard, Earl of Belfast. (A statue of the earl, who died in 1853, was erected in College Square East. Because of its colour, the statue became known locally as the 'Black Man'.) The chapel was completed in 1869 and consecrated on 20 December of that year with a service taken by the Bishop of the diocese, the Right Reverend Robert Knox. It was originally planned as a mortuary chapel and contained a white marble monument to the Earl of Belfast by Patrick McDowell. The interior was not decorated until 1891 when an altar, reading desk, organ and stained-glass windows were installed. The Chapel of the Resurrection was transferred without endowment to the Church of Ireland in 1938. The McDowell monument was moved to the City Hall and other fittings to St Peter's Church, Antrim Road.

The Antrim Road gate lodge, the Chapel of the Resurrection and Belfast Castle, at a time when the landscape allowed all three to be seen at once.

NATIONAL LIBRARY OF IRELAND

SEAT OF THE MARQUIS OF DONEGAL & CAVE HILL BELFAST. 826. W.L.

ESTATE BUILDINGS

As well as the chapel, the estate included a house called 'Martlett Towers' near the northern entrance from the Antrim Road, and an associated porter's lodge (this remains today at the Antrim Road entrance for the adventurous playground), Martlett Row (six workers' cottages), a private house called 'The Hill', a main gate lodge and post office, a gamekeeper's house, a walled garden and rose garden, a nursery area and stables with a coach house, harness rooms and a groom's house (now the site of the lower car park). There was a fish pond below the terraces of the castle gardens, and a quarry just above the building and beyond the Deerpark boundary wall. The former is now overgrown, the latter is a wooded valley.

GIFTS OF PARKS

The Shaftesburys were philanthropic patrons of Belfast and supported many charities. The ninth Earl became Lord Mayor in 1907 and Chancellor of Queen's University the following year. After a visit to Carrickfergus in 1901 he donated land for a public park there. The area, with its shamrock-shaped pond, was called after the family: Shaftesbury Park. The Shaftesburys also headed the subscription list of Belfast's new cathedral, St Anne's, while the gardens at Belfast Castle were frequently opened for public events such as garden fêtes.

The Shaftesbury family gave Belfast Castle and two hundred acres of ground to the Belfast Corporation in 1934, on the proviso that the Corporation purchased the various estate buildings and the walled garden for the sum of £10,750 (including legal fees). The agreement included the condition that Belfast Castle would not be used for a hospital for the treatment of infectious diseases, a mental hospital or any purposes likely 'to be objectionable to the vendor or the tenants'. The Tramways Committee agreed to this and the property was taken over on 1 February 1935. The Corporation made a number of alterations to the castle's interior to make it suitable for public use. The most dramatic of these was the combining of the former dining and drawing rooms into one long ballroom with a new maple wood floor laid on top of the original floor. Kitchens and cloakrooms were fitted out, some of the second floor rooms enlarged and tea rooms installed in the cellars (at ground level with the terraces outside). A new roadway and car park was also provided.

The site was officially opened to the public on 9 July 1937 by the Lord Mayor, Sir Crawford McCullagh. After speeches by the Lord Mayor and the Chairman and Deputy Chairman of the Tramways Committee, there was dancing in the ballroom, with cabaret acts from an accordionist, comedienne, baritone and a pianist. The artists were from a show, Fred Beck's *Modern Follies*, which was appearing at the Floral Hall at that time.

ESTATE PROPOSALS

At the time of transfer to the Corporation there were eight of Lord Shaftesbury's employees still living in the various buildings. Other tenants included Lady Baird, who lived at Park Lodge, and her chauffeur, who lived in the gate lodge. Before the estate opened to the public there were several ideas about how the grounds and some of the buildings could be put to good use. An open-air theatre was proposed, based on a successful one at Scarborough, which was attracting over 100,000 visitors per year in 1935. It was also felt that clay pigeon shooting and archery could be safely played on the estate, and that sites could be developed for tennis and squash courts, bowling greens and a pitch and putt course. Martlett Towers was to be used as a café, the coach house as public lavatories, a derelict farmhouse as a shelter for pedestrians, and the coachman's cottage for grounds maintenance staff. In the event very few of these proposals were carried through as many of the buildings would have needed considerable money spent on them. The Corporation decided in 1938 to demolish the gamekeeper's cottage, The Hill, and the stables and piggeries.

There was talk of linking the Shaftesbury Estate with neighbouring Hazelwood by means of a miniature railway. The idea was examined by the General Manager of the Transport Department, but he reported that the scheme was impractical. In 1951 the Corporation acquired further land beside the sheep's path from a Major Adeley, enabling visitors to walk unhindered right through from the castle to the zoo. This purchase increased the total area of Belfast Castle Estate, which was then fully contiguous with estates at Hazelwood and Bellevue, making it the largest single area of public open space in Belfast at that time.

10
During the Blitz

During the years of the Second World War the parks and open spaces in and around Belfast played an important part in keeping up the morale of those who experienced that traumatic period. The parks became places of refuge, away from smouldering and ruined buildings; they served as social gathering points; they were used for home-grown foodstuffs and they provided a source of raw materials such as iron railings for the war effort.

Even before hostilities commenced, the strategic importance of some park properties had been recognised. In the summer of 1938, trenches were being dug to serve as emergency air raid shelters. The first two specimen ones were completed at Ormeau Park.

ALLOTMENTS

Open parkland provided ideal opportunities for growing fruit and vegetables. In 1932 the Allotments Bill NI had given control of allotments to local authorities. At that time the rent for a plot covering one-sixteenth of an acre was 5s per year. Regulations governing the control and management of these allotments were drawn up in 1933. The Corporation was obliged to advertise any proposed allotment area, giving rents and closing dates, while successful tenants were required to 'keep and maintain allotments clean and free from weeds and well manured'. Plotholders were to prevent plants from encroaching on neighbouring plots and were forbidden to erect greenhouses or tool sheds without permission. Carpet beating and the drying of clothes on allotments were also banned, as was gambling or playing games of chance.

With the onset of war it was not long before existing vegetable allotment sites, such as those at Orangefield, Ardoyne (the forty-acre site opened in 1932) and Ballysillan, were being augmented. By early 1940, additional plots had been established in Ormeau, Falls and Musgrave Parks. In Botanic Gardens the low-lying area towards the river was also used for allotments, much as it had been during the First World War.

A Belfast Allotment Association was formed to give advice to plot-holders, and leaflets were printed with information on how to make best use of the ground, which vegetables to grow and where to take the produce after it had been harvested. Demonstration plots were laid out in Botanic Gardens and Ormeau, Woodvale, Alexandra, Falls and Musgrave Parks. Up-to-date bulletins on cropping plans, pest control and produce weights were displayed on noticeboards. The Ministry of Food organised displays and demonstrations in Botanic Gardens to illustrate how to cook with the most basic of ingredients. General horticultural advice was readily given by Parks Department staff on duty.

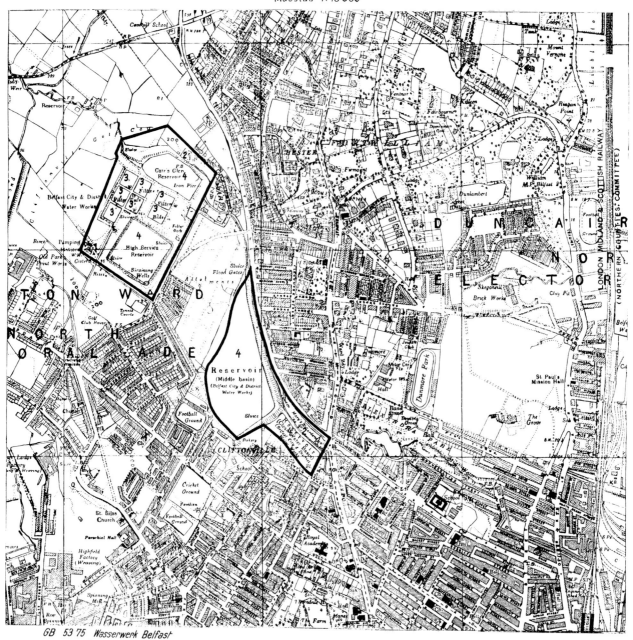

GB 5375 c

Nur für den Dienstgebrauch

n. Bild Nr. F 228/40/II/111 (I II. 5)

Belfast

Wasserwerk Belfast

Länge (wesll. Greenw.): 5° 56′ 55″   Breite: 54° 37′ 20″

Mißweisung: 14° 19 (Mitte 1940)   Zielhöhe über NN 50 m

Genst. 5. Abt.   Dezember 1940

Karte 1 : 100 000

Irl. 5

500   1000 m

Maßstab 1:10 000

GB 5375 Wasserwerk Belfast

1) Pumpanlage   etwa   550 qm
2) ansch. Pumpanlagen   etwa   400 qm
3) 7 Filterbecken
4) 4 Rohwasserbecken
                         bebaute Fläche   etwa   950 qm

Gesamtausdehnung etwa 350 000 qm

Luftwaffe map of Belfast showing the
Waterworks site on the Antrim Road which was
mistaken for the main dockland.

IMPERIAL WAR MUSEUM

TOMATOES AND BANANAS

As the war progressed the 'Dig-for-Victory' campaign became increasingly important until it encompassed not just original plot-holders but almost anyone with a
greenhouse or a piece of land or garden. In a report of 1942, the Ministry of
Agriculture stated that it was desirable that 'every endeavour should be made to
utilise all the space available for the production of tomatoes'. Any glasshouse space
not utilised for this crop was to be used to produce early vegetables for spring
planting. As a result, many shrubs and herbaceous plants were disposed of and the
bedding displays in parks and the City Hall grounds abandoned. About 75 per cent
of the glasshouse area in Botanic Gardens was given over to food production. The
1942 season alone produced over six tons of tomatoes and forty thousand early
vegetable plants including leek, onion, celery and cauliflower. Produce was distributed to wholesalers on a rota system at agreed prices.

The Tropical Ravine in Botanic Gardens was considered unsuitable for produce,
although bananas growing there were forwarded to the British Red Cross Society.

SCRAP METAL

During 1940 other early war preparations included the collection of scrap metal,
which was shipped across the Irish Sea to factories for melting down. In a personal contribution to the war effort, many grave-owners allowed the railings around
relatives' graves to be removed from cemeteries and included in these shipments. In
the early years of the war it was decided to keep park gates open at all times in case
emergency refuge was needed. This ruling became irrelevant as many parks, including Clara Street and Drumglass Playcentres, Willowbank, Queen Mary's Gardens,
and Falls, Musgrave and Woodvale Parks, lost both their railings and gates to the
scrap metal cause. Those at Musgrave had been put up only a few years earlier.
Many properties would have to wait a long time for replacements: Falls Park was
not enclosed with railings until 1960. Without their railings, parks were vulnerable.
Numerous reports of vandalism and damage were made and the police service was
asked to patrol more frequently.

NEW USES

The underlying threat of war was exemplified by the range of novel activities within parks. An air raid warden's post was established in the City Cemetery, and three
air raid shelters erected in Gallaher Playground, in east Belfast. Other air raid shelters were constructed in Dunville Park with the proviso that they would be converted into toilets and shelters for waiting tramcar passengers after the war was over.
Plans for fifty shelters in Victoria Park for the workers from Short Brothers were
abandoned after alternative accommodation was found. Grove Playing Fields,
Botanic Gardens, Dunville Park, and Clara Street and Hemsworth Street
Playcentres were authorised as assembly stations where people were to gather after
air raids.

The Auxiliary Fire Service used the pond in Ormeau Park for practice sessions
on Sunday mornings, and the Home Guard conducted rehearsals in Musgrave
Park, where incendiary bomb demonstrations were also held. There was a daily

Ceremonial Guard Mounting in Botanic Gardens, and from time to time instruction classes by the Air Training Corps. The latter took place on the lower ground of Botanic Gardens beside the allotments. Volunteers were asked to be fire watchers at the buildings within the parks and, as a precaution, important documents were removed from the City Hall in 1941 to purpose-built shelters in Botanic Gardens.

COOL AS CUCUMBERS

During the war years the Public Parks and Playgrounds Committee was kept busy with matters arising directly from the hostilities: everything from military problems to the requisitioning of premises (an estimated 215 acres of parks property were taken over by the Crown, including parts of Grove Playing Fields, Botanic Gardens and the sports grounds at Ormeau Park). However, the minutes reveal that there was still time to debate more mundane matters – such as the selling of cucumbers grown at Botanic Gardens.

AIR RAIDS

It was with the coming of the Luftwaffe bombing raids that Belfast citizens realised the full horror of war. Many left their homes and took shelter in the surrounding hills and countryside. Others slept rough in local parks such as Woodvale and Falls, feeling safer there than in their houses. Cave Hill was a particularly good retreat, where the lowest caves and gullies were used for shelter, and springs were tapped for fresh water. Many inhabitants armed with spades tried to unearth underground tunnels that were reputed to exist on the slopes behind the zoo. Others dug pits and trenches of their own and spent the nights of air raids looking down at Belfast, watching areas of the city burning.

During raids the parks were not necessarily any safer than residential areas. It is very likely that many open spaces were hit by bombs and debris and the incidents never recorded. On one occasion Grove Playing Fields received a direct hit by about six small devices near an anti-aircraft gun emplacement. This attack churned up the soil and impaled bowling green seats on nearby railings. Victoria Park, being adjacent to the dockland, would certainly not have been particularly safe, as there were anti-aircraft gun turrets within the park to help protect the shipyard. A line of bomb craters remained visible in east Belfast for many years on open ground that was later to be incorporated into Belmont Park (chapter 14).

Both Fernhill and Glencairn Houses in north Belfast, brought under Corporation ownership in the 1960s (chapter 13), were damaged by incendiaries. Members of the Cunningham family who lived there had to vacate Glencairn House because of a landmine. They did not return immediately: the Civil Defence took over the house until the end of the war. The building beside Glencairn, now a fire station, was used as a temporary morgue for air raid victims.

EASTER ATTACK

During the worst raid on the night of Easter Monday and morning of Easter Tuesday 1941, north Belfast was devastated by the Luftwaffe. It is possible that during a previous reconnaissance flight on 18 October 1940 the Waterworks site on

the Antrim Road was photographed and mistaken for the main dockland. Certainly the park and surrounding area were recorded in fine detail on Luftwaffe target files recovered after the war. Whatever the reason for the attack, because of the high population in the area, the results were devastating.

There was no real warning of an impending attack despite the fact that other major cities in England had been targeted by the Germans. The citizens of Belfast were enjoying Easter, flocking as usual to the zoo and Cave Hill. There was a dance on at the Floral Hall that Easter Monday evening, and when the raid began those returning from the dance had to get off the trams and head for shelter.

In the hours that followed, countless incendiaries and bombs fell on north Belfast, doing very little damage to the Waterworks, but having catastrophic effects on the surrounding streets. Casualties were heavy: an estimated 750 people died that evening. Ewart's Weaving Mill on the Crumlin Road, belonging to the Ewart family of Glenbank (chapter 7), was extensively damaged and burned for twenty-four hours. One bomb fell on to the miniature railway line at Bellevue.

WATER SUPPLIES AND SHORTAGE

Many fires burned well into daylight hours and attempts to fight them were hampered by a lack of water. The National Fire Service used water from the Waterworks and ponds at Alexandra and Woodvale Parks. On a subsequent overnight raid, on 4–5 May 1941, when the docks and east Belfast were worst hit, a shortage of water was a major problem. The turning of the tide had reduced the level of the Connswater around Victoria Park to a mere trickle. It was during this raid that the

The National Fire Service drew water from the ponds at Woodvale Park (shown) and Alexandra Park to supplement supplies. Woodvale Presbyterian Church in the background is now masked by the trees, and the pond site is a children's playground.

banqueting room of the City Hall was badly damaged. Some of those left homeless by the raids were permitted to use vacant buildings at Orangefield and Avoniel Playing Fields as temporary housing.

ANIMALS DESTROYED

In 1941, to 'reassure the public and calm fears of local residents', it became necessary to dispose of certain dangerous animals at Bellevue in case they escaped during bombing raids.

The difficult decision was taken by the Ministry of Public Security and on 19 April 1941 thirty-two animals were shot. Those destroyed included five lions, a tiger, two brown bears, two polar bears, six wolves, a hyena, a puma, a vulture and a giant rat. The shooting was carried out by Thomas Ward of Glengormley Police Barracks and Sergeant Murray of the Home Guard. Local press reports related how head keeper, Dick Foster, watched with 'tears streaming down his face, as the executioners proceeded from cage to cage'. For the destruction of a major part of the animal collection the government paid Belfast Corporation £815 compensation. Sheila the elephant beat the executioner's gun: she died from a heart attack during a raid, apparently after running wildly around the enclosure, trumpeting loudly.

BLITZ MEMORIAL

Services were held for unidentified victims of air raids. These took place at the markets at Cromac Street, which were used as a temporary morgue, as well as the Falls Road Public Baths. The bodies were then taken in covered military vehicles to cemeteries for burial. In November 1951 a memorial was erected in the City Cemetery to 154 unknown victims of the 1941 air raids, who were interred together in one plot.

In 1944 some of those living in north Belfast witnessed an American Flying Fortress crash into the side of Cave Hill in thick fog. Those that ran to the site of the crash, in the midst of the trees at Hazelwood, had to duck as the ammunition began to explode. Sadly the crew members lost their lives.

TEA DANCES AND BANDS

Efforts at normal life continued throughout this period. Outdoor recreational facilities were not only kept open but offered free to members of the armed forces. In July 1942 Bellevue and Hazelwood were reported as being as busy as ever. Blackouts were fitted to the dome and windows of the Floral Hall so that festivities inside could go on. Tea dances were held in the afternoon and bands played on the plateau. The Bellevue amusements were permitted to continue operating, but only during daylight hours.

Nissen huts beside the yew walkway at Wilmont, later Sir Thomas and Lady Dixon Park, were used by American troops from 1942 until the end of the war.
DESMOND McNEILL

The zoo was kept open and frequented by many, although most of the enclosures by then contained only farm animals. The Orange Order's Twelfth of July celebrations in 1943 were marked by a band performance by the Royal Ulster Rifles from the bandstand of Woodvale Park, broadcast by BBC Radio. These distractions, along with other entertainment such as Punch and Judy shows, doubtless helped many through the depressing years.

THE AMERICANS ARRIVE

As American troops began arriving in the province, several parks and properties in Belfast were used to host them. A camp was set up along the west side of Grove Playing Fields, while Wilmont Estate south of Belfast (later Sir Thomas and Lady Dixon Park – chapter 11), was requisitioned. There the lower ranks were billeted in estate buildings, while the officers were given quarters near and in Wilmont House, where General Collins, the Commanding General of the US Army, was based. The African invasion was planned in what General Collins described in 1942 as 'the private residence of a wealthy Irishman'. A chapel, Nissen huts (semicylindrical, temporary buildings, made from corrugated iron), a mess hall, enlisted quarters and a recreation building were all erected within the grounds of what is now Sir Thomas and Lady Dixon Park. Members of the Signals Communications Corps were stationed in the stable yard buildings where they were forced by cold weather to make crude chimney vents in the roof of the hayloft to accommodate their paraffin heaters.

Malone House (also destined for public ownership – chapter 11) was taken over by the Ministry of Aircraft Production in 1940 for use as drawing offices by Short Brothers and Harland. The Nissen huts in the grounds became known as Malone

House Camp, and the troops based there made roadways and trenches in the estate for training exercises. The overgrown remains of a few of these can still be found today in Barnett Demesne. An air raid shelter was built adjacent to Malone House (accommodating public toilets and a National Trust shop in the 1970s), while two further air raid shelters around the perimeter of the park later served as public shelters right up to 1987, when they were eventually demolished.

Belfast Castle was used by the Royal Navy from 1941, as the headquarters of the Flag Officer NI, who commanded control of all ships operating from bases in the province. The strategic importance of the ports in Northern Ireland had been stressed by Sir Winston Churchill, and so a lookout was constructed at the top of the east face of the castle tower, from where the whole of Belfast Lough could be surveyed. Belfast Castle was derequisitioned in 1946, whereupon the Ministry of Finance authorised the spending of £1,800 on the building's redecoration. The castle was reopened as a public building on 3 July 1946 by Deputy Lord Mayor Councillor R.B. Alexander, in the presence of the Tramways Committee.

HOLIDAYS AT HOME

The year 1943 saw the beginning of a 'Stay at Home' holiday campaign, which involved both parks and public venues. Punch and Judy shows, fancy dress parades, baby and beauty shows, outdoor concerts, performances by bands and individual musicians such as xylophonists, outdoor boxing tournaments and athletics events were organised in many parks including Woodvale, Falls, Grove Playing Fields, Clara Street Playcentre, Botanic Gardens and the City Hall grounds. By the following year aquatic galas in the Waterworks, Irish dancing and a cycle marathon in Falls Park, and displays by the Air Training Corps in Botanic Gardens had been added to the list of attractions. During 1945 twelve thousand children from different parts of the city visited Bellevue and the zoo over a two-week period. Each child was entitled to several free rides in the amusement park and free tram transport to and from the site. A garden party was hosted by the Government of Northern Ireland in Botanic Gardens on 18 July 1945 as part of the victory visits to the province of their majesties King George VI, Queen Elizabeth and Princess Elizabeth.

After the war the Stay at Home, or Holidays at Home, campaign formed the basis for a programme of summer entertainment in parks. The Belfast Water Commissioners gave permission for the use of the Waterworks site to be included in this programme. The first of these events included the victory celebrations held on 8 June 1946 to coincide with the victory parade through London. For this occasion a town versus country cricket match was played at Woodvale Park, and there were massed choirs at Botanic Gardens and Grove Playing Fields, water displays lasting two hours in the River Lagan alongside Ormeau Park, and sheepdog trials at Bellevue.

THE CLEAR-UP BEGINS

Many air raid shelters and damaged buildings were demolished after the war and suitable dumping grounds were sought for the tons of rubble. Several ponds within parks were filled in at this time, although it is uncertain whether this was due to an abundance of available infill material or whether the problems of keeping ponds hygienic would have made their continuation improbable in any case. Whatever the reason the ponds at Ormeau, Woodvale and Musgrave Parks all vanished at this time.

Some of the Nissen huts left by the forces were used for a time as changing facilities at Ballysillan and Orangefield, sites that were awaiting full development. One hut was erected at North Queen Street Playcentre for the use of children. Two other huts are still in place at Ormeau Golf Course today. Temporary housing, in the form of prefabricated bungalows on concrete foundations, was erected in the lower ground of Botanic Gardens for servicemen returning from the war. Many of the allotment areas were reseeded and returned to parkland.

A NEW STYLE OF PARK

The communities of Belfast turned away from war and its memories and looked forward to brighter times, and once again parks played their role in the rehabilitation and regeneration of a war-weary society. A new style of park emerged around this time: less formal than the Victorian parks, with less emphasis on active, organised recreation, and more reminiscent of the estate lands that the grounds had once been. Prime examples included two properties within the Lagan Valley – Barnett Demesne and Sir Thomas and Lady Dixon Park, both used during the war and derequisitioned in 1946, and soon to be freely open to all.

The Jaffé memorial drinking fountain, which originally stood in Victoria Square, was moved to Botanic Gardens in 1933. The temporary housing built at the end of the war – the 'prefabs' – can be seen in the background.

BELFAST CENTRAL
LIBRARY

11
The Lagan Valley Estates
Barnett Demesne and
Sir Thomas and Lady Dixon Park

The history of Malone House and Barnett Demesne, and Wilmont House and Sir Thomas and Lady Dixon Park, properties that came into public ownership in 1946 and 1959 respectively, has been extensively researched and documented. The character of these two estates, built up over successive generations of families that lived on them, is very different to that of the Victorian parks. Both have an air of informality about them, the feel of a country estate, a sense of the past – indeed many signs and remnants of their history can still be seen.

THE HILSBOROWE FORT

Barnett Demesne, with Malone House set prominently on top of rolling grassland, lies in the heart of the Lagan Valley. The site was first occupied in the early 1600s when Moses Hill built a fort called Hilsborowe on ground leased from Sir Arthur Chichester. This timber and brick house with a slated tower and drawbridge, surrounded by a palisade of stakes and earth ramparts, was on the site of the present Malone House. The sturdy defences proved inadequate during the rebellion of 1641 against the plantation settlers, and the fort was captured and burned down. Moses Hill moved to new estates in County Down, where he established the town of Hillsborough. The Chichesters soon found new tenants – the Legg (later Legge) family, which was to be associated with Malone for over two centuries.

THE SECOND MALONE HOUSE

Alexander Legg was listed in the hearth rolls of 1669 and built a new house on the estate in the late seventeenth century. This 'second Malone House', on the site of the present service yard, was three storeys high, with a tall roof and attic windows in the gables but no basement. It extended into a lower right-hand wing, which probably housed kitchens, while behind the dwelling were stables and buildings arranged around walled yards. The main entrance of Legg's house faced north and was reached by a short driveway through the estate from the Belfast to Dublin Coach Road.

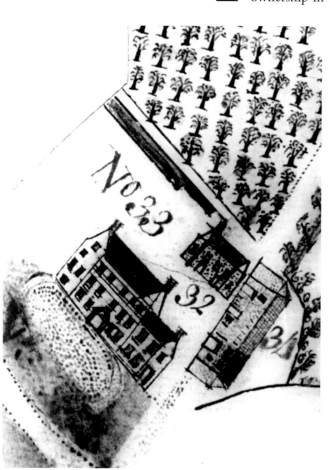

The 'second' Malone House and outbuildings (on the site of the present stable yard) are clearly drawn on this estate map *c.* 1780. The orchards are marked at the top right.

PUBLIC RECORD OFFICE OF NORTHERN IRELAND

The Legg family were merchants and prospered by participating in the growing trade of Belfast. They had connections in the West Indies and were part owners of the Old Sugar House in Rosemary Lane. Running from this lane to High Street was Legg's Lane, named because the family had a lease on property there. The road from Shaw's Bridge (built using some of the stones from the ruined fort of Moses Hill) up to Malone and past the estate became known locally as Legg's Hill. Details of the family in the late seventeenth and eighteenth centuries are sketchy and the exact lineage is uncertain. William Legg, a merchant, died in 1750, while Alexander Legg (1706–77), perhaps a grandson of the first Legg of that name, was described as a 'gent and linen draper'.

The new Malone House was captured by Edward Proctor in this engraving of 1832. Artistic licence may explain the dramaticised Cave Hill and Shaw's Bridge on the right (neither of which are visible from this viewpoint), but cannot excuse the main portico being shown on the south instead of the north face of the house!

MAGNI/ULSTER MUSEUM

A MOAT IN THE ORCHARD

It was Alexander's son, William Legg, who enlarged the estate by buying up leases of neighbouring lands, until in 1810 he owned about seven hundred acres (much larger than the present park). The lands immediately adjacent to Malone House and between the dwelling and the river included orchards, meadows, hayfields and bleachgreens. The rolling grassland of today's park was divided into small fields, many with intriguing names such as Mercer's Field, Fox Hole Hill, Nellie's Field and Haystack Hill. The site of Moses Hill's original fort was described in 1780 as 'a moat in the orchard'.

In 1810 William Legg had his leases renewed for sixty-one years for the relatively small sum of £700. He died without issue in 1821 and his nephew William Wallace inherited the estates at Malone, with the leases still good for a further fifty years.

THE THIRD MALONE HOUSE

William Wallace added the name Legge (now spelt with an 'e') to his own. He was a lawyer, High Sheriff of County Antrim and Deputy Lieutenant. With his uncle's wealth he was able to enjoy the life of a country gentleman and was encouraged to spend money on his estate. He built a new house and began to landscape the grounds. The exact date of William Wallace Legge's new dwelling (the third and present Malone House) is uncertain, as is the architect. It probably dates from the late 1820s and Legge himself may have had a hand in the design – he was something of an artist and drew sketches of local buildings and landscapes.

William Legge chose the site of Moses Hill's fort for the location of his new house, perhaps because of the panoramic views over the Lagan Valley. Looking north-west from the house he would have seen the Belfast to Dublin Coach Road, which followed the line of the present exit road of the park, crossed what is now Queen's University Playing Fields and rejoined the line of the Malone Road just at the entrance to the Mary Peters Athletics Track (chapter 14) at what is still called Old Coach Lane. Perhaps he took a dislike to the vagrants walking along the road or the carriages passing by, or perhaps it was down to pure egocentricity or aestheticism. Whatever the reason, William Wallace Legge (through his position as High Sheriff) arranged for the road to be realigned to the route of the present Upper Malone Road and out of sight of his new dwelling, thus ensuring that his view was not marred.

CLASSIC AND COLONIAL

The style of the new, late-Georgian Malone House was one of classic symmetry, five windows wide with the portico and main entrance on the north-west face. The cornice, parapet and prominent chimney stacks produced a stark appearance, contrasting with the more informal surroundings. On the south face there was a gentle bow, while shutters on the windows gave the house a colonial flavour.

Having completed the mansion to his satisfaction, William Wallace Legge then set about landscaping the estate grounds. By 1833 three screen areas of trees had been established between the north-east side of the house and Legg's Hill. The land between the new and old houses was laid out in orchards, bisected by a new straight driveway (now the tree-lined exit from the car park). In subsequent years, plantings approaching the house were established to frame vistas towards the main façades. A front gate lodge was built around 1840.

The estate map of 1871 shows specimen trees dotted on the estate to the front of the house, and also on the river side where most of the former fields had been removed. Near the south side of the house was a D-shaped formal garden containing two summer houses and a yew hedge walkway leading along the hilltop to the west. This feature was probably planted in the early 1900s. An east-facing walled garden served the house with fruit, flowers and vegetables, and originally contained several glasshouses. It was connected to the basement of Malone House by means of an underground passage, allowing tradesmen and servants to come and go unseen.

William Wallace Legge married in 1839 at the age of fifty. His only son, who bore the same name, began to squander his inheritance as soon as he came of age. He mortgaged the money settled on him when he married and ran up large debts. He was packed off to the colonies having killed a man in Malone House by flinging a plate at him, and ended up in Australia where in 1884, having married for the third time, he died of chronic alcoholism at the age of forty-four. With his son already disinherited, William Wallace Legge senior, who died in 1868, left Malone House and the estate in female hands, first to his wife and then to his daughter Florence.

BLOOMERS AND BICYCLES

Some years earlier in 1861 Florence had married James Spencer Pomeroy, who became Viscount Harberton. A circular ballroom was added to the south-east side of Malone House in the 1860s, probably for their wedding. It was a wooden construction with a minstrels' gallery and a pointed roof. One of the later tenants had it pulled down, although according to some accounts it had begun to fall apart shortly after the wedding anyway. Florence was a renowned feminist. She supported the campaign for votes for women, wore bloomers (a type of trouser suit designed by a Mrs Bloomer of New York) and rode a bicycle, all of which caused her to be regarded as rather an eccentric figure.

MANY DIVERSE TENANTS

Neither William Wallace Legge's widow nor the Harbertons lived at Malone House, but a Belfast solicitor, James Torrens, was appointed to act as agent. The steward, William Curry, was to manage the grounds and supervise the agriculture. During the fifty years after William Wallace Legge's death, there were numerous and diverse tenants at Malone House. The first of these was Thomas Montgomery, who was a distant relative of the Legges and a Director of the Northern Bank. He stayed for seven or eight years. The next occupant was Edmund Kertland, a Manager at John Shaw Brown & Co.'s mill at Edenderry, who agreed to make improvements and repairs to the estate. Kertland's association with Malone House was remembered nearly one hundred years later, when his daughter presented a fine watercolour painting of the Lagan by local artist George Trobridge to Belfast City Council for hanging in Malone House.

MRS HIGGIN'S PARTIES

The Higgin family took up the tenancy in 1896. By then other conditions had been attached to the rent agreement: the exterior of the house was to be painted every third or fourth year, no timber was to be cut without permission from the Harbertons, and only one crop of hay was to be harvested per year. William Higgin owned the Avoniel Distillery in Templemore Street. When he died his wife stayed on at Malone House. She became locally renowned for her entertaining and frequent theatre parties. In May 1920 the estate passed out of the Harberton family when it was bought by an insurance broker, J.M.K. McGugan. He retained Mrs Higgin as tenant and built a new front gate lodge, but unfortunately had to abandon the rest of the plans for his new property. He lost his fortune on the stock exchange and was forced to sell Malone House in July 1921, only a year after he had bought it. He sold it, along with 103 acres of ground, to William Barnett for £19,000.

The front of Malone House, *c.* 1952. The window shutters gave the building a colonial appearance. For many years ice cream and confectionery were served from the window on the far left, beside the wooden ramp.

BELFAST CITY COUNCIL

A DERBY WINNER

William Barnett was a grain merchant with a great interest in sport, especially horse racing. In 1929 his horse 'Trigo' won both the St Leger and the English Derby. For much of the time William Barnett lived alone in the house without family. He died in 1943 and left Malone House and the grounds to the citizens of Belfast.

Because of the previous stipulations and restrictions on tree felling and agriculture, Belfast Corporation inherited an estate that closely resembled the Georgian ideas of William Wallace Legge. The Corporation had to wait until the house was derequisitioned on 1 April 1946 (chapter 10) before any progress could be made.

Initially the park was called the 'Barnett Recreation Demesne'. The public was first admitted on 24 August 1946, but it was nearly five years before an official opening took place. During that time alterations were made to the house to facilitate public catering, and a car park was constructed in the grounds between the house and stable yards, where the Legges' orchard once blossomed. The adjacent land, now Queen's University Playing Fields, was the Malone Golf Course until 1959. This course, with the clubhouse site currently occupied by the House of Sport, extended right to the river beyond Barnett Demesne and into the arena that is now the Mary Peters Athletics Track (chapter 14). The club moved to Ballydrain in the 1960s when Queen's University bought the land at Malone.

AN AVENUE OF TREES

Extensive proposals for the new park were drawn up and included two nine-hole pitch and putt courses, a camping ground, a swimming pool, a paddling pond and sandpits, and a bowling green. There would be few citizens of Belfast who would regret the abandonment of such proposals – the park as it stands today has since been enjoyed by many as a semi-natural area. To mark the official opening on 14 May 1951 members of the Parks and Cemeteries Committee planted oak, sycamore and elm trees alongside the entrance driveway approaching Malone House.

ANOTHER LAGAN VALLEY PARK

Barnett Demesne is one of several former gentlemen's seats in the Lagan Valley. Eight years after it opened, Belfast Corporation received a gift of yet another estate in the area, one that was destined to become the jewel in the crown of the Parks Department. Until 1959 few people had heard of Wilmont Estate, but like that of Malone, its origins go back many years. The estate was formed during the mid-eighteenth century, and no fewer than five families were subsequently associated with the land. Each has made its mark on the shape and character of the parkland now known as Sir Thomas and Lady Dixon Park.

UPSTREAM TO PEOPLESTOWN

The Stewarts, a family of farmers with an interest in linen manufacturing, crossed from Scotland in the seventeenth century and settled in the Lagan Valley. In 1755 William Stewart leased twenty-nine acres at Drum Bridge from the Earl of Donegall, an area referred to locally as Peoplestown. A further fifty-four acres at Old Forge, adjacent to this ground, was leased by his father John Stewart, who lived at neighbouring Ballydrain (now the Malone Golf Club grounds).

THE FIRST WILMONT HOUSE

The Stewarts built the first house at Wilmont in the early 1760s. It stood on the site of the present barbecue area (below the children's playground) where some brick foundations can still be seen. An enclosed yard and some outbuildings (on today's lower car park) stood to the south of the house, and near Drum Bridge there was a bleachgreen and mill with a water race that remained in use until 1815. An ice house was dug out of a bank near the river to store foodstuffs under 'refrigerated' conditions. The family was among the first to grow carrots on a large scale in the early 1800s and one of the early threshing machines was erected on the property in 1811. The last Stewart to be associated with Wilmont was James, who mortgaged the property to the Northern Banking Company in 1844, ending almost a century of family connections.

TREE PLANTING ON A GRAND SCALE

During the nineteenth century the estate changed hands several times within a fourteen-year period. Alexander Mackenzie Shaw, a Belfast brewer, rented the house in 1847 and bought it two years later. Between 1847 and 1849 he landscaped the estate and planted 21,000 trees. He carried out improvements to the house but then, possibly as a result of this work, he fell into debt. He sold Wilmont back to the Northern Banking Company in 1856, having obtained it by Fee Farm Grant only a year before. Two years later, James Bristow, a director of the bank, was granted a lease to the property. He immediately decided the house was not grand enough and commissioned the building of the present Wilmont House.

WILMONT HOUSE

Bristow's new dwelling was designed by one of Belfast's most important Victorian architects, Thomas Jackson (1807–90), who also designed St Malachy's Church, Belfast, and the museum building in College Square North. Wilmont is typical of his designs for domestic premises: sensible, comfortable and relatively plain. James Bristow's initials are inscribed in stone on the north side of the house.

The building was, in fact, a large semi-detached house, the interior being divided into two halves. By 1860 James Bristow was living in one half, and his son James Thompson Bristow in the other. The son followed in his father's footsteps with a career in the Northern Banking Company. He was elected a member of the board in 1852 and after his father's death succeeded him as chairman in 1866. Elected President of the Belfast Chamber of Commerce in 1877 (again after his father), he declined the position due to ill health. He died that same year at Wilmont House.

As his eldest son, James Laird Bristow, was only fifteen, the estate passed into the hands of the trustees. On the death of James Laird at the age of twenty-eight, his sisters and mother ended the family's connections with the estate when they sold it to Robert Reade in 1897, having created a gentleman's estate out of a farming one. A walled garden with glasshouses had been built to provide fruit and flowers for the house, new driveways and gate lodges had been constructed, more formal gardens near the house planted and the farmyard extended to include stables, coach house, harness room, steward's house and hayloft. An inventory drawn up for insurance purposes in 1919 also lists among the outbuildings an acetylene gas plant house, used to produce gas for lighting.

BIG R.H.

Robert Henry Sturrock Reade, known locally as 'Big R. H.', paid £11,625 for 109 acres of Wilmont Estate. He was related on his mother's side to the original Stewarts of Ballydrain, and was Managing Director and Chairman of the Board of the York Street Flax Spinning and Weaving Co. Ltd. In 1906 he became the third owner of Wilmont House to be elected President of the Belfast Chamber of Commerce. Robert Reade's wife had died in 1883 and so never saw Wilmont, where Robert lived with their five children until his death in 1913 (see photograph, p.124). His son George sold it to Sir Thomas Dixon in 1919, for £21,500.

SHADY WALK

During the years of the Reades a double yew hedge was planted near the house to enclose a walkway that led from the lawn and tennis courts to a small ornamental pond near the walled garden. Beyond this were the apple and pear orchards. Sir Thomas Dixon kept these areas nearest the house separate from the main estate by iron fencing. They included the donkey paddock to the south of the walled garden, the field beyond the yew hedge (now the children's playground) and the pony field to the north of the house, which was separated by a small ha-ha near the building. His favourite path was 'Shady Walk', which ran beside and parallel to the Malone Road. He would not permit the gardeners to cut back the shrubs and allow more light into the path: he rather liked the secluded nature of the walk.

Wilmont House, as it looked when the Dixons took up residence in 1919.

POSTCARD

Sir Thomas Dixon had the two halves of Wilmont House knocked into one some time during the 1920s. Many of the agricultural buildings such as cattle houses disappeared over the following twenty years as the estate was used less and less for farming, although sheep were grazed on the meadows into the 1950s. Sir Thomas and his wife, Lady Edith Stewart Dixon, owned a yellow and black Rolls-Royce and had green-liveried footmen. Lady Dixon was very concerned about those in her employment – she reputedly bought all of the gardeners straw hats one very hot summer's day, and 'long johns' in the wintertime.

The Dixons were well known in public life. Sir Thomas became High Sheriff for County Antrim in 1912, and for County Down in 1913, and from 1924 to 1950 was His Majesty's Lieutenant for Belfast. Lady Dixon was created Dame of the British Empire after the First World War in recognition of her work for the forces. She held high office in the Royal National Life-Boat Institution and the St John Ambulance Brigade.

In 1935 Sir Thomas and Lady Dixon presented Larne Council with Cairndhu House, their former residence in Larne, as a convalescent home, and four acres of ground to be called Dixon Park. They served as Mayor and Mayoress of Larne from 1939 to 1941. Sir Thomas died in Harrogate in 1950. Lady Dixon's benevolence continued with bursaries to Queen's University, subscriptions to the Royal Victoria Hospital and funds for renovation of the former Technical College.

DISTINGUISHED GUESTS

Over the years Wilmont House played host to a number of distinguished visitors. In 1904 Captain Robert Scott, the famous Antarctic explorer, stayed there during his visit to Belfast. When Government House in Hillsborough was damaged by a fire in 1934, Wilmont served as a temporary residence for the Governor of Northern Ireland. The following year Prince Henry, Duke of Gloucester, was a guest of Sir Thomas Dixon. General Collins of the United States Army was billeted at Wilmont House during the Second World War (chapter 10). Some time after this, alterations were made to the building, which necessitated installing new windows. A dummy window was painted on to the brickwork on the south side to maintain the balance and symmetry of the exterior.

THE NEW PARK

Perhaps Lady Dixon's greatest act of benevolence was in 1959 when she presented Wilmont House and 134 acres of estate to Belfast Corporation in memory of her husband. The park was opened that same year. Wilmont House became a nursing home on 15 May 1963, and was opened by Mrs Terence O'Neill, her first official engagement as wife of the Prime Minister. Lady Dixon died in January 1964 at the age of ninety-two. The Corporation narrowly missed having to pay death duties, which were payable if a benefactor died within five years of making a bequest.

RESTRICTIVE COVENANTS

Countless visitors to Sir Thomas and Lady Dixon Park (originally referred to as Sir Thomas and Lady Dixon Park and Playing Fields) and Barnett Demesne have benefited from the generosity of the Dixon and Barnett families respectively. Both

Sir Thomas and Lady Dixon Park opened to the public in 1959. This area of open parkland was subsequently developed into the rose garden.

properties were given under strict instructions as to their future use. Barnett Demesne is held in trust 'to preserve same as a public park or for a playground for children and youths or otherwise for the recreation of the public'. Sir Thomas and Lady Dixon Park is held upon trust 'for the greatest good of the citizens of the City of Belfast'. Thanks to the foresight of the two families a considerable swathe of countryside within the Lagan Valley has been preserved for all members of the public to visit and enjoy.

12
Cemeteries Old and New

After the Second World War, Belfast Corporation realised that the City and Dundonald Cemeteries were filling up rapidly. Steps were thus taken to provide additional burial space. Sites at Carrowreagh, Dundonald (chapter 8), Whitehouse, Forster Green Hospital, Ballymaconaghy, Taughmonagh and Belvoir Park were considered, but were rejected as being too small or because their geographical position within the city was felt to be inappropriate. The Corporation turned its attention beyond the borough, and in particular to a piece of land at Crossnacreevy, which at that time was under the jurisdiction of Down County Council. Having decided that it would be suitable for a cemetery, Belfast Corporation applied for permission in October 1949 to purchase and develop it.

FARMLAND TO LAWNS

The agreed price of £32,750 was raised by means of loans sanctioned by the Ministry of Health and Local Government, on the basis that sixty-three acres would be used for a cemetery and five acres as a plant nursery. At that time there was also a suggestion of a crematorium, approved in principle by the Ministry of Health in 1952. The land at Crossnacreevy was a working farm, owned by a Mr McElroy, who was allowed to continue to use part of the grounds for grazing while the first phase of cemetery development began. The Corporation decided in January 1952 that the new cemetery should be laid out as a 'lawn' cemetery and by November of that year the name Roselawn had been chosen.

ROCKY GROUND

Development of Phase 1 necessitated the provision of water and electricity supplies, boundary walls, screen planting of trees and hedging as well as an integrated road and path system, particularly vital for the correct functioning of any cemetery. (By the time Roselawn was being developed there was already an estimated ten miles of roadway in the City Cemetery alone.)

Burials were due to begin in Section 1 towards the end of 1953 but the contractors found the ground there to be very rocky. Because of this Section 2 was utilised first. Despite the setback the cemetery was ready the following year and on 22 April 1954 the ground was formally consecrated. Roses were planted along the main driveway, thus completing the name of Belfast's new lawn cemetery.

It was a further seven years, however, before the idea of a crematorium became a reality. The City of Belfast Crematorium was the first of its kind in Ireland. The red, rustic Dungannon brick building, with its Chapel of Rest, floral display area and display room for the Books of Remembrance, was opened on 10 May 1961. The first cremation, that of a County Tyrone farmer, took place in July of that year.

EXTENSIONS

As well as finding unfavourable ground at Roselawn, gravediggers came up against boulder clay at the City Cemetery, resulting in ten acres being declared unfit for burial purposes. This ground was transferred to Falls Park in 1957, and earmarked for seven additional sports pitches. Hard ground was not the only problem encountered by gravediggers: they had to contend with extremes of weather. The diggers, and by 1965 there were thirty-five of them working in the municipal cemeteries, were supplied with three-quarter-length frieze coats, and portable tarpaulin shelters that could be set over a grave if one had to be dug when the weather was bad.

The pressure on land for burials was increasing in tandem with the population and as a result Belfast Corporation extended Roselawn Cemetery in 1979 by seventeen acres near the Ilford housing estates. Some years later yet another new area was developed, this time landscaped around a central lake.

In the twenty-five years after the opening of Roselawn in 1954, three historical burial grounds were added to the Corporation's list of properties – the graveyards at Balmoral, Shankill and Clifton Street.

A DO-IT-YOURSELF GRAVEYARD

There was a proposal to take over the Balmoral Cemetery, on Stockman's Lane, as early as 1918, but it did not come into public ownership until 1953. The graveyard, once called Belfast Cemetery, Malone, opened in 1855. It came into being through a rather unusual set of circumstances involving the Reverend Mackenzie of Malone and the Reverend Henry Cooke. The former owned a cottage and land on the Lisburn Road as far as Weston Drive in Stockman's Lane. The story goes that when these two gentlemen were refused permission to carry out a 'proper' Presbyterian funeral in another churchyard, Cooke remarked, 'It is a great pity we do not have one of our own.' Mackenzie supposedly replied, 'Well why not! I have the land if you want to go ahead.'

The cemetery was controlled by a board of trustees that included three

Roselawn Cemetery took its name from the open 'lawn' style of graves and the roses planted along the main driveway. The crematorium opened in 1961.

Presbyterian ministers. The burials were predominantly of Presbyterians, both sub-scribers and non-subscribers, but also included those from other denominations and faiths. The graves of a considerable number of Presbyterian ministers, several missionaries to India, William Batt, who designed the front gate lodge at Botanic Gardens, and Dr Arnold, the founder of the Presbyterian Orphan Society, all lie within the walls. Needless to say both the Reverend Cooke and the Reverend Mackenzie were buried there as well. The funeral of Henry Cooke, in 1868, was described some years later as probably the largest ever to take place in Belfast. His statue was erected in College Square East in 1876, where a statue of the Earl of Belfast had formerly stood. The local name of the 'Black Man' was transferred to Cooke's statue.

The 1858 prospectus for the cemetery claimed that 'as the ground of the ceme-tery will be chiefly in the hands of proprietors, it can never become a nursery for vermin, nor present the characteristics of old, overcrowded graveyards'. Good intentions, but reality turned out to be rather different. By 1922 the surplus clay dug from newly made graves was lying 'in uncouth heaps blocking the neglected paths'. A committee was formed to tidy up the cemetery before it was handed over to Belfast Corporation. The sum of £1,130 was also given over towards the ceme-tery's upkeep.

Clearing the vegetation from a very overgrown Shankill Graveyard during the early 1960s.

BELFAST CITY COUNCIL

SHANKILL GRAVEYARD

Shankill is one of the oldest known graveyards in Belfast. The first church on the

Shankill Road location was recorded in 1306, although evidence suggests that the site may have been used for a church and burials some three hundred years earlier than that. Many of the oldest stones at Shankill are unreadable or are missing; one of the earliest legible headstones is that of George McAuley who died in 1685.

From the seventeenth century onwards, the area around the graveyard gradually evolved from countryside into the industrial and housing sprawl of the early twentieth century, while the churchyard itself changed from a rural community graveyard to a town cemetery. In the eighteenth century burials were mainly of local people, while during the nineteenth century many residents from the linen settlements of Glenalina, Ligoniel, Oldpark and Springfield were buried there. An area was set aside for paupers' graves, the last of which was opened during the 1850s. For a time, around 1880, the gates of the graveyard marked the site of a terminus for horse-drawn trams coming up the Shankill Road.

A NEW LEASE OF LIFE

Although the opening of the City Cemetery in 1869 helped to ease the pressure for graves at Shankill, inevitably space became limited. The number of general burials declined from the mid-nineteenth century onwards, the last finally taking place in 1934. Subsequently Shankill Graveyard was closed by the Ministry of Home Affairs.

That same year the Rector of St Matthew's church suggested that the Corporation should take over the burial ground. The offer sparked off protracted

The new-look Shankill Graveyard after restoration. It was opened as Shankill Rest Garden in 1964.

R. CLEMENTS LYTTLE STUDIOS

negotiations between the church and the Corporation, resulting in the property eventually being transferred in 1958. At that time there were 129 burial rights still outstanding. These rights were publicly advertised but no responses were received. Thereafter all remaining rights were rescinded. As burials had been infrequent even before that, the site had became very overgrown. Belfast Corporation staff cleared the vegetation away from headstones. Most of the 1,310 stones uncovered had been vandalised and were beyond salvaging, but 174 were retained, some remaining upright and others repositioned alongside the memorials set into the walls.

After renovation and tidying, the graveyard was opened as the Shankill Rest Garden on 3 June 1964. Two years later the garden received a commendation in the Civic Awards Scheme for County Boroughs.

CURES AND PLAGUES

As with any graveyard many stories and traditions came to be associated with Shankill. One of the most interesting items discovered in the churchyard during the nineteenth century was the Wart Stone or *Bullaun* Stone. It was moved the short distance to St Matthew's church in 1911. The stone may have served as a font, possibly in the original church at the White Ford, which tradition states was founded by St Patrick in the year 455 on his way to Slemish. The stone was reputed to have magical properties. In his *History of the Town of Belfast* of 1823, George Benn dismissed this by saying that 'the power of healing trifling diseases is superstitiously attributed to it by some old people'. There is evidence that the stone was commonly used by children to heal warts, but none to illustrate how effective it was. A pin would be stuck into the wart and then dropped into the hole in the stone, so effecting the cure. In the early twentieth century, solid layers of rusting pins were found lying in stagnant water inside the stone.

There was also a tradition of children being sent to cough three times through the railings while saying 'My cough go with you.' This practice may well have begun in the days when consumption and similar diseases were commonplace. Many burials took place as a result of pestilence such as the 'Black Death', the local name for the cholera epidemic of 1832–3. This plague was so dreaded that the part of the ground used for victims was ordered to be closed over and never reopened for fear of releasing the disease.

THE CHARITABLE SOCIETY'S CEMETERY

Fifteen years after acquiring Shankill, Belfast City Council obtained another of the city's important historical burial sites – Clifton Street Graveyard. This ground, which contains the graves of many prominent Belfast citizens, was transferred from the Belfast Charitable Society in 1979. As with previous graveyards, the site came along with a significant slice of Belfast's history.

When the old Corporation churchyard at High Street was declared unfit for use (chapter 5) a 'New Burying Ground' was established beside Clifton House. The ground, once owned by the Vicar of Belfast, the Reverend William Bristow, was made available by the Marquis of Donegall. Both Clifton House, which was founded in 1776 for the relief of the aged poor and the control of beggars, and the new graveyard, which opened in 1790, were run by the Belfast Charitable Society. There was a reluctance on the part of some to give up on the old High Street church-yard, so much so that a clause had to be included in the Act of Parliament 1800 stating that 'every person who shall dig, or assist in digging any grave, for the pur-pose of interring any dead body within the said church-yard, shall forfeit the sum of five pounds'.

THE RESURRECTIONISTS

Once the graveyard at Clifton Street was established, the Society built a wall around it so that 'what had been formerly an open field, in that noisome state to which open fields near centres of population are usually reduced, became a more tidy and useful place'. The wall also helped with security. In both Shankill and Clifton Street Graveyards, fresh graves were vulnerable to looting. Newly interred bodies were prone to being dug up during the hours of darkness by body snatchers, sometimes called 'resurrectionists', who made money by selling their 'loot' to students of anatomy for dissection. A watchtower was built at Shankill in 1834 by William Sayers and Israel Milliken to ease the burden on families guarding new graves. For a small donation this watchtower could be used by 'respectable persons'.

At Clifton Street there was no such tower and relatives were forced out in all weathers to guard for several nights after a funeral. Despite this the first attempted theft occurred in 1824. A reward of £50 was offered for information leading to

A quiet and green oasis near Carlisle Circus, Clifton Street Graveyard contains graves of many prominent families of late-eighteenth- and early-nineteenth-century Belfast.
ROBERT SCOTT

conviction of the 'person or persons guilty of the atrocious offence of entering the Burying ground behind the Poor-House, on Monday Night, 12th January, and raising an Infant's Coffin, several years interred'. The fact that the coffin was unopened would have been little comfort to the relatives. To deter such desecration some families resorted to using a coffin guard, a heavy cage of iron fixed around the coffin before burial. Professional watchmen were employed by those who could afford to pay them. There was acrimony in later years over whether or not these watchmen should be permitted to carry firearms.

COMMON GROUND

As the area for paupers' graves at Shankill filled up, Belfast Charitable Society set aside a portion at the east end of its New Burying Ground for poor graves and for anyone who died while under the Society's care in Clifton House. This practice ceased in 1882 when the ground was assumed to be full: subsequently the poor were interred in an area specially purchased at the City Cemetery (this plot filled up by the mid-1920s). There was also a plot at Clifton Street for victims of cholera, typhus, dysentery and smallpox. It is unmarked.

Disease followed the famine years of 1845 to 1849. Many who did not die from starvation died from ailments like dysentery, scurvy, cholera or bacillary dysentery, a horrible disease brought on by a diet of raw turnips, old cabbage leaves, seaweed and half-cooked meal. Although Ulster suffered less from diseases during the famine than other parts of Ireland, the cholera mound in Friar's Bush Graveyard at Stranmillis is a grim reminder of how victims were disposed of outside the town boundary.

FINANCIAL BURDEN

With the exception of the common ground, the original field at Clifton Street was full by 1819. A second area was opened, doubling the size of the cemetery, and became known as the lower ground. By 1854 all of the vacant plots in this area had been sold and so, instead of being a source of income to the Charitable Society, the graveyard became something of a financial burden. (The cemetery was originally planned as a money-making concern and therefore the ground was never consecrated.) Despite this, attempts were made to keep the graveyard as tidy as possible. The Society built a lodge in 1840 for a resident caretaker whose job included general maintenance. His lodge had to be replaced by a 'properly built house' before the turn of the century. The replacement was later occupied by the Society's engineer, who was responsible for opening and closing the gates. Money was found to plant trees and shrubs within the cemetery and this was done in 1874 through A.J. Macrory, then Chairman of the Royal Belfast Botanic and Horticultural Company.

PROMINENT CITIZENS

Clifton Street Graveyard is the burial place of many well-known citizens who played a vital role in the political, cultural and professional life of Belfast in the late eighteenth and early nineteenth centuries. They include United Irishmen the Reverend William Steel Dickson and Dr William Drennan; Valentine Jones, a West

Indian merchant and a founder member of the Charitable Society; William Ritchie, who established a shipyard on what is now Corporation Square; Robert and Henry Joy, one-time proprietors of the *Belfast News-Letter*; and John Templeton of Cranmore, the famous naturalist who put forward the idea of a botanical garden in Belfast (chapter 1).

Perhaps the most notable grave is that of Mary Anne McCracken, sister of the famous Henry Joy McCracken, who was hanged for his part in the United Irishmen uprisings. His bones are believed to have been discovered in the church-yard at High Street and reinterred at Clifton Street in the same grave as his sister (beside the wall on the Antrim Road). The inscription on the simple block of red sandstone says that 'She wept by her brother's scaffold, 17th July 1798'. Mary Anne herself had been keenly involved with the work of the Charitable Society. She died in 1866 at the age of ninety-six.

PARKS' FAMILIES

There are also links between the parks of Belfast and families buried at Clifton Street. One of the most striking monuments is the mausoleum of the Dunville family, famous for its whiskey production and presenting Dunville Park to the city (chapter 3). The vault originally contained ceramic images of the family but unfor-tunately these have been vandalised. Also buried in the graveyard are members of the Ewart family, formerly of Glenbank Park (chapter 7), the Sinclairs, who once owned the ground that is now Falls Park (chapter 2), and the Bristows, who lived for a time at Wilmont (now Sir Thomas and Lady Dixon Park – chapter 11).

George C. Hyndman, one of the founder members of the Belfast Botanic and Horticultural Society, showed his rather eccentric nature by having a statue of his pet dog put on top of his memorial. It looks down on his final resting place. A man called Thomas Ash marked his grave with four ash trees, one planted at each cor-ner. One of these specimens has been removed but the other three flourish, per-haps to the detriment of adjacent graves: they are now quite large trees.

'UNHINGED AND FALLEN'

Despite the efforts of the Charitable Society to maintain the increasing number of graves, a report of 1884 recorded that 'headstones and monuments were dilapidat-ed, railings eaten with rust and gates unhinged and fallen'. Funds were not available for the proper upkeep of the graveyard and appeals were made to families of those buried there. Accordingly a sum of £400 was raised, which enabled some improve-ments to be carried out. In 1930, after further deterioration, a fresh appeal was made but this time there was little response. Money was found, however, to employ a full-time groundsman, a post that was occupied until 1969. In that year the mil-itary took over the gate keys, being billeted at Glenravel Street Barracks next to the cemetery until 1973. The last burial took place in June 1984, by which time Belfast City Council had taken ownership of the site. The graveyard had been heavily van-dalised before the takeover and continued to be the object of much wilful damage for some years afterwards.

In 1987 a local action team funded by the Department of the Environment NI carried out renovation work, which involved cleaning of headstones, clearing paths and making repairs to the perimeter walls. Unfortunately this clean-up did not provide immunity from further vandalism and the authorities were forced to introduce restricted opening hours for the cemetery.

OTHER GRAVEYARDS

Within Belfast there were other burial grounds that did not fall under municipal responsibility. The largest of these, Milltown Cemetery, was consecrated in 1870 and run by the Catholic Church. Discussions between the Catholic authorities and Belfast City Council were held at various times over the future of Friar's Bush Graveyard on the Stranmillis Road, at one time the only Catholic burial ground near Belfast, but to date it remains the property of the Church. Other sites included the Friends' Burial Ground at Balmoral Avenue and a burial ground connected with the Wesleyan Methodist chapel at Ballymacarrett, which was closed for new burials from 1869. A former paupers' graveyard on the Donegall Road, run by the Board of Guardians, was developed into a playground (chapter 14).

THE SMALLEST GRAVEYARD!

There is another very small graveyard in Belfast – this one actually within the confines of a public park. Down by the walled garden at Sir Thomas and Lady Dixon Park lie the remains of three pet dogs: Spark, Pinty and Dandy. Three simple headstones mark the spot. Spark was an Irish terrier and belonged to a member of the Reade family (occupants of Wilmont between 1897 and 1919) who died in action in South Africa. The dog was adopted by the rest of the family and lived to the age of ten before being killed in a railway accident. His headstone, dated 1905, describes him as 'brave, faithful, wise, gentle and affectionate'. Dandy, a 'faithful and devoted follower of Sir Thomas Dixon', died in 1952. Pinty, a 'devoted companion' of Lady Dixon, died in 1958 – the year before she donated the park to Belfast.

The Irish terrier 'Spark' (front row, middle)was the Reade family pet, seen here at Wilmont House (now Sir Thomas and Lady Dixon Park) where they lived from 1897 to 1919. The dog, along with two pets of the Dixons, is buried by the walled garden.

ROBIN READE

13
A Period of Change
1950s–early 1980s

George Horscroft retired in June 1956, having given over twenty-seven years of service to horticulture and outdoor recreation in Belfast, firstly as Superintendent of Parks and then as Director of Parks when the title was changed in 1948. His successor was Reginald Wesley, who was aged forty-four when he took up the directorship. Born in Kent, he was a cousin of former Lord Mayor of London Sir Frank Alexander, and was one of the first candidates in Britain to obtain the Diploma of the Institute of Park Administration. His interests included writing, gardening and fishing.

Wesley came to Belfast from Southgate, north London, where he was Superintendent of Parks, and remained until 1972. In the year before his retirement he was appointed President of the Institute of Parks and Recreation Administration, and was partially responsible for bringing the organisation's National Conference to Northern Ireland for the first time. Part of this took place in Malone House and Barnett Demesne, where the nineteenth Parks and Recreation Exhibition was held under canvas and featured exhibits from play equipment manufacturers, nurserymen and horticultural suppliers.

During his time in charge Reginald Wesley saw many changes, both to the Parks and Cemeteries Department itself (by then commonly abbreviated to Parks Department) and to the properties it looked after.

NEW OFFICES

As well as a new director, the Parks and Cemeteries Department gained new offices in the early 1960s. Having moved to the front gate lodge of Botanic Gardens in 1933 and then to the curator's house near the Tropical Ravine in 1951 (once the home of the Superintendent of Parks), the Department was forced to move once again. This was due to the increase in the number of staff and to the fact that the curator's house was scheduled to be demolished to make way for the extension to the Ulster Museum. The front entrance gate lodge, the Department's previous accommodation, was also taken down at this time (1965).

An area of Ormeau Park service yard (previously the head gardener's private vegetable patch) was selected as a suitable site and plans were drawn up for office accommodation. Coinciding with this proposed move, however, was the acquisition of a new property in north-west Belfast, which became known as Glencairn Park. Ormeau Park, as a possible venue for headquarters, was abandoned in favour of Glencairn.

Fernhill House, former home of the Cunningham family, was the headquarters of the Parks Department from 1975 until 1990.

MAGNI/ULSTER MUSEUM

Glencairn was the former home and estate of the Cunningham family. At one time it covered over one hundred acres, more extensive than the present seventy-acre park. Two houses, Glencairn and Fernhill, were positioned on hilltops, one on each side of a sloping valley, while a third house, Glendivis, stood between the Ballygomartin River and Glencairn Road, just beyond the present entrance to the park. A smaller house, called Four Winds, was sited farther up Glencairn Road and modest mid-nineteenth-century gate lodges served Fernhill and Glencairn Houses.

A TALE OF THREE HOUSES

The Cunningham family came from Scotland to Ireland during the plantation and settled at Killead, about ten miles north-west of Belfast. The Cunninghams were involved in the West Indian trade; one descendant, Barber Cunningham, established himself in business in Belfast as a tobacco manufacturer and importer. Barber's son, Josias, founded a stockbroking and insurance company at 41 Waring Street in 1843. He acquired the estate lands at Glencairn in 1855, and is listed in the Belfast Street Directory of 1858–9 as the occupant of Glencairn House.

On his death in 1895, Josias Cunningham left three sons – James, Josias and Samuel – and five daughters. In 1899 the youngest son, Samuel, was able to move into a new house called Fernhill, built across the valley from Glencairn. From his home some three hundred feet above sea level Samuel would have had views of Belfast, the Mourne Mountains and, weather permitting, the family's home country of Scotland.

The Cunninghams continued to live on the Glencairn Estate for the greater part of the twentieth century, with both houses (and from 1935 Glendivis) being inhabited. Glencairn was the main house and was, by 1906, surrounded by extensive lawns and gravel pathways, mature trees including conifers, formal gardens, vegetable plots and a croquet lawn. Just behind the house was an ancient rath or fort, some 120 feet in diameter with ramparts and surrounding trench. During the Cunninghams' time the trench was filled in and the site used as a ring for training horses.

There were shrub borders and a rock garden around Fernhill House, which had a backdrop of conifers and Divis Mountain. A white wooden railing separated it from the sloping grass valley to the front. Behind Glendivis were orchards, tennis courts and a row of cottages. Members of the various households may well have walked alongside the Glencairn River, on a path edged with ornamental metal fencing, and crossed over using one of several bridges. Near a hollow in the ground, known locally as the 'inkpot', there was a small cottage from which the occupant sold ice creams and refreshments to passers-by.

The Ulster Volunteer Force stored guns and ammunition in the stable yard beside Fernhill prior to the First World War. On one occasion the coachman set alight a car that was being used for transporting the arms, resulting in fire damage to the yard. The UVF paraded in the grounds in 1914 (chapter 7). Both houses were damaged during the Second World War (chapter 10) and when Colonel Cunningham returned home after the war he found Glencairn House empty and abandoned and his family living in part of Fernhill House.

The last of the family to live on the estate was Lieutenant-Colonel James G. Cunningham, OBE, DL. He was born in the room that later became the office of the Parks Director. As a young boy he was tutored by an uncle of Craig Wallace, who succeeded Wesley as Director of Parks (see p. 144). In yet another link with the past, one of the family's descendants, Penny Cunningham, worked as a student in the 1980s for the Parks Department.

THE PARKS DEPARTMENT MOVES PARK

In 1962 the property at Glencairn was acquired by Vesting Order Procedure by Belfast Corporation. The Parks and Cemeteries Department moved its headquarters from Botanic Gardens into Glencairn House in 1964. Three years later Glendivis House was knocked down, along with nearby cottages, while Four Winds House was rented out. It too was demolished, when the tenant moved to Woodvale Park in 1974. The Parks Department transferred its offices across the park and into Fernhill House in October 1975, at which time the future of Glencairn House came under consideration. The suggestion of a college of music was raised but rejected. Instead the building became the training centre for Belfast City Council.

TRANSPORT AND IMPLEMENT

With the increase in mechanisation after the war, vehicles took on an increasingly important role, both for transporting plants and materials, and for horticultural jobs such as grass cutting. With this came the task of maintaining the machinery itself. At first, the work was contracted out, but eventually Belfast Corporation decided to employ its own mechanical workforce. A base at Botanic Gardens was chosen: a corrugated iron shed on the Stranmillis Embankment near Southview Cottages, which at that time were also owned by the Corporation. This shed had served as an auxiliary fire station during the war, and the brick building to the rear of it had been a decontamination unit, where anyone suffering from exposure to mustard gas could be washed down and cleansed. After the war these buildings were used to store equipment for the Holidays-at-Home programme (chapter 10).

In 1951 the site was turned into a vehicle repair base and became known to staff as T & I (short for Transport and Implement). The responsibility for this mainte- nance function switched between various sections of the Corporation, including Transport, Technical Services, and Parks and Cemeteries. The depot was extended in the mid-1960s to cope with an increasing workload, which included the serv- icing of the Parks Department's staff car. For many years this was a 1954 Ford Prefect, until it had to be scrapped after an accident in 1963.

The rise in the number of vehicles in the fleet corresponded to a widening remit for the Parks and Cemeteries Department. By 1964 it was responsible for the care and maintenance of some 417 sites throughout Belfast. As well as the principal parks and playing fields, this total included open spaces, street trees, traffic islands, housing estates, library sites, fire station grounds and school grounds. Many of these were maintained on an agency basis for other public bodies.

SCHOOL GROUNDS

The Parks and Cemeteries Department began to look after the playing fields and land around some of Belfast's schools as early as 1945. A school grounds supervisor was first appointed in 1955 to oversee this work, which at its peak involved care of over two hundred school and library sites. The work included grass cutting, prepa- ration and marking of pitches, some tree and shrub planting, and general mainte- nance. During the 1980s cutbacks in the Belfast Education and Library Board's budget brought about a reduction in the service that could be provided. One result of this was an overstaffing problem for the Parks Department, which was alleviat- ed by transferring some manual workers from school grounds maintenance to the general parks workforce. The Council's responsibility for school grounds ended in 1986 when the Education and Library Board put the work out to contract.

KEYS TO THE WATERWORKS

From the 1930s right up to the 1960s, the Waterworks continued to be a venue for informal recreation with diving and swimming galas, boating and model yacht rac- ing. A single track miniature railway ran from Queen Mary's Gardens, along the perimeter of the park parallel to the Cavehill Road and then along the north-west- ern boundary of the upper lake. A steam train operated by the Model Engineers' Society of Northern Ireland could carry as many as eight hundred children in one afternoon, often raising money for charity.

Perhaps as a reminder of earlier days when entrance to the Waterworks was restricted to those willing to 'sign on' (chapter 4), a system of keys operated until the mid-1950s. Keyholders made an annual subscription, which gained them admittance to the grounds whenever they wanted.

On 1 May 1956 the property was transferred to Belfast Corporation for the sum of £4,000. Over one thousand keyholders were permitted to retain their keys, although the main gate at the Antrim Road was opened during daylight hours for use by any member of the public. The Corporation wrote to keyholders asking them not to leave other gates open behind them as young children were finding their way into the property and were in danger of drowning in the open water. The rules of the Waterworks clearly stated that children under twelve were not allowed access unless accompanied by an adult.

FISHING AND FILLING

Anglers were also supplied with keys. The Belfast Reservoir Anglers' Association held the fishing rights to the two ponds, on the condition that it made day tickets available to the public. The group's duties included stocking the lakes with fish. Fly-fishing was popular, possibly because the fish were attracted to the many insects near the water. There were numerous complaints about these insects from other users, particularly those playing water polo on the upper pond.

When the Corporation took over ownership of the Waterworks, it was decided that the upper reservoir was too deep to be safe – in parts it was almost forty feet to the bottom – and that four feet would be a more appropriate depth. The lake was drained in August 1958 and opened to allow infilling with hardcore material. No charge was made for this dumping. Those supervising the process estimated at the onset that it would take about five years to fill the pond. In the event the dumping was not completed until 1965, by which time some 685,000 tons of material had been deposited. The depth of the lower pond was also reduced from twenty-seven feet to just under three. The practice had been to drain this pond during the school summer holidays when more children were about the park.

THE BELFAST LIDO

In 1966 proposals were put forward to develop the site as a 'Pleasure Resort'. The concept was that of a lido, which would bring 'the atmosphere of the seaside right

For safety reasons, the depth of the former reservoirs at the Antrim Road Waterworks was greatly reduced during the site's development as a public park in the 1960s.

BELFAST CITY COUNCIL

into the heart of the city'. The ambitious plans included major planting and land-scaping, the resiting of the railway, the provision of changing accommodation and the incorporation of Queen Mary's Gardens into the main park. The upper pond was to be developed for adult boating and fishing (stocked with brown trout), the lower pond for children's bathing and model yachting. The work was carried out under the relief of unemployment scheme, and employed thirty men for three years. The new park was opened in three stages. The first section, comprising the lower waterfall area (and costing about £144,000), was opened on 27 June 1968 and the second, comprising the lower pond and tea garden (and cost-ing a further £14,000), two years later to the month. The third phase included planting around the upper pond. Plans had to be altered to include the former allotment area (seventeen acres) adjacent to the fire station, which had been trans-ferred to the Parks Committee from the Improvement Committee in 1966.

Considerable damage was done by vandals only six weeks after the opening of the first phase. Belfast Corporation closed the park to effect repairs, but there was an outcry from local residents, who drew up a petition against the closure. The Corporation agreed to reopen the gates for restricted hours: between 1.00 p.m. and closing time. The rule about unaccompanied children was reinforced, and no one was per-mitted to bring bottles into the property. Despite this setback the first phase was award-ed a commendation in the Civic Awards Scheme in 1969. It was the only local author-ity project throughout the United Kingdom to receive recognition in that year.

The floral clock, with its face marked out in carpet bedding, was installed in the City Hall grounds to commemorate the Queen's Silver Jubilee year, 1977.

BELFAST CITY COUNCIL

FLORAL TIME

One of Reginald Wesley's many innovations as Director was the installation of a floral clock at the Waterworks. Work began in the spring of 1971, under the watchful eye of James Ritchie & Son of Edinburgh (builders of the famous floral clock in Princes Street Gardens, Edinburgh). At an estimated cost of £550, plus installation fees, the outdoor floral-decorated timepiece was constructed on the site of the ice house, which had been demolished in 1960. Unlike very early mod-els, which were weight-driven, the clock was electric – which was just as well, as the arms when planted out were extremely heavy. The hour and minute hands of a typical clock could weigh up to 50 lb and 80 lb respectively when dry.

The clock at the Waterworks kept time for a number of years before vandals forced Belfast Corporation to move it to a more central site. Work on its transfer to the gardens in front of the City Hall began in the latter part of 1976 and was completed in time for the Silver Jubilee celebrations of Queen Elizabeth II the following year. The clock ran for several seasons, and then had to be removed, again because of vandals. The circular bed with stone surround that had housed the clock continued to be planted out with seasonal bedding displays.

TRACKS FOR RUNNING, CYCLING AND PONIES

Under Reginald Wesley, the Parks Department applied itself to increasing and improving sports facilities within the city. The cycle track at Orangefield was opened by the Lord Mayor in 1957, one year after the athletics track in Ormeau Park. By this time the twenty-year-old cinder track at Grove Playing Fields was no longer being used by cyclists. After a suggestion by the local horse-riding fraternity, permission was given for the Grove track to be used for trotting ponies.

HOLIDAY CAMPERS

A portion of land at Oldpark was acquired by the Corporation in 1956 at a cost of £6,300. The Ministry of Education offered grant aid towards half the cost, so that the site could be developed with two soccer pitches, a pavilion and a playcentre. Thanks to a generous contribution of £4,000 towards the pavilion raised by holiday campers through the Butlin's Holiday Games, the cost to the Corporation and the Ministry was reduced. Oldpark Playing Fields were officially opened on 2 August 1963 by the Earl of Clanwilliam, Chairman of the NI Branch of the National Playing Fields Association. He unveiled a plaque to mark the contribution of the holidaymakers. The pavilion itself was called the Butlin's Holiday Campers' Pavilion. The opening ceremony was followed by a lunch at Belfast Castle.

MODEL TRAFFIC AREA

Moves were finally made to develop the land at Avoniel, which had been in the Corporation's ownership since 1939 (chapter 8) and derequisitioned from the military authorities in 1958. The site was a mixture of poor topsoil, foundations, disused roadways, the ruins of Avoniel House and two large water dams. Development plans had to take the state of the ground into consideration, and included netball courts, a roller skating rink, a playground and a model traffic area. This last item consisted of a road layout designed to encourage proper road use and cycling proficiency skills among children. It was fitted with electric traffic lights, and the Corporation purchased a number of bicycles, tricycles and toy motor cars to be used there. Avoniel Playing Fields were officially opened on 19 October 1967 by the Chairman of the Parks and Cemeteries Committee, Councillor Charles McCullough, JP. As a result of a deposition by hockey's governing body, three hockey pitches were added to the plans. Some twelve years later Avoniel Leisure Centre was built on part of the site and the model traffic area transformed into the main car park.

There are few clues today to reveal what the area once looked like. The leisure centre is built on the site of the two water-holding tanks, and nothing remains of the original Avoniel House which stood near the entrance to the centre. The Flora Street Walkway, which joins the leisure centre grounds to the Beersbridge Road, was once laid out as allotment gardens.

THE WHINS

Despite the opening of Oldpark and Avoniel Playing Fields (and of King George V and Dixon Playing Fields in 1960 and 1966 respectively – chapter 8), the appetite for sports facilities was not satisfied. Following a survey of existing properties Belfast Corporation reckoned that nineteen acres of the agricultural land at upper Glencairn could hold five football pitches. Due to difficulties in obtaining grant aid these were never constructed. Further proposals were then made for pitches at Barnett Demesne, on land held at Belmont and Musgrave, and at Falls Park. The first two were rejected, the second two accepted. This decision was made in the light of the purchase of ground beyond Glengormley. One hundred and ten acres at Mallusk, known as 'The Whins', were bought for £18,500 in 1960 for the sole purpose of providing pitches: no fewer than thirty-seven of them, at a total estimated cost of £140,000. The site, later called the City of Belfast Playing Fields, was not officially opened until 1975, by which time football, hockey, rugby and cricket matches had been played for two seasons. The Lord Mayor, Sir William Christie, performed the opening ceremony. He dismissed the suggestion to call the site the William Christie Playing Fields, preferring the 'City of Belfast' title.

LAND EXCHANGE

A twenty-nine-acre site at Cherryvale had been acquired by Queen's University as its main sports ground in 1920. The area was sold to Belfast Corporation as part of an exchange deal in 1967, which involved the simultaneous transfer of a piece of Botanic Gardens to the university for the building of a new leisure centre. This took place after five years of negotiation that involved not only the two parties but the public, the press and the courts. Finally a deal was struck that allayed the fears of the public over the future of Botanic Gardens.

Along with the sports grounds at Cherryvale, Belfast Corporation inherited two small pavilions for cricket and hockey, a covered stand facing the main rugby pitch, a derelict and partially ruined Cherryvale House, a gate lodge and an avenue of lime trees from the former entrance to the site (on the Ravenhill Road) – the last two are all that remains today of this part of Cherryvale's history.

FROM DESKS TO BENCHES

Cherryvale House served the university as the main changing accommodation of the playing fields for over forty years. Staff from Belfast City Council inspected the house and decided that it was in such a state it should be demolished. But not before some of the benches had been rescued. Because of limited funds back in 1920 the wooden benches in the changing rooms had been made out of old lecture room desktops from the university. They had been reversed to serve as benches, and were found to be heavily inscribed with names and initials of past pupils. Extensive research identified twenty of these students who had attended the university between 1880 and 1913. A piece of one of the benches was framed and presented to Queen's University on 24 October 1978, the day that the new pavilion, staff quarters and yard buildings on the site of the old house were opened by the Parks Department.

A WORLD RECORD

Three years later a plaque was unveiled in the pavilion to mark the twenty-fifth anniversary of Thelma Hopkins breaking the Women's World High Jump record at Cherryvale. This achievement took place on a dull day in May 1956 when, representing the Queen's University Ladies' Athletics Club, Thelma jumped a height of 5 feet $8^1/_2$ inches. She went on to win a silver medal at the Melbourne Olympics later that year. The plaque at Cherryvale was unveiled by her sister Moira McKelvey.

The Cherryvale site was often used for athletics: the Amateur Irish Championships were held in 1923, and each year the university's own athletics club held its sports day and an inter-varsity match between Dublin and Belfast Universities.

ULSTER '71

After the exchange of Cherryvale for part of Botanic Gardens, Queen's University began work on its new leisure centre. The building was utilised as part of the 'Ulster '71' exhibition before being finally converted to full recreational use. This major exhibition to mark the fiftieth anniversary of the Stormont parliament was held on the lower ground of Botanic Gardens near the river. Before any construction work could be carried out, workmen had to clear away the prefabricated bungalows built there after the war, which had provided homes for many during the intervening years. These were grouped in an area below Botanic Primary School, with a single row extending along the embankment road as far as the Jaffé Fountain. They had a postal address of 'Botanic Bungalows'.

For the Ulster '71 extravaganza new fencing and gates were erected along the embankment and a total of forty-nine 'grown-on' nursery trees were planted in the grounds of Botanic Gardens. In and around these was a major funfair. Some of the larger rides were purchased from Miss Pauline Barry, who operated the amusement park at Bellevue, and were moved over from the plateau for the event. During those summer months thousands of visitors flocked to the attractions at Botanic Gardens. It cost a considerable amount to reinstate the ground after the event was over.

FLOWERS OF SUMMER

As part of the Ulster '71 celebrations a Flowers of Summer Festival was held on the centre lawn in front of the Palm House. This flower show ran for four days in July and contained over one hundred classes including ones for roses, cacti and succulents, general flowers and exhibits from members of the Women's Institute, the Townswomen's Guilds and the Business and Professional Women's Clubs. The schedule cost 12p, more than the admission, which was 10p for adults and 5p for children. The secretary and organiser was a man from the Ministry of Agriculture, Craig Wallace, who was to join the Parks Department as Director a year later (see p. 144).

CENTENARY PARK

The year 1971 also marked the centenary of the opening of Belfast's first public park – Ormeau. During a week in April, games, band performances, and army and navy displays were organised, with a pageant and fireworks display on 15 April, the actual centenary day.

WEDDINGS AND DANCES

During the 1950s and 1960s both Malone House and Belfast Castle were used for wedding receptions, dinners, functions or simply for afternoon tea. The catering was franchised out and for a time was run by the Hastings Hotel group. There was a small ice cream and sweet shop in the kitchen wing of Malone House, and customers walked up a shallow outdoor ramp to be served through a window. In the late 1950s museums were very much on the agenda. There was a proposal to create a local history museum on the top floor of Malone House, and a folk museum at the new property of Sir Thomas and Lady Dixon Park. Neither proposal was followed through.

In 1959 the Floral Hall was redecorated and, because of new safety regulations, its capacity was reduced to 1,100. It did not diminish the enthusiasm of patrons for the musicians who played at the hall, such as Sam Glover's Dance Orchestra and the Fred Hanna Band. The 1950s and 1960s saw the rise and fall of the showband era when bands such as the Chris Barber Jazz Band, the Joe Loss Orchestra, the Plattermen and Candy all took their turn. Because of changing social trends and the coming of the disco scene, attendances at the Floral Hall gradually dropped. In an attempt to revive interest in the venue, roller skating was introduced in 1965. It was so successful that extra sessions had to be organised almost immediately.

A view of Ormeau Park showing a cricket match – and the prevailing fashion in trousers!

BELFAST CITY COUNCIL

DEMISE OF THE HALL

Gordon Connolly was appointed manager of the Floral Hall in May 1966 at a salary of £20 per week. He was given an extra 21s to 'compensate him for the additional expense of appearing on duty in evening clothes'. Thanks to his efforts dance attendances doubled. However, it proved to be only a temporary respite and when usage of the building in the early 1970s reached an all-time low, decisions about its future had to be taken. The Floral Hall was closed for a year from 1 April 1972, during which time a number of private entrepreneurs expressed interest in running it. In March of the following year the building was used as a counting centre for the Northern Ireland Border Poll. Occasional dances were still held, the last on 4 January 1974 with Teddy Palmer and the Rumble Band providing the music. The hall, which was granted listed building status later that year, quickly became nothing more than a hay store for the animals in Belfast Zoo (chapter 15).

In 1953 the familiar 'toast-rack' buses used to conduct visitors at Bellevue from the Antrim Road to the top plateau were replaced by two Leyland TD4 double-deckers, rebodied as single-deckers. The amusement arcade and rides at the northern end of the plateau were resurrected by Miss Barry in 1952 (the previous amusement park had closed in 1949 – chapter 9). The rides included a speedway, an American Whip and a Peter Pan railway. During the summer months the music from a huge fairground organ could be heard throughout the site. In 1973 the funfair was taken over by the Wallace brothers, who ran it until 1980 on a much smaller scale.

At the height of its popularity during the 1950s, the amusement park at Bellevue occupied the entire plateau.

BELFAST ZOO

AN AIR OF ABANDONMENT

The children's section of Bellevue Zoo included a Noah's ark (seen in the background) for rabbits and small animals.

A small children's playground was laid out at the southern end of the plateau, next to the entrance to the zoo itself, and included a maypole with chains and rings and a sandpit. Near to this was a fountain and pond. Belfast Corporation tried an experiment in 1959 by giving permission for a drive-in cinema to be held on the Bellevue plateau. The event was not repeated, presumably due to lack of enthusiasm from filmgoers. The grounds around the Floral Hall had their attractions as well. There was a miniature nine-hole golf course on the sloping ground to the south-east, which had been laid out in the 1930s, and there were pedal boats on Ballygolan Lake. Visitors not wishing to play golf or go boating could always stand and enjoy the panoramic views of Belfast Lough and the Antrim hills.

In April 1962 the Parks and Cemeteries Committee took over the management of Bellevue Zoo, the Hazelwood site and Belfast Castle Estate from the Transport Committee. By then the zoo was rather run-down, public interest in it having waned, and consideration was given to closing down the facility. Many enclosures lay empty, others were wrongly labelled or contained animals that were not named at all, and the cages for many of the animals were cramped and unsuitable. The former rockery was overgrown and untidy and the whole site had an air of abandonment. There were still some interesting features, such as the racoons in the former bandstand, the polar bear pacing its white rock enclosure, and the 'Noah's Ark' boat in the children's section, where visitors climbed on board to view the rabbits, guinea pigs and birds. The large red-brick monkey house with its curved roof (this feature was not originally part of the building) was a major landmark near the centre of the site – although not many visitors realised that it housed the zoo staff as well as the monkeys!

When the new zoo development began on the Hazelwood site (chapter 15) in 1978 the boating on the lake and use of the nearby pitch and putt course ended. The Bellevue amusements were discontinued soon afterwards to make room for a car park for the zoo.

The pedal boats on the lake beside the Floral Hall during the 1960s.

"SUNDAY MUSIC IN THE PARKS."

PERSECUTOR: 'Your worship, the Prisoner (Mr Bird) is charged with creating Music in the Parks on Sunday (cries of horror). He has outraged our principles and has committed a most heinous crime. I demand his extermination.'

NORTHERN LIGHT, MAY 1938

TO OPEN OR NOT TO OPEN

The question of whether or not parks facilities should be open on Sundays was debated on many occasions over the years. As early as the 1870s the Royal Belfast Botanic Garden had to be closed on Sunday evenings during church services because of 'grossly indecent goings-on among the bushes' reported in the press. In 1887 George McCann, the superintendent of Falls Park, was instructed to do his best to deter boys from playing football on Sunday evenings, until a bye-law banning such use could be drawn up. A subsequent proposal in 1920 to allow football to be played in the park on Sundays was defeated. The sale of refreshments, which took place in a number of parks including Ormeau, was banned on Sundays during the 1930s, and police were asked to move ice cream vans from the entrances of some parks because of the nuisance they were causing. In contrast Drumglass Playcentre and Queen Mary's Gardens were open on Sundays during the summer months from 1932 onwards.

From its inception Bellevue Zoo was open seven days a week for visitors, although questions were raised about whether children would be allowed to 'leave the Sabbath schools to spend the afternoon looking at animals'. The zoo's policy, introduced in 1933 after a secret ballot of the Tramways Committee, was later extended to the Hazelwood pitch and putt course and amusements at Bellevue. From 1942 the offices at Dundonald and City Cemeteries were opened for one hour on Sunday afternoons, between 4.00 p.m. and 5.00 p.m., to 'facilitate the general public'. In 1956, when the Corporation took over the Waterworks, the Parks and Cemeteries Committee rejected a call to ban the use of the miniature railway and boating ponds on Sundays, and by the mid-1960s playground equipment that had been previously chained up every Sunday was left unlocked. The debate was

Grosvenor Hall Military Band plays for visitors to Sir Thomas and Lady Dixon Park, 1977.

BELFAST TELEGRAPH

fuelled by the presentation of Sir Thomas and Lady Dixon Park to the city by Lady Dixon, who insisted that any swings put for children should be available on Sundays. Around the same time Councillor John O'Hare led the successful campaign to allow Sunday bathing at the Falls Park cooler.

In 1984 the Parks Committee held a review of Sunday opening of playing fields, in light of the new policy for leisure centres that permitted Sunday use. There had been unauthorised use of certain pitches for many years and the Council decided to open some sporting facilities on a trial basis. This provoked a petition from residents living near Wedderburn Park, resulting in this property being excluded from the trial. The Parks Committee's attention was later drawn to those using the aero-modelling circles at the City of Belfast Playing Fields on Sunday afternoons. One member forestalled any debate by announcing that fathers and sons were using the circles side by side and 'not doing anyone else any harm'. And so the aeromodel-ling areas remained open.

The playing of bands on Sundays in parks was permitted in 1957. In subsequent years this practice seems to have faded out, because by the mid-1970s the question of whether or not music should be provided on Sundays was again being asked. Objectors were appeased by the Council's insistence that the bands include sacred music in their programme.

MONITORING MUSIC

In February 1967 it was announced that band performances in Falls Park would cease because of hostility shown to bands playing the national anthem at the close of their concerts. By then the outdoor music scene was a well-established tradition, with the bands programme being organised in conjunction with the Northern Ireland Bands Association. Attendances during the 1970s, however, did decline. Staff monitored performances closely and found at times the bands were playing literally to 'two men and a dog'. In an effort to boost the popularity of the concerts, an 'Entertainments' championship was held in 1974 in Botanic Gardens. Eight local bands participated. The Corporation moved some of the midweek performances to weekends, including Sundays, and used busy venues such as Corn Market and the City Hall grounds. Attendances began to be measured in hundreds of listeners instead of only a few.

Two early cast-iron drinking fountains, sited at Alexandra Park (above) and Woodvale Park (below).

BELFAST CITY COUNCIL

SHELTERS FOR ALL AGES

In 1963 Lady Dixon presented a shelter for the playground at the newly opened Sir Thomas and Lady Dixon Park. The idea of having some form of shelter in a park is almost as old as the idea of parks itself and over the years both temporary and more permanent shelters were erected. Many of them, including those in Falls, Dunville, Ormeau and Woodvale Parks, Queen Mary's Gardens and Botanic Gardens, became fondly known as elderly men's shelters. They were meeting places: somewhere to sit quietly and read the paper, or to have a game of dominoes, quoits or cards with friends. A coal fire was lit every day to provide a warm and welcoming environment.

Further shelters were proposed for Orangefield and Grove Playing Fields in 1969, and an open-air theatre was built in Victoria Park in 1968. At the same time additional public conveniences were planned for many parks, including Glencairn, Ormeau and Shankill Rest Garden. By the mid-1980s some of the elderly men's shelters were reported to be in a bad condition. Those at Falls Park, Grove Playing Fields and Alexandra Park were demolished and the men's clubs moved their activities into the relevant bowling pavilions.

TIME FOR A DRINK

Drinking fountains were also common in parks from early days. The first ones were elaborate cast-iron constructions, the more recent ones made of enamel and stainless steel. The fountains in Ormeau and Woodvale Parks, among others, had a metal drinking cup attached to the fountain with a chain. On hot summer days there would be quite a queue to get a drink – with hardly a second thought about everyone drinking out of the same cup!

PERSONAL ATTACKS

Unfortunately features such as shelters and drinking fountains were easy targets for vandals. This was exemplified when the small summer house in the walled garden at Sir Thomas and Lady Dixon Park was burned down in early 1967. Playground equipment was also vulnerable, despite the presence of the park rangers who, armed with a stick and whistle, commanded respect and fear from most park users. Signs such as 'Keep off the Grass' were religiously observed by some but ignored by others – unless the ranger was close by. The park rangers had many nicknames: to some they were 'parkies', to others 'wakkies'. Doubtless there were some unprintable names as well.

Being an employee of the Corporation did not bring immunity from attack – in fact the opposite was often the case. One employee was assaulted by a pitch and putt player at Grove Playing Fields after trying to stop him damaging a green. The Council minutes recorded that the 'injuries to his dentures were replaced free under the National Health Service Scheme'. Another incident resulted in two stewards at the Floral Hall being reimbursed for damage to their clothing sustained during a disruption at a dance one evening.

It was a commonly held view that most of the vandalism was wrought by children and teenagers, but not every member of the younger generation was bent on destruction. In 1969 twenty-five bullocks were spotted in Musgrave Park. Seven youths assisted a park employee to remove the animals and were each rewarded with a letter of thanks and a £2 voucher.

The province's unpredictable weather also brought headaches for those in charge of horticulture and parks maintenance. Newly planted bedding plants would dry out easily in hot weather; bulbs would rot in waterlogged soils over winter. During the very hot summer of 1968, fears grew that irreparable damage would be done to some of the bowling greens because of drought. The Fire Brigade came to the rescue and pumped water on to the greens to keep them from drying out. But not all bowling problems were dealt with so easily. On several occasions greens were wrecked by vandals, who cut into the turf with spades. This type of damage can often take up to five years to repair fully.

FIRE

Over the years there has been a catalogue of arson attacks on park buildings. On the night of 21 April 1969 the boathouse and boats in Victoria Park were damaged by fire. Twelve boats were completely destroyed and a further twelve severely damaged. The same fate overtook the boats and boathouse at the Waterworks in March 1975, when a blaze caused £5,000 worth of damage. Malone House was burned to the ground in 1976 (chapter 15) in the worst single incident, the bowling pavilion in Musgrave was burned in December of the same year, and the following summer the Hazelwood café was damaged by a terrorist attack. In 1981 a fire caused considerable damage to the tennis pavilion at the Waterworks. Fernhill House, the Parks Department's headquarters, also suffered several arson attacks.

THE 'TROUBLES'

The Hazelwood café incident was one of numerous ways in which the 'Troubles' affected parks. During civil unrest, parks and open spaces unfortunately became venues for rioting and violence. Parks that lay between conflicting communities, for example Alexandra Park, suffered particularly badly with nightly sectarian battles raging at one stage. Extra night patrolmen had to be employed during rioting. Machinery was often stolen from the storage yards or the stores themselves burned out. There were several bomb attacks at Belfast Zoo, and in March 1987 an explosion at the gate to Roselawn Cemetery resulted in extensive damage to the gate house.

The most serious incident was the murder of zoo gardens' foreman Ricky Connolly, in October 1981. A member of the Ulster Defence Regiment, he was shot at the doorway of his Hazelwood home. A small rose garden at the zoo was opened in his memory two years later.

FRIENDSHIP SUNDAYS

In the mid-1970s the concept of Friendship Sundays was started at the City Cemetery to provide relatives with freer access to the cemetery through what had become a troubled part of Belfast. The initiative came from the local Catholic and Church of Ireland churches. Clergy from both denominations were involved with Belfast City Council in publicising the special days, organising buses, providing extra staff to be on duty and opening additional gates. The Friendship Sundays ran until the early 1980s and allowed many relatives from both sides of the community to visit graves in safety.

EDUCATION VERSUS VANDALS?

General vandalism continued to be a problem, costing the Council several thousands of pounds each month. The total bill for 1980 was exacerbated by a single act – the destruction of the mortuary chapel at the City Cemetery in July of that year. During the same period some £5,000 of damage was reported at Shankill Rest Garden alone, a comparatively small site. The Council bravely kept going, replanting trees, replacing bedding plants (sometimes two or three times in a single season), refitting playgrounds and rebuilding damaged property if possible. The Hazelwood café was replaced by the Ark restaurant, but sadly the cemetery chapel proved too costly to replace and the remains were removed in 1985. The tower was left to mark the site.

This ongoing problem was one of the reasons for the Parks Department employing an education officer in 1980, as it was felt that working with schoolchildren and the general public to raise awareness of the value of parks, both socially and historically, would help to alleviate vandalism. In addition a security patrol service was introduced in 1985 to combat the gangs of drinkers, glue sniffers and motorcyclists that were becoming an all too familiar scene within the parks.

OUTDOOR FACILITIES

The never-ending catalogue of vandalism did not deter efforts to provide as wide a range of outdoor facilities as possible. These were, and always had been, subject to the fickle moods of popularity. The use of some facilities waned while others rose to replace them. Pony and donkey rides were a feature at Sir Thomas and Lady Dixon Park and Grove Playing Fields for several summers in the late 1960s, the animals being stabled at the zoo during winter. In support of European Conservation Year 1970, a nature trail and waymarked posts were erected in woodlands around Belfast Castle. By the end of the decade 'trim trails' had been set out at Belfast Castle Estate and Cherryvale Playing Fields, with wooden exercise pieces set at intervals throughout the grounds. These were heavily vandalised and remained in fashion for only a short time, but were perhaps the forerunners of the orienteering courses of the late 1980s and 1990s that were laid out in parks such as Ormeau, Sir Thomas and Lady Dixon and Barnett Demesne.

Some activities had their moment and then vanished totally: the crazy golf courses have gone from Ormeau Park, Wedderburn Park and Ballysillan Playing Fields, the pitch and putt courses from Victoria Park and Grove and Orangefield Playing Fields, and the netball courts from Orangefield and the City of Belfast Playing Fields. Other facilities such as putting greens and BMX tracks remain but are used much less than they once were.

All of these facilities, with the exception of the BMX tracks, were charged for. In 1973 an adult wanting to play tennis on a grass court, such as those at Musgrave Park, had to pay 10p an hour for the privilege. It cost a full £1 for a game of football, a price that included use of pitch and pavilion. The admission price for an adult to the zoo in the same year was 14p, and for children 8p. By comparison, ten years later the zoo costs had risen to £1.00 and 50p respectively.

At one time all sports pitches were closed from the end of March until the beginning of September each year, to rest the playing surfaces. To extend the playing season and to accommodate more matches, the Corporation changed its ruling in the early 1970s, and permitted games to be played on pitches right up until the middle of May. Other pitches were set aside especially for summer use.

A former manager of the Floral Hall, Mr Smyth, was engaged to organise entertainment at the outdoor theatre in Victoria Park. In the early 1970s this took the form of a Starways Disco Show, variety acts and children's entertainment such as Punch and Judy shows. A bid was made to revive interest in this facility during the early 1980s by allowing local pop bands free use of the theatre, but without much success. It was just one example of a facility suffering from changing trends and ideas. Another was the use of parks for motor events.

CHANGING EVENTS

Until the early 1980s motor events were permitted in certain areas. Auto tests were held on the car parks at Belfast Zoo and the City of Belfast Playing Fields and at Barnett Demesne and Ormeau Park, where go-karting also took place. For a number of years one of the early timed stages of the prestigious Circuit of Ireland Rally was held on the roadways through Ormeau Park.

The outdoor boxing tournaments at Woodvale Park (see photograph, p. 79), so well attended in the 1940s and 1950s, were replaced by summer league football matches and running festivals. Circus performances were held at Woodvale and

Ormeau Parks, Botanic Gardens and Orangefield Playing Fields. These were not always popular, at times causing damage to the park and disturbance to local residents. Belfast's very first outdoor folk festival took place at Botanic Gardens in 1981, and the lower ground on the embankment was used for events such as gymkhanas. Parks also provided the venue for religious gatherings such as outdoor summer tent missions and campaign meetings – in 1981 the Campaign for Nuclear Disarmament held a 'March for Survival' in Botanic Gardens.

Following voluntary subscriptions from the workers of James Mackie and Sons, who collected £364, it was possible to revive the practice of guided bus tours through the parks. This was largely as a result of the efforts of Councillor Herbert Ditty, who encouraged the idea and organised the collection. Several tours were conducted during the summer of 1981, and they became an annual event of the parks summer programme.

THE END OF THE POOLS

Around the same time some well-known sights vanished from the parks. The outdoor swimming pool at Falls finally closed in 1979, having been enjoyed by countless hordes over its fifty-five-year life, including one, a Mr Keenan, who had been authorised to use the pool for training towards his goal of swimming the English Channel in 1970.

Some of the parks became sites for indoor leisure centres, including parts of Avoniel, Ballysillan and Loughside Playing Fields. Because of the new heated pool

Belfast's first outdoor folk festival attracted many fans to Botanic Gardens in 1981.

ROBERT SCOTT

at Avoniel Leisure Centre, the outdoor swimming pool at Victoria was used less and less. In 1980 and 1981 only a few hundred tickets were sold and although over one thousand people used the pool the following year, presumably because of better weather, it was decided in 1982 to close it. The decision was delayed while water samples were tested, repair costs investigated and users drew up a petition, but the reprieve was short-lived. The pool was declared unsafe. The water was contaminated and there were cracks on the concrete floor. No one was to swim in the outdoor pond at Victoria Park again. The site was filled in and levelled in the early 1990s.

ANOTHER NEW DIRECTOR

The span of thirty years or so from the mid-1950s into the 1980s, which had begun under Reginald Wesley's leadership, finished with a different man at the helm of the Parks Department. Following Wesley's retirement in 1972 (he died ten years later), Craig Wallace was selected as his successor. Born in Belfast, Wallace worked for a time with the rose firm of Samuel McGredy and Son, which inspired his love of this flower. He was educated at Ballymena Academy, Greenmount College and Reading University before joining the Ministry of Agriculture in the Horticultural Education Service. During his time as Director of Parks he was made an Associate of Honour by the Royal Horticultural Society (1981) and a Fellow of the Institute of Horticulture (1986). He received an MBE in 1987 for his contribution to horticulture.

The post of Director of Parks was altered to Director of Parks and Recreation to take account of the growing number of leisure centres in Belfast, although the responsibility for these and general indoor leisure was transferred to a separate Leisure Department in June 1976.

Like his predecessor, Craig Wallace witnessed a major transformation during his time in charge of the Parks Department. Under his guidance the number of staff and the number of major properties more than doubled. The total area of public open space rose to almost three thousand acres. The period of his directorship, between 1972 and 1988, proved to be one of unrivalled development and expansion for the Parks Department – a time when financial and social circumstances created opportunities that would have been undreamed of only a few years earlier.

14
The Expanding Empire
New Properties
1970s–1980s

During the 1950s the Parks and Cemeteries Committee had bought up land with the intention of keeping it in store, as it were, until the opportunity arose for its development. During the time of Craig Wallace, Director from 1972, that opportunity presented itself. He was able to finally oversee the landscaping and opening of areas that had lain dormant, some for as long as twenty years. At the same time new land was acquired by the Corporation, both by direct purchase and transfer from other bodies. As a result the number of parks and playing fields increased rapidly during the 1970s.

This 1864 painting by J.H. Connop, of land to the east of Belfast, encompassing the present Knocknagoney Linear, Blanchflower, Alderman Tommy Patton Memorial, Belmont and Victoria Parks.

BELFAST HARBOUR COMMISSIONERS

FINLAY PARK

A small piece of ground off the Whitewell Road was bought in 1946 from Greencastle and Whitehouse Recreation Centre for the purposes of providing an open space to be called Finlay Park. It cost the princely sum of £515 16s 3d, but because the agreement included a right to claim for a pavilion damaged by enemy action during the war, just over £167 of this cost was recouped. The ground lay undeveloped for many years, partly because of road proposals that threatened to affect the site. Finally, after the construction of the approach road to the new M2 motorway, the Corporation was left with two small bits of land divided by the road, each less than two acres. One was given over for housing, the other developed as a playground.

BELMONT PARK

It was proposed in 1951 to form a park near Schomberg House at Belmont. After the initial acquisition of ten acres from the NI Hospitals Authority in 1953, further land in the same area was added piecemeal until the total area reached thirty acres. The site, which cost the Corporation £12,000, lay undeveloped for many years, a wilderness of scrub and wild flowers – scorned as wasteland by some, enjoyed as a natural wilderness by others.

Ideas for possible playing fields and a municipal golf course came and went until development plans were finally drawn up in 1962. Proposals for the outer ring road east delayed progress for seven years until a three-year work programme began in the park under the relief of unemployment scheme. The land immediately around Schomberg House was never included in the plans (it is now housing: for example, Schomberg Avenue), but proposals for the remainder of the land allowed for lawns, gardens, a lily pool with fountain, a playground and a refreshment pavilion to the east of the new ring road with sports pitches laid out to the west. The long narrow strip of land to the north-west of the site was thought suitable for archery. A proposal for a par 3 golf course was still being considered in 1970, but as with many other sites the plans were changed in the light of financial constraints and public demands. The park was finally laid out with informal pathways and tree planting, with much of the work being carried out by Enterprise Ulster, a government training scheme set up in 1973 to alleviate unemployment. Areas of gorse and hawthorn already on the site were left as landscape features. The two halves of the park were linked by a footbridge over the ring road that bisected the property. Belmont Park was opened on 3 May 1985 by the Parks Committee Chairman, Councillor William Corry.

DOG TOILETS

Belmont Park acquired the somewhat dubious honour of being one of the first parks to have a dog toilet. This consisted of a fenced area where the grass was left to grow long, and where dogs were encouraged and members of the public were not! Similar areas were then set aside at other venues including Cherryvale Playing Fields, Barnett Demesne, Woodvale Park and the Waterworks in an effort to combat the problem of dog fouling.

PETROL DEPOT TO PLAYING FIELDS

Ground at Sydenham was acquired by the Corporation in 1957–8. A limited amount of levelling work and controlled tipping was carried out for a time but this was abandoned in 1966 pending road proposals. Some years later, in 1973, the Corporation added a further twelve acres lying between the Holywood Road and Sydenham Bypass and beside the original land. The site had been a petrol supply depot for the Ministry of Defence. A consulting engineer was appointed in 1974 to oversee the dismantling of the fuel storage units, but the work itself did not begin for a further two years.

In April 1978 plans were approved for a junior international soccer stadium with grandstand, terracing and floodlighting, other soccer pitches, a cricket square and two aeromodelling circles. Again there were delays, but work finally began in 1982. The Football Trust gave a grant of £40,000 towards the facility; the cheque was officially handed over by the Irish Football Association at Malone House. The site was named Sydenham Playing Fields and opened in May 1985 (the same day as Belmont Park), almost thirty years after the initial land acquisition. Some of the original brick buildings were retained and used as a foreman's office and stores. The property was later renamed after one of Northern Ireland's best-loved soccer stars, Danny Blanchflower – Sydenham Playing Fields and the junior stadium became the Blanchflower Park and Blanchflower Stadium respectively.

MUSGRAVE PLAYING FIELDS

Although the playing fields at Musgrave were opened in 1971 their formation had taken almost twenty years. At a joint meeting of the Welfare Committee and the Parks and Cemeteries Committee in 1954, it was decided to set aside twelve acres of the Balmoral Boys' School lands for recreation. This was originally separate from Musgrave Park, although in 1959 the Corporation purchased a strip of land from the Ulster Transport Authority to connect the two properties. A scheme was drawn up to accommodate three rugby pitches, a cricket square and a pavilion, but the tendering process was halted by the subsequent exchange of four acres of land to the NI Hospitals Authority. The plans were redrawn and in 1969 the machinery moved in. Development of the playing fields cost the Corporation £33,000.

Because a resting period of two years was required to allow the newly sown grass to become properly established for play, the property was not opened until 9 December 1971. The Chairman of the Parks Committee, Mrs Grace Bannister, JP, performed the opening ceremony, after which the guests had lunch in Malone House.

LOCAL GOVERNMENT UPHEAVAL

A major upheaval in local government in 1973 resulted in many local authority responsibilities being siphoned off into new bodies. The former Belfast Corporation became Belfast City Council, which held its first meeting on 12 June 1973. The original twelve committees (Gas, Improvement, Estates and Markets, Police, Police [Road Safety], Libraries, Parks and Cemeteries, Health [and Baths], Town Planning, Finance, Education, General Purposes) were reduced to five (General Purposes and Finance, Town Planning and Environmental Health, Technical Services, Gas, and Parks and Recreation). The Parks and Recreation Committee became responsible for parks, playing fields, leisure centres, baths, play-centres, cemeteries and the crematorium, as well as the continuing maintenance of school grounds on behalf of the newly formed Belfast Education and Library Board. Three departments (Parks, Recreation and Baths) reported to this committee, whose total expenditure for October 1973 to March 1974 was £738,714.

The Parks Department was the largest of the three, employing eighty-three white-collar workers and nearly six hundred manual staff. Subsequently, in 1976, responsibility for baths and indoor recreation was transferred to a Leisure Department under a Leisure Committee, and the Parks and Recreation Committee became simply the Parks Committee.

PARKS FROM LISBURN

The borough boundary lines were redrawn and Belfast acquired a number of existing parks that had previously fallen under the jurisdiction of Lisburn Rural District Council. These included Suffolk Playing Fields, the forty-acre site of Glen Road Playing Fields, Wedderburn Park and several playgrounds. Wedderburn Park, named after Councillor Andrew Marr Wedderburn, was a small neighbourhood park, equipped with a bowling green, tennis courts and a children's playground containing a small rectangular pond. The ground, in the parish of Drumbeg, had been acquired by the former Lisburn Rural District Council from the Diocesan Trustees of St Anne's Oratory in 1949.

Prior to 1973 Lisburn Council had started work at Glen Road on pitches earmarked for Gaelic football. Work was halted when a community of travellers moved in. Despite attempts by Belfast City Council and the Gaelic Athletic Association to solve the impasse the contractors moved out and no further work was possible. The site was transferred to Belfast City Council's Community Services Department in the mid-1980s.

CLOGS TO CANNED FRUIT

Belfast City Council obtained another ready-made park when it took ownership of land within the Lagan Valley at Newforge. The public had been allowed access to the ground for a number of years before it was formally opened as Clement Wilson Park.

At the beginning of the twentieth century the site was occupied by a factory producing clogs, which were once worn extensively by the labouring classes. A mill-race that started beside Shaw's Bridge fed water from the River Lagan to the factory. In 1929 it was bought by a company called Wilson Management Ltd, which gained twenty-five acres of land north-east of Shaw's Bridge in the deal. Further pieces of land were annexed in 1943 and 1960, bringing the total area to fifty-four acres. Wilson's firm used the factory to produce soft fruit for canning, some of which was grown in orchards that stood on what are now the grasslands of the park beside Newforge Lane. From 1945 onwards the factory also supplied frozen fruit, which was sold from the first retail freezer unit situated in Brands Arcade, Belfast.

Because the factory was located out of town, it was impossible for employees to travel home for lunch. Therefore it became their custom to walk the nearby fields. The chairman of the company, Robert Clement Wilson, decided to follow an idea that was prevalent in England and had the grounds landscaped into gardens for the benefit of his employees. Thus the area became the province's first factory garden.

After the war the millrace was filled in using rubble from demolished air raid shelters and buildings. The sunken waterway became a raised walkway, known locally as the 'Burma Road'. This is still the main path through the property today.

Negotiations between the Clement Wilson family and Belfast City Council over forty-five acres at Newforge began in spring of 1974. Several amendments were made, resulting in a reduction to forty-one acres. The total cost was £51,000 and the family stipulated that the park should be called 'The Clement Wilson Park'. The Council agreed to the purchase, which was grant-aided by the Department of Community Relations. The park was officially opened on 30 October 1975, with a ceremony conducted by Councillor William Corry, a former Chairman of the Parks and Cemeteries Committee. The factory garden adjacent to Clement Wilson Park, which by then belonged to Spillers Foods Ltd, had also been open to the public, and from 1975 the Parks Department maintained this garden on a contract basis for the company.

Most of the old factory buildings and adjacent farm buildings had already vanished when the Council took over ownership. One farmhouse remained, however, near the River Lagan. It was used for ten years by the Belfast Canoe Club before it too was demolished in 1985.

GREENVILLE PARK

Seven acres of land between Orangefield Playing Fields and Dunraven Park were designated as open space in the Belfast Urban Area Plan of 1969. This area, comprising Greenville House and grounds, was purchased by Belfast City Council in 1976 at a cost of £32,000. The house was demolished and the site, which was

A 'green' Ulster Transport Authority bus crosses Shaw's Bridge, *c.* 1960. Behind the bus are the factory buildings on what is now Clement Wilson Park.

POSTCARD

continuous with Orangefield Playing Fields, developed under the Environmental Improvement Scheme – grant-aided 100 per cent by the Department of the Environment, NI.

The same improvement scheme subsidised the development of eight acres alongside Shore Road beyond the Fortwilliam roundabout and an east Belfast playground site on the Lower Newtownards Road. Greenville Park and the ground at Shore Road, which became known as Loughside Park, were opened in November 1983. A year later nearby Loughside Playing Fields were added to the growing list of properties.

LINEAR PARKS

The 1970s saw the introduction of the term 'linear park' to describe long narrow stretches of open space, usually along a river or stream valley, or a disused railway line. The first, called Ballymacarrett Walkway, was on part of the former County Down Railway line between Manderson Street and Dee Street. Proposals were made in 1973 for another linear park on land at Knocknagoney that had been transferred from the Northern Ireland Housing Executive. The scheme was grant-aided under the Urban and Rural Improvement Campaign. Enterprise Ulster began development work on Knocknagoney Linear Park in 1976.

The estate lands around Forth River House, including ground alongside Forth River, were purchased by the Council in 1975 for £8,800. It was felt that this ground, adjacent to property at Glencairn, would make 'worthwhile open space' and was suitable for a linear park. A grant of £4,800 was given by the Department of Housing, Local Government and Planning. Forth River House was let to a member of staff for a short time but was demolished a year later.

Progress at Forth River and Knocknagoney was painstakingly slow, with both developments finally being completed and named in 1984. Knocknagoney was officially opened on 3 May 1985; Forth River Linear Park had no official opening. One year later yet another linear park was ready, this time on forty acres at Carr's Glen, which had been acquired in 1978. The first stage of development involved the removal of cars, prams, shopping trolleys and other rubbish from the Carr's Glen Stream that flowed through the park – the same stream that fed the ponds at the Waterworks and Alexandra Park.

Within the confines of the park there were two sites of archaeological interest. These raths, or forts, were indications of early settlements in the area. There were also signs of an industrial past in the form of two ruined farmhouses and a mill, beside which was a water sluice – a pit lined with uncut stone. Early pictures show the mill's large waterwheel in position. The two ruined gable walls of the mill, over-looking the glen and the city, were known to local children as the 'old castle'.

LIGONIEL PARK

The Northern Ireland Housing Executive approached Belfast City Council in 1975 with regard to seven acres of land due to come into its ownership, suggesting that the land might be suitable for development as a park. Negotiations with William Ewart Properties Ltd resulted in adjacent land also being considered, increasing the area to nineteen and a half acres. This included the open water

known as Boodles Dam, and Ligoniel House, the former home of the manager of Ligoniel Mill. Belfast City Council agreed to purchase the land for a sum of £13,750, plus £1,000 for reducing the depth of the pond to allow it to be used as a paddling pool. As with other purchases it was partly grant-aided. Before the sale was completed the house and some of the trees were vandalised. The building, like many before it, had to be demolished before the park landscaping could begin. Boodles Dam never became an official paddling pool, but instead remained a potential danger. It was later fenced off from the rest of the park.

A DOCTOR'S PARK

Dr John Pitt Memorial Park, on the Lower Newtownards Road, was formed in memory of the well-loved family doctor who practised in Ballymacarrett from 1932 to 1973. A stone plaque at the entrance was donated by grateful patients and unveiled by Mrs Pitt on 29 May 1982. After the ceremony a local ladies' group provided tea and refreshments in a nearby church hall. The doctor was held in such high esteem that a former patient wrote a poem about him.

> A great doctor he, a man of great skill
> Curing patients of illness with medicine and pill;
> Long may the memory remain in our mind
> Of John Pitt, so skilful, so courteous, so kind.

The park included raised flower beds, seating, a small kick-about area and a playground. It formed an ideal template for other community areas such as Clara Street Playground, in east Belfast, which was landscaped along similar lines in 1985.

Many parks contain relics of an industrial past. In Carr's Glen Linear Park only a few stone walls remain of this water-powered mill.

POSTCARD

EDUCATION AND LIBRARY BOARD SITES

In 1987 the Department of Education transferred lands that were surplus to the requirements of the Belfast Education and Library Board to Belfast City Council. In a single transaction, 160 acres of open space, primarily playing fields, were transferred into public ownership. Some of the sites were derelict, with pitches no longer serviceable, while others gave a much-needed boost to areas of the city lacking in sporting facilities.

The transfer included playing fields at Shore Road, comprising four hockey pitches; Clarendon Park, which included former allotments towards the northern end; Cliftonville, the old Cliftonville Cricket and Hockey Club ground; Boucher Road, with all-weather pitches and tennis courts; Woodlands, once the grounds of Woodlands House and former field for the Orange Order's Twelfth of July parade; Strangford Avenue, which was used annually as an overflow car park for the Royal Ulster Agricultural Show; Clara Park, once attached to Robert Bell Primary School; Ormeau – the former Ulster cricket ground and Ulidia school grounds (later called Ulidia Playing Fields); and Inverary, an area of disused all-weather hockey pitches.

SPORTS GROUNDS AT INVERARY

The present park at Inverary, Sydenham, came into being through two separate agreements over two parcels of land. The smaller portion, the former IEL Sports Ground and Social Club premises, came on to the market in 1975 and was purchased by the Belfast Education and Library Board for the use of schools in the area. At that time the Parks Committee expressed an interest in the site, and for many years it managed the bowling green and pavilion as the Education and Library Board had no use for it. Following an agreement between the Board and the Council in April 1981, the Parks Department took over the property on a lease, pending grant aid for purchase being made available by the Department of the Environment, NI.

Events overtook these plans when the second, larger portion of ground was transferred in 1987 along with the other Belfast Education and Library Board sites, bringing the total area at Inverary up to forty-five acres. This area had been bought by the education authorities in 1951 and had, at one time, been considered for a par 3 golf course. The new site, known locally as Cranfield Park, was officially called Inverary Playing Fields. It was later renamed Alderman Tommy Patton Memorial Park, after a local councillor. The indoor pavilion on the site was used for a time as a playcentre, for after-school children's activities and for indoor games during park summer schemes.

NORTHERN IRELAND'S GOLDEN GIRL

One consequence of Mary Peters's famous gold medal pentathlon performance in the 1972 Munich Olympic Games was the increase in the profile of athletics as a sport. The culmination of this was the opening of the Mary Peters Athletics Track in 1975 on a site near the River Lagan – an area that was formerly part of Malone Golf Course (chapter 11). At that time there were no modern synthetic running tracks in the province. Funds to provide up-to-date training facilities were raised by public subscription enabling the six-lane track to be constructed. Mary Peters attended the opening ceremony, where local primary school children formed up on the track and spelt out her name, to the delight of the spectators, all of whom had tramped across Queen's University Playing Fields to reach the site. It was five years later before public access was improved and a car park provided. Enterprise Ulster undertook this programme of work, which also included the installation of trackside fencing, paved terracing and a discus and hammer cage. After prolonged negotiations and the acknowledgment that the property needed constant management and maintenance, the facility was transferred from Queen's University to Belfast City Council in 1985 on a ninety-nine-year lease, along with thirty acres of conifer woodland that had been planted out as a shelter belt. One of the first tasks taken on by the Council was the resurfacing of the track.

In the same year a new nine-hole, par 3 golf course was opened at Mallusk, on rough farmland beside the City of Belfast Playing Fields. Former British Open champion Fred Daly played the opening round on 30 August 1985. It was officially titled Belfast Parks Golf Course, but with time this became abbreviated to Mallusk Golf Course. Despite being some miles outside of the city boundary, it remains Belfast's only true municipal golf course.

Local schoolchildren release balloons to mark the opening of the Mary Peters Athletics Track in 1975.

ROBERT SCOTT

OPEN SPACES

Despite the development of facilities in and around the outskirts of Belfast, the number of open spaces and general sitting areas within the city centre remained low. Such sites can do much to make a city attractive to visitors and residents alike. The main problems associated with their acquisition and development were, and still are, lack of availability and high land cost. Notwithstanding these difficulties, some open spaces were provided within Belfast. The ground beside St Anne's Cathedral was first landscaped during the 1960s, but was later redesigned by the Parks and Technical Services Departments in 1977. At that time new trees and shrubs were added, along with beds for seasonal bedding, seating and a centrepiece of three large buoys and basal fountains, one of the most striking features in that part of Belfast. The fountains were switched on by Councillor Andy Cairns, JP, Chairman of the Parks Committee, on 21 November 1983, when the site was given its official title of Cathedral Gardens. On the same day the Department of the Environment, Roads Service, handed over Bloomfield Walkway to the Parks

Manderson Street Garden was developed under a scheme for the relief of the unemployed, using land regained by culverting the Connswater River, c. 1964.

BELFAST TELEGRAPH

Department on a fifteen-year maintenance lease (Greenville and Loughside Parks were also opened on that date).

The possibility of obtaining another city centre open space at the junction of Victoria Street and High Street was brought to the Parks Committee's attention in October 1974. After negotiations with the owners, the corner site was bought for £73,500 the following year. The Department of the Environment, NI grant-aided the purchase by 75 per cent under its Open Space Grant Scheme. Clearance work was paid for under the Spruce-Up Campaign, and the site was landscaped with seating, raised beds, and a fountain that, unfortunately, has seldom worked. It also contains a wall mural made from a mosaic of tiny squares, each representing one person killed during the 'Troubles' up to that time. The open space was named Jubilee Garden to commemorate the Silver Jubilee of Queen Elizabeth II and was opened on 10 May 1977.

Other open spaces throughout the city included small established parks such as King William Park and Finlay Park, unfenced areas such as Sharman Road Open Space and Manderson Street Garden, flower bed sites in the city centre, car parks such as those at Stranmillis and Ormeau Avenue (the site of Tower Buildings, the former Gas Department property), various traffic islands, road landscaped sites such as Westlink, and ground around leisure centres. Some of these areas were owned by Belfast City Council, others maintained on an agency basis on behalf of the Department of the Environment.

Since the early twentieth century the grounds of the City Hall have been a prime open space within the centre of Belfast. Although many of the elements of their original Victorian design have been removed, the grounds still provide a lunchtime haven for countless shoppers and office workers, particularly during good weather.

MISCELLANEOUS SQUADS

These open spaces, along with other sites throughout Belfast, were maintained on a day-to-day basis by gardeners grouped in what were known as 'miscellaneous squads'. Each squad had responsibility for a specific area of the city. Their role included general horticultural maintenance, such as grass cutting and planting, and more specialised work such as the care of the street trees – including planting new ones. Pollution levels in the late 1960s had declined sufficiently to allow a greater diversity of tree species to be used in the city: hazel, hornbeam, cherry, birch and rowan all proved successful.

The squads were called upon from time to time to carry out more unusual tasks, including the repair of tarmac paths damaged by weeds and replanting of hedges and lime trees that were slowly being poisoned by gas leaching from ageing underground pipes. A landscape development squad toured the city, under the direction of the Parks Department's landscape architects, carrying out tasks such as bulb and shrub planting on new sites, some of which were owned by the Department of the Environment, NI.

Two further squads, each of two people, inspected all of the playgrounds on a daily schedule to check for vandalism and to ensure equipment was kept to the highest standard of safety. This checking became more and more vital as the range and versatility of playground apparatus increased and as instances of claims and litigation procedures became more frequent.

PLAY FOR CHILDREN

Children's play equipment was an important feature of parks and open spaces. In February 1963 some innovative equipment was purchased for Glenbank Park. It included a Wendy House, a spaceship and a 'Wyndsor' motor launch. It is easy to imagine the excitement this must have caused among children who up until then had known only traditional swings and slides. Many pieces of play equipment that became popular around that time, however, were subsequently banned for health and safety reasons. The witch's hat, the plank swing, the spider's web and the rocking boat have all disappeared from the playground arena.

CENTRES OR GROUNDS

Play equipment was generally positioned at playgrounds, where there was no staff supervision, and at playcentres, a term that gradually came to be associated with buildings where staff supervised indoor activities for children. Playcentre staff were trained in a range of disciplines including mime, drama, games, arts and first aid. The centres catered mainly for five- to twelve-year-olds, although toddlers' groups were later introduced into morning sessions while the older children were at school. Throughout the year the children participated in a host of other activities such as games, arts and crafts, exhibitions, costume making, fancy dress and pet shows. Coming up to Christmas broken toys were collected, repaired and

By the end of the 1960s Belfast had twenty playcentres, at which staff organised games for local children, such as this ball game at Scotch Row Playcentre in east Belfast, *c.* 1960.

repainted, and then forwarded to Dr Barnardo's homes and to children in Lissue Hospital, Lisburn. Each centre held an annual open-air display to highlight the year's work. An accordion player was engaged to provide music, and the audience included parents, local councillors, education and library board members and press.

'CREATIVE CHANNELS'

In 1952 there were eleven playcentres operating within twenty-five square miles in the city. By the end of the 1960s this number had risen to twenty, although almost immediately it fell again to eighteen when Hemsworth Street Centre was closed and Boundary Street Centre destroyed during civil unrest. This total was short of the National Playing Fields Association's recommendation that no child should live more than one quarter of a mile from a playground, a figure that was more of an ultimate goal than an achievable target. In 1970 the Director of Parks, Reginald Wesley, presented a report to the Parks and Cemeteries Committee stressing the importance of playcentres and suggesting that they were more than merely areas where children went to play. The report described them as places of safety, where 'superfluous energy is diverted into creative rather than destructive channels' and where 'lonely children find companionship and where many of their emotional problems are resolved through their relationship with the Playleader, who becomes a second mother to the youngest and an older sister to the rest'. At that time up to four hundred children were using the centres on a daily basis, especially in good weather during the school holidays.

CHANGING RESPONSIBILITY

Back in 1951 the responsibility of the city's playcentres had been transferred to the Education Committee so that the Corporation could qualify for the 65 per cent grant available under the Youth Welfare, Physical Training and Recreation Act of 1947. The Parks and Cemeteries Department operated the centres on behalf of the Education Committee, with the exception of Donegall Road which remained under the direct control of Parks. With the local government reorganisation in 1973 ownership of the playcentres was transferred to Belfast Education and Library Board. Because it was felt that the work of these centres was more appropriate to the work of the City Council, their ownership was transferred back two years later.

The Department of Education generously offered 75 per cent funding up to a total of £100,000 for expenditure on playcentres and playgrounds for the 1975–6 financial year. By then the number of centres had dropped to sixteen (Avoniel, Ballysillan, Beechfield Street, Castleton, Clara Street, Donegall Road, Drumglass, Gallaher, Loop River, North Queen Street, Oldpark, Queen Mary's, Midgley, St Leonard's Street, Willowbank and Stanhope Street), but rarely were they all operational at the one time. This was due to high instances of vandalism and difficulties in recruiting staff.

By 1980 only four playcentres were still running, namely those at Clara Street, North Queen Street, Loop River (opened without any official ceremony in 1959) and Queen Mary's Gardens. The number rose to six in 1982 when new buildings at Avoniel were opened and those at Ballysillan reopened. New centres at Olympia (Grosvenor Road) and Whiterock followed, but the total number remained unchanged when Clara Street and Queen Mary's Playcentres finally closed their doors to local youngsters. Clara Street was later redeveloped as a playground. The leisure centre at Olympia (originally referred to as the Bog Meadows Leisure Centre), which included the playcentre, was built on what had been known as Midgley Park. This park, comprising a playground and one all-weather pitch, had been named after Alderman Midgley, who had campaigned for a playground in the area in the 1930s.

Although the idea of staffed playcentres was in decline, the number of playgrounds was on the increase. In the early 1970s the army erected playground equipment on numerous sites but made no provision for maintenance. As a result many were vandalised and unusable. However, the trend had been set. By the end of the decade there were thirty playgrounds in Belfast (excluding those associated with playcentres), a number that was to more than double within the following fifteen years. Some of these were sited within parks, some were on open space, and others were within housing estates. Names such as Highfield, the Hammer, Horn Drive, Northlink, Slievegallion and Taughmonagh became familiar to children. The playground in Ormeau Park beside Park Road was designed by a five-year-old local boy, Thomas Stevens, as part of a competition. It was opened in the mid-1980s but was called Ormeau 2000.

PAUPERS' GRAVES TO PLAYGROUND

The playground and playcentre at Donegall Road had a more unusual history than most. In 1915 the Board of Guardians, administrators of the poor laws, offered the

Corporation a portion of land at the Union Workhouse on the Donegall Road that had been acquired in 1848 for use as a paupers' burial ground. As it was no longer required for this purpose the Board felt that it would make a suitable open space. The Donegall Road burial ground was deconsecrated and developed as a children's playground and playcentre. Much later, in 1984, it came under scrutiny again. A deal was struck permitting the use of this site for housing development (it is now Prince Andrew Gardens and Park), while Belfast City Council received compensation to purchase land nearby belonging to the Northern Ireland Transport Holding Company. Access to this ground was from Bythe Street. A new playground was constructed and opened as Bythefield Park in 1985. The Council issued a licence for the human remains found at the original site during development to be reburied at the City Cemetery.

A poster advertising the summer scheme organised in Orangefield Playing Fields in 1974.

BELFAST CITY COUNCIL

SUMMER ENTERTAINMENT

In 1974 Easter Recreation Schemes for children and young people were introduced in Botanic Gardens, Victoria Park, Drumglass Playcentre, and Ballysillan, Orangefield and Grove Playing Fields. Ten schemes were run during July and August with activities such as swimming, cycling proficiency, fancy dress and five-a-side football. Minibuses were hired to take children for 'out-of-parks outings'. A five-week camp was held in Newcastle and thirty children from different areas taken to it each week. A Gala Week for all the summer schemes was held in Ormeau Park in August, and included 'Miss Playcentre' and 'Miss Park' competitions. The Parks Department employed a full-time Recreation and Entertainments Officer from 1975.

The popularity of summer schemes peaked around 1980 with the organisation of Play Schemes for five- to twelve-year-olds and Opportunity Schemes for teenagers, grant-aided by the Department of Education. These involved over sixty staff and fourteen parks. Organised games, bouncy-castles, puppet shows and sports were provided for the younger age group, while the activities for teenagers included educational elements such as constructing wooden bird boxes that were subsequently placed in parks.

HOW FAR ON?

In 1986 a survey of the land within and around the fringes of the Belfast Urban Area Plan recorded that some 5,041 acres of land comprised open space and was recreation-based. This figure included private open space such as golf courses. Only 40 per cent of it consisted of public open space. This represented a major step forward from the situation as assessed in 1969 – in the space of seventeen years, twenty-six new parks or amenity areas and twenty-four playing field sites had been developed. Although Belfast City Council owned and maintained the largest proportion of open space, there were a number of other heavily used public parkland areas. These included Colin Glen Forest Park along the Glen River (run by the Colin Glen Trust), Belvoir Forest Park (owned by the Forestry Service), the grounds of Parliament Buildings at Stormont, and municipal parks and playing fields within the jurisdiction of neighbouring councils of Newtownabbey, Castlereagh and Lisburn.

Despite this rapid increase Belfast still did not compare favourably with other cities in the United Kingdom. In 1989 the total amount of open space available to the public was significantly less than in Dundee, Cardiff, Coventry and Middlesbrough, all of which had a smaller population than Belfast's estimated 800,000. Belfast had fewer walking linkages with the surrounding countryside, fewer allotment sites, and fewer opportunities within built-up areas for development of further open space.

15
The Restoration Period

Belfast Corporation took decisions to spend considerable sums of money on public facilities, particularly buildings, during the 1970s and 1980s. Belfast Zoological Gardens was in line for not just a facelift but a total renewal: a new zoo was to be developed on the former Hazelwood Estate. Belfast Castle was in poor condition and was to be renovated. Malone House was even worse off. In November 1976, two terrorist devices and an ensuing fire had reduced the building to a mere shell. It stood roofless and open to the elements for a number of years before the decision was taken to restore it. The two Victorian gems in Botanic Gardens, the Palm House and the Tropical Ravine, were also badly in need of repair, so much so that the Corporation considered demolishing the Palm House at a time when there were almost as many plants growing outside on the roof and in the guttering as were on display inside.

As money became available from a variety of sources, these superb public facilities received the attention they deserved, representing as they do a sizeable portion of Belfast's social and horticultural history.

A NEW ZOO

An exciting resolution was taken by Belfast City Council in May 1974: Belfast was to get a new zoo. This decision was taken in the light of changing public opinions towards zoos and a growing awareness of the importance of nature conservation and the value of captive animal breeding programmes. Hitherto Bellevue had been primarily an entertainment venue and, although any new development would still be considered a major visitor attraction, emphasis this time round was firmly placed on education, conservation and animal welfare. The architect firm McAdam Design Ltd was appointed consultant and under its leadership extensive and innovative plans emerged. Enclosure design was based around the needs of the animals in terms of behaviour, social grouping and physical activity, encouraging the occupants to behave as naturally as possible in front of visitors. This was balanced with keeper requirements – so that the animals could be looked after to the highest standard, and visitor enjoyment – providing unobstructed viewing where possible with panels of information about the animals and their natural habitat. The animal houses were of a particularly high architectural standard, for example, the elephant house. The importance placed by the Council on the overall project was underlined when it created a new post in 1979 – that of zoo manager.

The first exhibit in the new Hazelwood site was opened on 12 December 1979 by the High Sheriff, Councillor Mrs Grace Bannister, JP. The initial phase of enclosures included large paddocks for antelope and deer, on and around the grassy slopes below the Floral Hall – where the buses once ferried visitors from the Antrim Road to the plateau entrance. The next phase included a children's farm,

spider monkey enclosures, and a wildfowl and flamingo collection around the pond area behind the Floral Hall. A temporary education centre on the site of the original Hazelwood House (chapter 9) was later transformed into the Ark restaurant when a permanent education classroom was set up in the children's farm.

The lake at Hazelwood is one of the main features of the new zoo.

HOUSTON GREEN PHOTOGRAPHY

FIFTY YEARS

A colour guidebook was published in 1984 to mark the fiftieth anniversary of the zoo. It contained an artist's impression of the proposed aquatic enclosures that were still under construction. Their intended occupants were penguins, sea lions and polar bears. The completion in 1985 of this complex, based around a natural limestone amphitheatre, greatly boosted visitor numbers to the zoo. To celebrate its opening a penguin party was held, just as twenty-one gentoo penguins were acclimatising to their new home at Belfast. Visitors were fascinated by being able to watch for the first time both penguins and sea lions swimming underwater. Considering that three of the sea lions were sightless (they had been obtained from the Californian Marine Mammal Rehabilitation Centre – after one had been shot in the face and two had been clubbed), it was a marvel how easily they found their way around the pool and managed to catch fish thrown in by their keepers.

The later years of the 1980s and early 1990s saw the finishing of the big cats' area, a free flight aviary, and enclosures for elephant, giraffe, zebra and the primate collection. Bellevue had always contained chimps, but in very inadequate cages. To see a group of these primates in much superior surroundings was, for staff and visitors, very satisfying. The enclosure was endorsed by Dr Jane Goodall, world-renowned zoologist, when she visited Belfast Zoo in August 1991. The chimpanzee troop was upstaged somewhat that year when two gorillas arrived to take up residence next door. This was the first time that gorillas had been exhibited in Belfast. The male silverback, 'Kéké', had been rescued as an infant from poachers in the Cameroon, his mother having been killed.

By the mid-1990s the new zoo was considered to be more or less complete, with only minor projects left unfinished. The old Bellevue site finally closed to the public in June 1989.

Belfast Zoo has established a world wide reputation of breeding successes, particularly with endangered species. The first agonising steps towards the ultimate goal of such a programme – to return captive bred animals to the wild – were taken when one golden lion tamarin (a species of small monkey), born at Belfast Zoo, was released into the wild in Brazil. Over the years many animals have been born at the zoo: perhaps the culmination of this breeding programme was the birth of the first baby gorilla 'Djamba' in 1994 (only the second gorilla to be born in Ireland) and that of a baby Indian elephant, called 'Vishesh', which is Hindi for 'special', in May 1997.

An animal adoption scheme was introduced early in the new zoo's development, through which individuals, schools or firms could sponsor a favourite animal. Sponsors were often able to choose a name and tried hard to come up with appropriate ones: for example, 'Wash' and 'Tumble' for two polar bear cubs, 'Hop', 'Skip' and 'Jump' for three kangaroos and 'Ice' for one of the penguins. Fun days, behind-the-scenes visits, sponsors' evenings, educational visits, photographic competitions and a regular newsletter *Zoo Crack* have all helped to maintain interest and support for what is now one of the most modern zoos in Europe, and one of only two zoological gardens in the United Kingdom to be managed by a local authority (the other being Blackpool). The setting is superb. The attractive landscaping around the enclosures and the panoramic views over Belfast Lough and County Antrim add to the enjoyment of a visit.

Perhaps as a throwback to the nineteenth century when crowds gathered on the slopes of Cave Hill at Easter (chapter 1), Belfast Zoo always has its highest daily attendances on Easter Monday and Tuesday – as many as ten thousand in one day. That's a lot of enthusiasm for what is now officially called the City of Belfast Zoological Gardens, a project that cost Belfast City Council £10 million and took over fifteen years to complete.

BELFAST CASTLE

From 1937, when it first opened to the public, until 1971, when the catering franchise ran out, Belfast Castle was used for wedding receptions, dances and afternoon teas. These functions generally occupied the main rooms on the ground and first floors. Some of the second floor rooms were used for a rather unusual purpose for a time: to quarantine smaller animals for Belfast Zoo. (The animals were in quarantine boxes, not just allowed free run of the rooms!) The heavy demand on space at the castle took its toll on the decoration and fabric of the building until, in the late 1960s, the pigeons were reported to be literally 'flying in and out of the windows'.

PUBLIC INQUIRY

Belfast City Council examined possible uses for the castle including a library, a welfare home, a museum or art gallery, a youth hostel and a mansion house for the Lord Mayor. The Council opted to sell the building and five acres of ground for development as a hotel. There was widespread objection to the sale and a public inquiry was held in 1971, as a result of which the Ministry of Development recommended that the proposal should be abandoned. The Council then decided to embark on an alternative road – that of a major renovation programme.

The castle had just been designated as a listed building, an important step as it meant that any restoration work would be eligible for grant-aid. The Council commissioned a firm of architects, Hewitt and Haslam Partnership, to produce a report on the condition of the building, which made for dismal reading: a tale of timber decay, wet and dry rot, missing roof flashing, subsidence in some of the retaining walls and deterioration of the sandstone. The first phase of restoration was to repair and restore the roof and to eradicate any timber decay. After that came the cleaning of and repairs to the exterior faces of the sandstone walls. In 1982 the castle was attacked with a firebomb that caused damage to flooring and windows in the

Belfast Castle reopened in 1988 after its £2 million renovation.
ROBERT SCOTT

main ballroom. Fortunately this did not undo any of the exterior restoration work already completed.

The firm William Dowling Ltd was appointed to carry out the interior restoration, beginning in 1985. This involved work to the entire building – from the cellars to the tower levels: a total of eight different floors, connected by three separate staircases. All 100 interior doors were replaced, and each of the windows had to be resashed and painted. There are reputedly a total of 365 windows – one for each day of the year, with a round bullet window in the south tower to signify a leap year. Two new lifts, a skylight over the stairwell (designed to hide the emergency fire vents) and miles of cablework were installed without disrupting the historical appearance of the castle. Sections of the maple wood ballroom floor and the entire carved oak staircase and oak panelling in the first room were retained and restored.

During the restoration some interesting building techniques of the past came to light. Energy conservation must have been on the agenda back in the 1870s as the walls of the castle were found to be three feet thick in places and insulated by plaster lathes. The roof was also well insulated using layers of plaster, lathes and horsehair. Water was conserved and recycled through rainwater tanks that were filled from the run-off from the many-angled roofs – a good idea, but costly in the long run as leaks and condensation from interior pipework were found to have taken their toll on the fabric of the building.

The restoration of Belfast Castle lasted ten years and cost £2 million. One-third of the cost came from a grant supplied by the Historic Monuments and Buildings Branch of the Department of the Environment, NI. The building was reopened to the public on 11 November 1988, when the various rooms were renamed to commemorate the Donegall and Shaftesbury connections (chapter 9).

The final part of the project was the transformation of the basements into a cellar restaurant, antique shop and bar facilities. This was done in the style of a Victorian street with paved floors, shopfronts and gas lighting, and was finished in 1990. The machinery that operated the original water-powered lift was preserved in the basement. Part of the lift shaft can still be identified in the oak-panelled reception room – it is a booth for a public telephone. A far cry from the days of the Shaftesburys who were among the first to own a telephone in Belfast, with a number of Belfast 2.

In 1994 a Cave Hill Heritage Centre was opened on the second floor, while the grounds around the castle were landscaped with gardens and a central fountain – all thanks to funding from the European Regional Development Fund. The gardens were given an intriguing cat theme with feline statues, mosaics, poems and even footprints concealed in the pathways and flower beds. The theme was inspired by the castle cat, although no one seems quite sure if there ever had been one. A castle cat may be a distinct possibility, but a castle ghost? The nightwatchman once reported that in one of the upstairs rooms his dog had suddenly started baying and had hidden under a table. He claimed that 'things were mysteriously thrown about'!

MALONE HOUSE

From April 1971 the National Trust leased Malone House as its headquarters. When the house burned down on 11 November 1976, the Trust lost a lot of its records and the Ulster Museum lost its costume collection, which was stored in the attic. Between 1976 and 1980 the ruined shell of Malone House stood abandoned on the hilltop, in much the same manner as Moses Hill's original fort must have done after it was burned over three hundred years earlier (chapter 11). It became obvious to Belfast City Council that the local population wanted to see the house rise from the ashes and so in 1980 the rebuilding project was put in the hands of contractor H. & J. Martin Ltd and architects McKinstry & Brown. It was to take two and a half years to return Malone House to its former grandeur.

THE PHOENIX RISES

The damage to the house was so severe that only the basement walls, some ground floor walls, the entrance portico and kitchen wing survived. Everything else was gone or had to be pulled down and rebuilt. A repair grant from the Historic Buildings Council was put towards work on these original pieces, but could not be used for the new sections such as the roof, second floor walls, interior walls and decorative plasterwork. With the exception of one piece of the half-landing, the entire staircase had to be replaced. The fireplace currently in the Malone Room was in storage in the basement at the time of the fire and was saved.

Particular care was taken to ensure that the restoration work, which was carried out by local craftsmen, followed the original as closely as possible. Moulds were cast from fragments of plasterwork rescued from the ruins and used to make new cornices and door frames. The interior decoration was based on photographs taken of the house before the fire. The decorative plasterwork in the largest room, now called the Harberton Room, was cast from moulds taken directly from the late-eighteenth-century plasterwork in Mount Panther House near Clough, County

Thanks to the renovations of 1980–3, Malone House once again enhances the hilltop within Barnett Demesne.

ROBERT SCOTT

Down. The chimney piece also came from this house. Above it was placed a painting depicting a symbolic rebirth of Malone House, by Cherith McKinstry, wife of one of the architects.

The building was officially reopened in June 1983, and used for public and private functions, exhibitions, trade shows and meetings. Wedding receptions were not permitted at first, but this decision was later rescinded. The rooms were given titles recalling people and place names associated with the house's past: the Barnett Restaurant and the Harberton Room after previous owners, the Malone Room after the original estate name, the Montgomery Room and Higgin Gallery after tenants, and the Hilsborowe Room after the original fort name (chapter 11). The first owner and builder of the house, William Wallace Legge, was remembered in the Legge Lecture Theatre, as it was thought inappropriate to have a Legge Room!

VICTORIANA RESTORED

In the early 1970s the future of the Palm House came under close scrutiny. It had not been painted for over a decade and plants were sprouting from the exterior guttering. There was talk of demolition, but in 1975, European Architectural Heritage Year, this was changed to restoration. The promise of a grant from the Historic Monuments and Buildings Branch of the Department of the Environment, NI, together with the preservation order on the building, doubtless contributed to the change of heart. The task of restoring this unique piece of Victoriana was given to H. & J. Martin Ltd.

Before any work could commence on the Palm House many of the plants had to be moved to other greenhouses or into the Tropical Ravine. Large specimens that could not be shifted were covered with plastic sheeting to protect them from the reconstruction work and from the cold. Initial survey work indicated that the majority of the glass panes were cracked or broken, particularly in the dome, and that there was extensive corrosion in all the main roof glazing bars and the valley gutters. The wrought-iron glazing bars had succumbed to the ravages of time more than the cast-iron features such as gutters. Decay in the two wings seemed to be less advanced than in the dome: the wrought-iron columns and the cast-iron pilasters with scroll heads were in reasonable condition.

All of the metal that was not perished was grit-blasted and treated with zinc. Where the ironwork had corroded badly it was replaced: moulds and templates were taken and replacements cast locally. Welders on site made any necessary final adjustments. One of the restoration workers uncovered the date 1852 stamped on one of the top bars of the dome with the original workman's initials (Wm. M.) beside it. This was an exciting discovery as previously it had only been possible to estimate the dome's completion date as early 1850s.

The stonework at the entrance to the Palm House and along the window sills was restored and finally new glass was cut to size on site and inserted. The metalwork was then painted white.

The complete project, including a new heating system, painting, lighting, plant staging and new nursery glasshouses to the rear of the main house, cost a total of £850,000. For the restoration work the Palm House was awarded a British Tourism Award, Certificate of Distinction.

A NEW ROOF

During this restoration of the Palm House the Council decided to give the Tropical Ravine a new lease of life as well. The roof consisted of timber-framed glass on a superstructure of fan-type steel lattice trusses, set in cast-iron shoes. The ridge formed a lantern light which housed the ventilation system. On inspection the wood was found to be badly rotten and much of the glass was damaged. A cocoon of timber and plastic sheeting was erected over the plants to protect them, as some

The luxurious 'jungle' growth in the Tropical Ravine makes a visit to this unique building an unforgettable experience.

ROBERT SCOTT

of them were quite valuable specimens – the tree ferns, for example, were estimated to be over one hundred years old. Once this was in place, work began in August 1980 on stripping the roof.

A new aluminium-framed roof was constructed and set on to the original trusses. About 10,000 square feet of glass was then inserted into the framework. The total cost of the work to the Tropical Ravine, which also involved installing a new sprinkler system, heating system and additional lighting, was £200,000. The pond over the boiler house was renewed to facilitate the growing of the giant water lily, destined to return to Belfast after an absence of nearly half a century (chapter 6).

A GRAND REOPENING

The renovation work on the Palm House and Tropical Ravine was completed simultaneously and so the houses were both reopened to the public on the same day – 5 May 1983. The Palm House was officially opened by the Parliamentary Under-Secretary of State, David Mitchell, MP, the Tropical Ravine by the Chairman of the Parks Committee, Councillor Andy Cairns, JP. There were speeches and refreshments in a marquee on the main lawn, a throwback to Victorian days. In another link with former times the grandson and great-granddaughter of Charles McKimm, the curator who built the Tropical Ravine (chapter 4), attended the reopening.

After the restoration the plant collections were assessed and supplemented where necessary with seeds and cuttings donated by Kew Gardens, London, and the National Botanic Gardens, Glasnevin – as in the early days of the Belfast Botanic and Horticultural Society (chapter 4). Although many plants survived all the disruption, some sadly did not. The large date palm in the central dome of the Palm House perished due to frost damage during one of the winters when the heating was not operational. However, the cloud had a silver lining. The tree had cast heavy shade and its removal meant that there was more light for other species to be grown. It had also been a haven for sparrows that chirped all day long and left a mess of droppings on the leaves and floor below them!

PAVILIONS

Other renovations being carried out by Belfast City Council had a lower profile but were no less valuable to the local users and communities. They included changing pavilions at Grove, Cherryvale and Suffolk Playing Fields, opened in 1977, 1978 and 1981 respectively, and four new bowling pavilions opened on a single day in May 1980 at Alexandra, Victoria and Woodvale Parks and Grove Playing Fields. The ceremonies, performed by the Lord Mayor, Mrs Grace Bannister, JP, were followed by a luncheon at the City Hall.

At that time a ruling was passed that male and female bowlers were to be treated equally. Prior to this, female bowlers had been allowed to use greens only during restricted afternoon sessions and had been barred from evening bowling altogether.

BEYOND REPAIR

Despite the huge expenditure on facilities, not every project proposed was realised.

The one disappointment among the exciting new enclosures and landscaping of the zoo was the Floral Hall. It was originally planned as the showpiece of the new zoo, with an interpretative centre, theatre seating, multi-screen projections and extensive exhibition areas on the world of nature. Subsequent ideas included a tropical exhibit with raised walkways over crocodile pools and other jungle features, with appropriate planting and exhibitions, and a theatre-style showcase. Sadly, due to lack of funding, none of these plans ever came to fruition.

Many pavilions within parks have suffered at the hands of vandals. This bowling pavilion at Musgrave Park was burned down in the late 1960s. Its successors met with the same fate in 1976 and 1995.

ROBERT SCOTT

WILMONT HOUSE

Across the city the hayloft in the service yard at Sir Thomas and Lady Dixon Park was being transformed into a public coffee shop. This became known as the Stables restaurant. The main building within the park, however, was not so fortunate. By the end of the 1980s restraints on local authority spending had begun to take their toll. This meant that opportunities for restoration work such as those taken ten years earlier were no longer an option for Belfast City Council. Wilmont House, in the centre of Sir Thomas and Lady Dixon Park, unfortunately exemplified this change in circumstances.

Given to the city by Lady Dixon in 1959 (chapter 11), Wilmont House served for many years as a nursing home run by the Eastern Health and Social Services Board. In the early 1990s the facility was closed and the house reverted to the ownership of Belfast City Council. The Council produced ideas as to its possible use – including an information centre for the Lagan Valley Regional Park, an outdoors pursuits centre and a base for local craftspeople – but was unsuccessful in its attempts to attract appropriate funding.

DUNVILLE FOUNTAIN

The fountain in Dunville Park also missed out on the period of affluence. It had long since ceased to be a spectacular water feature and had become little more than a novel climbing frame for local children. The base was kept filled with water for many years after the fountain had stopped functioning, and was used unofficially as a paddling pool when the park ranger was not about. At some point a drinking fountain was inserted into the wall. Over the years the terracotta base degraded as a result of vandalism and exposure to the elements.

CHANGE OF USE

Many smaller buildings such as public toilets, 'elderly men's shelters' and some sports pavilions, such as the former bowls pavilion at Victoria Park, were demolished after their serviceable life was over. Other buildings were used, rather mundanely, as stores. The ladies' pavilion at Cherryvale, however, was put to a much more interesting use. From 1983 the Northern Ireland branch of the Conservation Volunteers moved in and established its local headquarters within the building. It was not the only voluntary body to be housed for a time within the parks. The National Trust leased Malone House from 1971 to 1976 and, for a number of years from 1984, the Ulster Wildlife Trust (formerly the Ulster Trust for Nature Conservation) had its offices in a house attached to the yard buildings in Barnett Demesne. Previously this house had been home to an Assistant Director of Parks.

It may seem strange that a Parks Department has so many buildings to maintain, but historically this has always been the case. Everything from the oldest (Malone House), the grandest (the Palm House), the most unique (the Tropical Ravine) and those with the most unusual inhabitants (the zoo buildings) to the more modest pavilions, shelters, bandstands, gate lodges and public conveniences have all had their place within the public parks in Belfast.

16
Green Fingers

The Parks and Cemeteries
Department's entry for the Ulster
Festival in 1957, in front of a Palm
House in need of some attention.
BELFAST CITY COUNCIL

Despite the resources devoted to the maintenance of buildings, despite the requirement to provide recreational and sports facilities, and despite the continuing problem of malicious damage to plants and property, Belfast Corporation continued to uphold the tradition of good horticulture and gardening practice. The number of bedding displays in the 1960s and 1970s may not have reached the extent of Victorian times, but the quality remained high. Each autumn hundreds of thousands of spring-flowering plants and bulbs were planted out into display beds; each June they were replaced with the same number of summer-flowering plants. The tropical houses at Botanic Gardens were kept at a high standard, the cool wing of the Palm House with a changing display of colour that would surely have pleased Charles McKimm. On a smaller scale the greenhouses in the walled garden at Sir Thomas and Lady Dixon Park were opened to the public on Wednesday and Thursday afternoons from 1963. These lean-to buildings were

Horticultural apprentices
learned their craft at
Grovelands Training Centre,
Musgrave Park, which was
kept to a very high standard.
The pillar in the background
was moved to Grovelands
from Fortwilliam Park in
north Belfast.
ROBERT SCOTT

stocked with cacti, orchids and house plants.

The care of indoor plants in the greenhouses was only one of many aspects of horticulture that required professional expertise and training. The Parks Department's work ranged from the planning of bedding displays to the keeping of bowling greens, from the preparation of soccer pitches to production of high-quality lawns, and from care of trees to maintenance of rose gardens. Each area possessed its own problems, each required specialised skills. Because of this it was important to keep the workforce well trained. It was also vital to provide some means of encouraging new gardeners to join the staff.

A CENTRE OF EXCELLENCE

A training scheme for horticultural apprentices was initiated during the early 1960s. For many years the trainees led an itinerant lifestyle, with no permanent base for lectures or classes. These were generally held wherever space could be found: in potting sheds or greenhouses, and in an area beside the walled garden in Ormeau Park that came to be looked upon as an unofficial training garden.

All of this changed on 24 September 1974 when the house and gardens at Grovelands, in Musgrave Park, beside Stockman's Lane, were officially opened as the Parks Department's Horticultural Training Centre. Previously the house had been occupied by George Horscroft and Reginald Wesley during their time as Director, but it had become vacant in 1972 when the new Director, Craig Wallace, decided to live elsewhere. It provided a badly needed indoor centre and was adapted into a lecture room, office and staff quarters. The trainees had finally got their permanent base.

Under the watchful eye of the training officer, the apprentices soon outgrew the rather small garden around the house. And so the training area spread out into Musgrave Park until nearly five acres of parkland had been transformed into superb shrub and herbaceous borders, bedding displays, a heather garden, a rose garden, a bog and water garden, and demonstration gardens – set among lawns of the highest standard and worthy of a centre of horticultural excellence.

The central pillar from the lower gateway at Fortwilliam Park in north Belfast – removed to make way for increased traffic – was 'planted' in a flower bed just inside the Stockman's Lane entrance to Grovelands. The pillar dates from the 1870s and features the monogram of James William Valentine, the last owner of the Fortwilliam Estate before it was divided up. This little piece of Belfast history, rescued from the growing demands of traffic, complements the floral displays around it.

Initially Grovelands was not open to the public on a regular basis. People did have the opportunity to visit the site on 16 August 1975 when it opened as part of the National Trust's 'Ulster Garden' scheme. On that occasion 50 per cent of the entrance fees were donated to the Lord Mayor's welfare fund. Gradually the public was given freer access and Grovelands was opened during daylight hours like any other public park (although the house garden was open only during working hours when staff were in attendance). The grounds have become a popular site for wedding photographs, the record standing at thirteen different bridal parties visiting on a single Saturday.

BOYS OF GOOD PARENTAGE

All of this was a far cry from the days when gardening apprentices were trained at the Royal Belfast Botanic Garden. Around 1840, boys between fourteen and sixteen, who were 'reasonably well educated and of good parentage', were taken on at the garden. They started at 4s a week and stayed for four or five years. During the winter and spring months they were tutored in school subjects. For the rest of the time they learned horticultural crafts – such as how to grow melons and cucumbers in special pits behind the Palm House. They lived in the upstairs bothy, adjoining the rear wall of the Palm House, and the wife of one of the gatekeepers looked after them.

ROSE TRIALS BEGINNING

Of all the horticultural aspects of the Parks Department's work, it was perhaps the International Rose Garden at Sir Thomas and Lady Dixon Park that, more than anything else, made the name of Belfast familiar throughout the gardening world. The idea of a rose trial ground in Northern Ireland was first put forward by Sam McGredy at a meeting with Craig Wallace on the nursery premises of the famous Portadown rose firm. The suggestion was taken up by local horticulturists in the autumn of 1963, when a number of potential sites, including Glencairn Park, were examined. Sir Thomas and Lady Dixon Park was chosen as the most suitable place for a large rose display garden that would incorporate an area for trial roses. The Rose Society of Northern Ireland was founded by Craig Wallace in March 1964 to assist with the organising and judging of the trials. That year marked the beginning

of a long association between the Rose Society and Belfast City Council. Plans were drawn up for the rose garden, and the bushes planted in the winter of 1964–5 included varieties submitted for the first trials to be judged through 1965 and 1966.

These first trials were very nearly a total disaster. During a single weekend in May, rabbits in the park reduced the bushes to stumps literally only inches high. Fortunately the roses recovered sufficiently for informal judging in late July. The following season, in memory of the incident, each of the twenty or so international judges presented the Director of Parks, Reginald Wesley, with a white furry bunny. Wesley later donated these toys to a local children's home. In subsequent years the rose gardens were extended, with many thousands of favourite blooms bringing colour to the park each summer. The name Sir Thomas and Lady Dixon Park was to become almost synonymous with roses and the International Rose Trials.

A small stone entrance patio with a framework for climbing roses was opened by Pat Dickson, the rose breeder from Newtownards, in July 1977. Belfast Rose Week was inaugurated in 1975 with the aim of promoting the rose gardens and encouraging interest in the rose trials. The event was timed to coincide with the final judging of the international roses. It proved such a success that both Rose Week and a Summer Rose Show, with exhibits from local amateur growers, quickly became established as annual events. That first summer over 2,700 entries were received for the innovative 'Choose Your Rose' competition, in which the public was asked to select its favourites from among the trial roses.

WORLD ROSE CONVENTION

The highlight for local rose enthusiasts was the coming of the Rose Convention of the World Federation of Rose Societies to Northern Ireland in 1991. Such was the importance of this event that the Parks Department decided to redesign the rose garden at Sir Thomas and Lady Dixon Park. Old beds were ripped out and weaker varieties of roses scrapped in a daring redevelopment programme. New circular areas were laid out for the roses, with trees and shrubs planted around them to provide shelter. There were new trial areas for hybrid teas and floribundas, and an Irish Heritage Garden, in which the best of locally bred varieties from the Irish McGredy and Dickson stables were displayed. Beside Wilmont House a spiral garden was laid out to trace the development of the rose. The redesigned rose garden was opened in time for the 1990 flowering season.

NURSERIES AND FARMING

At one time plants for use in the parks were grown and propagated in several nursery sites, including areas of Ormeau Park, Botanic Gardens, Bellevue and a nursery in the old walled garden at Belfast Castle. Plants were also grown under glass at

The International Rose Garden at Sir Thomas and Lady Dixon Park attracts thousands of visitors each summer.

ROBERT SCOTT

Dundonald Cemetery and there were glasshouses and a propagation house behind the gate lodge at the City Cemetery. In 1980 the aluminium-framed greenhouses at Ormeau Park were transferred to Botanic Gardens to replace wooden-framed houses that were in a bad state, having served the garden since 1901.

Increased demand and growing problems of transporting material from site to site led the Council to think of a single main nursery for the Parks Department. Having been authorised to explore possible sites, the Director of Parks reported in 1975 that a 136-acre farm was up for sale at Beechvale, Gransha, near Comber, County Down. Belfast City Council paid the owners, the Robinson family, £98,750 for the land, which was much more extensive than the estimated 60 acres required for a nursery. While discussions over the use of this extra ground were being held, it was let under conacre for grazing.

The farm nursery at Beechvale was developed by Gilbert Ash Ltd, at a final cost of over £400,000, which included the building of a staff bungalow. 'The Farm', as the site became known within the Department, incorporated an extensive tree and shrub nursery and almost half an acre of glass. This comprised a mist propagation house for shrub cuttings, a seed propagation house for sowing bedding plants, and houses to grow indoor plants, exhibition material and seasonal flowers. There were also two side-ventilated tunnels used for hardening off bedding plants and a potting shed for mixing compost. The nursery supplied trees, shrubs, up to 400,000 bedding plants per year, and plants and cut flowers for indoor displays and decoration. This included material used by the city florist, a full-time member of staff, whose role was to provide floral decoration for the City Hall, civic functions and shows.

The Farm was in use for some seasons before the official opening ceremony, which finally took place on 23 April 1982 and was followed by a luncheon in the City Hall. Once the nursery had become established, an annual open day was held to permit members of the public to see behind the scenes. The days attracted a good number of visitors, but invariably seemed to attract very heavy rain as well. The programme included horticultural demonstrations, guided tours and a digging competition, in which competitors had to dig over a plot of a certain size in a given time. A prize was awarded for the best-dug plot.

With the introduction of compulsory competitive tendering (CCT, chapter 18) it was decided that it was no longer viable to maintain a farm nursery, and that it was cheaper to buy in plants through a tendering process. Consequently, after a relatively short life, Beechvale Farm ceased to produce the Department's plants from the mid-1990s.

TREES AND BULBS TO REMEMBER

The nursery provided many of the trees that were used in the remembrance scheme initiated at Roselawn Cemetery in 1978 whereby a tree, or a selection of spring bulbs, could be planted in memory of those who had died. Over three thousand trees and many thousands of bulbs were planted as a result. As the available space for trees within the cemetery became limited, planting was carried out in copses rather than as individual trees.

Commemorative tree planting was also introduced in connection with the small

arboretum established at Barnett Demesne in 1992. Having paid the appropriate fee, anyone can plant a tree to mark an anniversary, birth, death or other significant date. This arboretum replaced a tree collection that had been started some years earlier at Sir Thomas and Lady Dixon Park. Some of the trees planted there were subsequently moved to Barnett Demesne, others were left as landscape features.

Each spring the daffodil garden at Barnett Demesne provides 'golden hosts' in the parkland around Malone House.

ROBERT SCOTT

FURTHER TRIALS

Less well known than the International Rose Trials are the International Camellia Trials, organised in association with the International Camellia Society. The trials began in 1979, when the first camellia bushes were planted in and around the walled garden at Sir Thomas and Lady Dixon Park. During subsequent seasons the area of camellias was extended to include more varieties. In 1982 yet another horticultural trial was set up in the walled garden at the same park, this time for summer bedding species. These 'Fleuroselect' annual seed trials provide a blaze of summer colour within what many regard as a secret garden. In the field below the walled garden a fourth trial area, for daffodil cultivars, was begun as recently as 1997.

A GOLDEN HOST

In 1990 Belfast City Council established a daffodil garden at Barnett Demesne. A representative selection of all of the divisions of daffodils was planted in and around Malone House, and in the surrounding parkland. Many were grouped under existing trees in natural glades. Some were sponsored by the Marie Curie Foundation (in connection with its Field of Hope campaign), others were planted by schoolchildren. The aim was to illustrate the full range of the daffodil form, from miniature to small-cupped, from large trumpet to double-flowered. Each cultivar was labelled and educational leaflets and signs provided to raise the profile of the delightful *Narcissi*. Of course, daffodils depend on weather conditions and do not always bloom at exactly the same time each year. So visitors to the garden at Barnett Demesne might walk past 'February Gold' in March, 'March Sunshine' in April and 'April Tears' in May. In some seasons, flowering of the main varieties coincides with Mother's Day, resulting in pirate armfuls being gathered the day before!

This garden was the culmination of a daffodil-planting programme initiated some ten years earlier. In 1980, under a scheme grant-aided by the Department of the Environment, NI, Belfast City Council began mass planting of daffodils, measuring the bulbs by weight rather than by number. Tons of bulbs were planted under trees and in grass banks in Ormeau Park, Falls Park and sites within the Lagan Valley. Each autumn more bulbs were added in these and other parks, open spaces, road islands and roundabouts as Belfast City Council fine-tuned the art of mass daffodil planting.

The Japanese-style garden at Sir Thomas and Lady Dixon Park is designed for quiet contemplation and relaxation.

ROBERT SCOTT

JAPANESE GARDEN

In the early 1990s the Parks Department transformed the site of a former spring at

Sir Thomas and Lady Dixon Park into a Japanese-style garden. The water and stone features, and the planting of oriental azaleas, maples, bamboo and other plants, were designed to provide a place for quiet reflection and contemplation. On a hot summer's day, with children and dogs about, it can be anything but quiet. Unfortunately the Japanese Garden, as with other planting in the park, has suffered at the hands of sophisticated vandals – those with a gardening background who know which choice shrubs to steal!

The positioning of the lake in this garden is rather appropriate. In the days when Wilmont was a private estate owned by the Bristows (chapter 11), and when Wilmont House itself was being built, it was fashionable to allow visitors a glimpse of one's estate as they travelled up the driveway, and to cross water on the way. Either a river or a lake would do but, alas, Wilmont had neither. The Bristows were not put off – they had a false bridge constructed on the driveway to give the impression of passing over a stream. Thanks to the Japanese Garden it is now possible to look down on to water from this 'bridge', the parapet of which was once adorned with stone urns.

HANGING FLOWERS

During the 1980s there was a move to brighten up the centre of Belfast. Security bollards were replaced by flower tubs at sites such as the rear of the City Hall (Donegall Square South) and the Albert Bridge Road. Belfast City Council, the Belfast Development Office and the Belfast Chamber of Trade began a joint floral

In the mid-1980s the city centre was decorated with some 1,300 summer hanging baskets, such as these at Cathedral Gardens.

ROBERT SCOTT

basket scheme, which at its peak involved over thirteen hundred colourful hanging baskets being put up between June and September to enhance buildings and streets alike. Initially baskets were supplied to premises free of charge, and maintained throughout the season by parks staff, but in later years a small charge had to be levied to offset some of the costs. Many favourable comments on this floral scheme were received from the press, traders, tourists and residents alike. Some of the baskets were prepared at Beechvale Farm, others were bought in from private nurseries to meet the demand.

One of the main problems of the scheme was that of watering the baskets, which even in wet weather needed watering every day, or every other day at least. During hosepipe bans enforced in hot summers, water had to be piped into a tanker from the pond at Alexandra Park, and the baskets watered from this. At the height of the scheme it proved physically impossible for the staff to travel around all of the sites due to the volume of vehicle and pedestrian traffic. And so they turned nocturnal, watering the baskets throughout the night from 10.00 p.m. until 6.00 a.m. the following morning. Naturally they wore the traditional green overalls of the Parks Department: so those who claimed to have seen green men moving around Belfast late at night may not have been suffering from delusions after all!

Because of funding restrictions the floral basket scheme was cut back during the early 1990s, and the number of baskets brightening up Belfast in the summer was greatly reduced.

HORTICULTURAL MEDALS

Staff at Botanic Gardens, under the guidance of one of the area managers, worked from time to time on show displays, in which a theme or message was worked out through flowers, plants, water features and accessories. On one particular occasion these took the form of large metal butterflies and lengthy 'caterpillars' made out of stacked flowerpots laid flat and painted black. The 'Show Team', as it became known, set up display gardens at the Royal Ulster Agricultural Show, Balmoral, and the Garden Fair at Greenmount College during the 1970s, before venturing across to Scotland and England.

The first success outside the province was at Ayr Flower Show in 1982, when the team won a Large Gold Medal. Subsequently the Department won many trophies and medals at flower shows and garden festivals including those at Glasgow, Gateshead, Liverpool and Stoke. One of the highest horticultural honours in this type of work is to be invited to exhibit at Chelsea Flower Show: Belfast Parks Department was asked for the first time in 1986 and returned from the famous London show with a Silver Gilt Flora Medal. The Department won the Wigan Cup at the Royal Horticultural Show at Birmingham in 1996. This was presented for the best exhibit from a municipal authority put before the Royal Horticultural Society that year.

CARPET BEDDING

The idea of carpet bedding arose from a nineteenth-century attempt to emulate expensive Turkish carpets in the garden. Low-growing plants would be arranged in complex patterns and designs, often with rather garish colour schemes. The

technique was once described as a 'good example of Victorian bad taste'. For many years carpet bedding schemes (more tasteful ones!) were planned and exhibited in some of the parks, including Ormeau, Victoria and the City Hall grounds (see photograph, p. 130). The plants were grown in trays and set out according to a carefully drawn plan into a prepared site. The design often marked a special occasion such as an anniversary or centenary year of a charity or voluntary organisation.

Plot-holders at Belmont allotments spend many hours tending their vegetables and flowers.

EDWIN OXLADE

FOREMEN TO SUPERINTENDENTS

After the Second World War many staff joined the Parks Department having served their time as gardeners on Belfast's larger estates. They were the 'old brigade' – with an enormous amount of experience and expertise in traditional horticultural methods. As these men retired, much of their knowledge sadly left with them. The staff who remained were still of good calibre, but their background and training were different and the type of work they were required to carry out was changing.

From the very early days staff were generally based at one site with a foreman in charge. Even small parks such as Dunville Park had their own foremen. In the search for greater efficiency, properties were grouped together and foremen and staff given responsibility for several parks. For example, Dunville was combined with Falls Park, and Barnett Demesne with Clement Wilson Park and Drumglass Playcentre. The foremen in turn reported to one of three area managers. During the 1980s the foremen were gradually replaced by superintendents, who were expected to have a greater input into the management and future planning of their parks and properties.

ALLOTMENTS

One area where professional horticulture and amateur gardening have conventionally sat side by side is the allotment sites. At Belmont, for example, parks staff maintain the parkland on one side of the boundary while private plot-holders work the ground on the other. The two groups have one thing in common, however – vulnerability to vandalism. The plot-holders at Belmont were pestered for a number of years by youths breaking in and causing damage to plants and greenhouses. The problem was solved by the Council's planting of a hawthorn hedge along the boundary; after only two years' growth this barrier was impenetrable.

Many areas of the city have been used for allotments and garden plots in the past, some in connection with the home produce campaigns of the two world wars (chapters 7 and 10). These temporary plots have long since been returned to parkland, while others have subsequently disappeared under urban expansion and development. For example, plots to the south of Schomberg House at Belmont were worked for a time during the 1960s, but now houses stand where vegetables once grew. Some sites, such as those at Ballysillan and Belmont, have been reduced in size. A small percentage of the plots at Belmont vanished under the East Link Road development, having previously survived a proposal to build a primary school on top of them at a time when they were administered by the Education Committee. (The land was transferred to the Parks Department in 1973.)

The allotments at Seaview, on the Shore Road, were tidied up by Belfast City Council in the early 1980s, as they were badly overgrown and full of derelict sheds and outhouses. They were reopened to plot-holders in 1987, one year after the attractively sited allotments at Annadale Embankment had passed into Council ownership. The plots at Annadale are still worked; alas, those at Seaview were closed in the late 1990s.

During wartime the allotments proved vital in terms of both keeping up morale and providing much-needed food supplies. In peacetime they have furnished those who work them with countless hours of pleasure and tons of produce. They remain popular: there is always a waiting list of potential plot-holders. Perhaps in the future, with modern emphasis on sustainable development and organically grown produce, allotments will once again increase to meet the demand from those keen individuals who, like the local authority professionals, have green fingers.

A BEND ON THE LAGAN, BELFAST.

01636

17
A Natural Approach

Boating on the River Lagan, *c.* 1900, beside Lagan Meadows.

POSTCARD

By the end of the twentieth century the reasoning behind public open space had changed radically from that of Victorian times when parks such as Ormeau and Falls were first opened. No longer was it the norm to enclose areas with iron railings, to mow every blade of grass short, to plant trees in neat rows, or to plant formal bedding displays by well-edged paths. While this type of formal park management was retained where appropriate as an example of the city's horticultural history, emphasis was also placed on more informal landscaping and maintenance – a type that benefited wildlife and was in line with the ideas of nature conservation, environmental improvement and sustainability.

The semi-formal parks of the mid-twentieth century, such as Barnett Demesne, Sir Thomas and Lady Dixon Park and Belmont Park, represent a transitional stage between the precision of the Victorian era and the wilder, natural appearance of more recently acquired areas such as Lagan Meadows in south Belfast and the Cave Hill Country Park in north Belfast. Long before falling under municipal care, these two properties were playing an essential role in supporting wildlife within the city.

They were also providing, and will doubtless continue to provide, first-hand experiences of nature to a population faced with the ever-increasing pressures of urbanisation.

LANDS AT DERAMORE

From 1977 Belfast Parks Department maintained an area of undeveloped land at Deramore in south Belfast on an agency basis for the Department of the Environment, NI. The following year it was suggested that the Council take ownership of this land, which bordered the River Lagan and was a sizeable area within the Lagan Valley. The site, originally to be called Deramore Country Park, was not transferred until early 1983. The Council paid £56,000 for it, 75 per cent of which was in the form of grant aid from the Department of the Environment. The park was officially named Lagan Meadows in 1985 and thereafter was promoted as Belfast's first nature park.

The 120 acres cover a variety of habitats: grazed pasture, woodland, hay meadow, damp grassland, willow scrub and marshland. The preservation of these habitats, together with their rich variety of fauna and flora, was given preference over amenity horticulture. One-time plans for sports pitches were rejected and the Council decided on a complete absence of gardening influences within the park – or at least that was the intention. When a wild flower seed mixture was sown near the entrance, a good crop of highly bred, ornamental daisies emerged, much to the embarrassment of the management staff and the seed company that had supplied the mixture. Fortunately this variety reverted to the wild type after only one or two seasons. Apart from this, and one or two 'garden escape' species growing on the site, Lagan Meadows has lived up to its name of a nature park.

A SOURCE OF WATER

The park has had a watery past. Towards the end of the eighteenth century the job of providing water to Belfast was given to the Charitable Society. Previously the task had been in the hands of private individuals such as 'Pipewater Johnston' (William Johnston of Newforge), who had a lease from 1733 to 1762 to supply water and did so by means of wooden pipes constructed from hollowed-out tree trunks. In 1795 the Society inherited a limited system of wooden pipes and fountains in very bad condition and totally inadequate water sources. It engineered a new supply from Lester's Spring (also spelled Lister's, Leister's or Lyster's) at Malone, which was named after local landowner John Lester, and now lies within Lagan Meadows.

An earth bank was constructed (in a valley near the Knightsbridge Park entrance of Lagan Meadows) to dam the spring (Lester's Dam). This created a reservoir capable of holding one million gallons of water. A small pump house nearby held machinery to force the water along an open aqueduct that ran parallel to the River Lagan towards Belfast. The water then travelled by gravity until it reached two small holding ponds at Mount Pleasant (now in the grounds of the Queen's University Vice Chancellor's Lodge at Lennoxvale). From there water was ducted along University Street and Conduit Street (hence the name) to a reservoir at Basin Lane (now Bankmore Street). From this service point it was distributed through wooden pipes to public fountains in Cromac Street, Fountain Lane and others. This water scheme was transferred from the Charitable Society to the Belfast Water Commissioners in 1840.

Some two hundred years after the Lester's Dam scheme was instituted, the present-day Department of the Environment Water Service went back to Lagan Meadows and tapped into the same spring to supplement Belfast's water supply. A new pump house was built, this time to the south of Lester's Dam. The foundations of the original pump house and the remains of the dam wall and aqueduct can still be seen at Lagan Meadows today. The former reservoir now lies partially overgrown, a haven for wildlife.

GREENS AND TEES

The ground towards the northern end of Lagan Meadows once formed part of Malone Golf Course, before the club moved to a new site beside Barnett Demesne (now Queen's University Playing Fields – chapter 11). A number of flat greens and tee areas can still be identified among the clumps of gorse and recent tree planting. The Council began to let this land for grazing shortly after the property opened.

MORELANDS MEADOW

A section of Lagan Meadows is in fact an island. A low-lying flood meadow was already bordered to the east by the meandering river when, in the 1760s, the Lagan Navigation Company constructed a straight canal cut along its western perimeter. The intervening land became known as 'The Holme', and later as Moreland's

The former lock-keeper's house at the corner of Moreland's Meadow and the upstream end of the canal cut. Footbridges now span the silted-up canal and the river, allowing access to and from Lagan Meadows and Belvoir Forest Park.
POSTCARD

Meadow. Several oaks and cedars, now mature trees, were planted on the land, possibly by the Batesons who lived at the Deramore Estate (Belvoir) across the river. The second lock on the Lagan navigation system was at the northern tip of Moreland's Meadow (the downstream end of the cut) while the lock-keeper's house was sited at the southern end, beside a weir that controlled the flow of water into the canal. This house was known as 'Mickey Taylor's', after a former occupant. Careful inspection of the ground at this point will reveal some remains of the foundations. A footbridge joining Belvoir Forest to Moreland's Meadow was put across the river in 1995 beside the retaining walls of the original weir.

LAGAN LANDS EAST

Across the river from Lagan Meadows at the Sharman Road entrance lies about seventeen acres of ground with the rather unromantic title of Lagan Lands East. Accessed from Annadale Embankment, the ground was originally zoned in 1948 as open space within the green belt around the city. In 1985 it was transferred to Belfast City Council from the Belfast Development Office for a nominal sum (although Belfast Corporation had previously owned it up until 1973). The Council planted copses of trees and drew up grazing agreements for the site. Otherwise, like Lagan Meadows, the land was left very much to nature.

NATURE RESERVES

Thirty-three acres of the central, low-lying portion of Lagan Meadows beside the towpath was established as a nature reserve to be managed by the Ulster Wildlife Trust in association with Belfast City Council. This represented one of the first partnerships between voluntary groups and local authorities that were set to become more commonplace (chapter 18). Because of this reserve status, nature conservation was given top priority, with a view to creating a balance between public usage and the sensitive needs of wildlife. Photographs taken early in the twentieth century show haystacks in the main part of the reserve, but the ground today is damper, and attracts wetland birds such as lapwings and herons, and hordes of frogs during the spawning season in February.

In 1992 Belfast City Council designated two Local Nature Reserves on Cave Hill: one at Hazelwood and one at Ballyaghagan. The former, just above the new zoo devel-

The peacock butterfly is one of many species that thrive on the 'wilder' areas within parks.

ROBERT SCOTT

opment, was considered important for its hazel woodland and the presence of some rare plants such as wintergreen (*Pyrola* sp.) and wood vetch (*Vicia sylvatica*). It is one of only three sites in Ireland where a particular parasite of woodlice has been recorded. The reserve at Ballyaghagan, above the Hightown Road, was once an upland farm and comprises meadow, heathland and marsh, where over eighty species of wild flora were recorded in a site survey. The dry meadowland is rich in butterflies during the summer.

CAVE HILL

The Cave Hill Country Park is the largest area of open space managed by Belfast City Council. It came into public ownership somewhat piecemeal: Bellevue in 1911, Hazelwood in 1922, Belfast Castle Estate in 1934, land adjoining the castle estate in 1951 (chapter 9) and Carr's Glen, which was opened in 1986 (chapter 14). The catalyst for the formation of the Cave Hill Country Park, however, was the acquisition in 1988 of 350 acres from the Wallace Estate. This area on the top of Cave Hill stretched back from the skyline along McArt's Fort to Hazelwood, as far as the Hightown Road, the Crumlin Road at the horseshoe bend, the higher ground at Carr's Glen and the Upper Cavehill Road. It was acquired from the trust fund of former quarry owner Captain W. F. A. Wallace, at a cost of £125,000. Like many before it, the purchase was grant-aided to 75 per cent by the Department of the Environment, NI.

The concept of the Cave Hill as a country park was introduced in 1992 when a sizeable grant from the European Regional Development Fund allowed for the relandscaping of the gardens around Belfast Castle, the establishment of a Cave Hill Heritage Centre on the second floor of the building, and the setting up of way-marked trails throughout the area. The Cave Hill Country Park consists of 750 acres of moorland, heath, grass meadows, rock face and woodland, an unsurpassed natural asset so close to the city.

The Country Park is not only important for wildlife, however. Within its confines are many relics of its archaeological and industrial past. There are also many traditions associated with the hill (chapter 1) and legends and stories too numerous to list. It would be impossible to do justice here to this wealth of material – one could write a book on the Cave Hill alone. Suffice it to say that the following paragraphs are intended to give a flavour of what is to some the most interesting and valuable open space around Belfast.

EARLY SETTLERS

The highest point of Cave Hill is 1,182 feet above sea level, and affords superb views over the city and the surrounding countryside. Early settlers on top of the hill must have enjoyed that view, although the landscape they overlooked would have been very different from that of today. Spearheads, flint arrowheads and jewellery have all been found on the hill, along with traces of where those early settlers once lived. The remains of a stone cairn lie on the summit. This circular structure, in its day some 65 feet in diameter and almost $6^{1}/_{2}$ feet high, probably dates from the New Stone Age (c. 4500–2500 BC) or early Bronze Age (c. 2500–1500 BC). Late Bronze Age settlers (c. 1500–500 BC) favoured the south-facing slopes of the hill in preference to the exposed summit.

Signs of settlement during early Christian times (AD c. 400–1200 approximately) include several raths or ringforts, each comprising a bank and outer ditch to protect the central houses and farm buildings from wild animals and hostile

neighbours. A stone cashel, near the Hightown Road entrance, would have had walls 8 feet thick enclosing an area about 150 feet in diameter, where people and livestock lived side by side. The builders of the crannog or lake dwelling at Ballygolan, Hazelwood (now with spider monkeys in residence), also had defence firmly in mind. In the early 1900s several archaeological surveys were carried out at this settlement. Fragments of pottery were found at what was then described as a 'conical mound surrounded by a marsh' – created when the original lake had drained away. This lake was reinstated during the development of Hazelwood in the early twentieth century.

There were several forts in the area, including one at Drumnadrough (near the entrance to the zoo), but McArt's Fort is probably the best known of all the early sites. Situated on a high rocky outcrop, it was defended to the rear by a bank and ditch, with access via a causeway on the north-west side. In a report to the Belfast Naturalists' Field Club in 1893–4, the secretary, Francis J. Bigger, described it as the 'pride and glory of our landscape'.

WHAT'S IN A NAME?

The origin of the name McArt's Fort is uncertain. It may be connected with the mythical character Cormac MacAirt, with the derivative McArt possibly arising during the nineteenth century. F. J. Bigger referred to a 'MacArt O'Neill' but also admitted that the fort's 'first occupation was lost in the mists of time'. Another earlier name for the fort was *Dún Matudháin* – the Fort of Matudan, after an Ulster king of the ninth century. The hill was referred to as the peak of Matudan, a name that forms the derivative, Ben Madigan. McArt's Fort is often mistakenly referred to as Napoleon's Nose: in fact it forms the emperor's tricorn hat. His upward-looking profile continues northwards, the nose lying over the caves, the chin formed by a drop in the headland just north of the caves.

McArt's Fort, Ben Madigan, Cave Hill and Napoleon's Nose are all familiar names around Belfast in connection with the skyline that dominates the city, but some of the unusual features elsewhere in the park have also been given names: the Devil's Punchbowl for the steep-sided valley below the first cave, the Sheep's Path (or Pad) for the track up from the Antrim Road to the top via the caves, Jacob's Ladder for the ascent from the south via the remains of the Donegalls' boundary walls, the Volunteer's Well for a spring in the woodland – so named because of the associations of the United Irishmen with the area. It is reported that in 1795 Wolfe Tone and his fellow United Irishmen met on the summit of Cave Hill, where they 'took a solemn obligation never to desist in their efforts till they had subverted the authority of England over their country and asserted her independence'. Another version claims that the meeting took place within one of the caves.

CAVES

There are five caves in all, two of them having been discovered as recently as 1874. They are probably man-made, and may well have been early iron mines. Only the lowest cave is accessible with care. It goes back about twenty feet. The caves themselves have often served as a retreat: in early times to watch for invaders coming up Belfast Lough, and more recently during the Second World War (chapter 10). There is a story told that prisoners were at one time kept in the upper caves and that there was a secret entrance to these from the top of the hill – unfortunately it is so secret that no one knows of its whereabouts.

LIMESTONE RAILWAY

Signs of mining and quarrying can be seen on the plateau below the caves, where there are numerous spoil heaps, and there were quarries at Bellevue and on the southern slopes of the hill. The most extensive of these is the old limestone quarry above the Upper Cavehill Road. Here, between 1840 and 1896, the Belfast and

Cavehill Railway Company operated a quarrying business, hewing the white lime-stone out of the rock face and transporting it to the docks via a railway system. Loads of rock were placed into trucks and sent down the hillside. The first trucks, on the steepest slopes, were operated on a continuous rope and pulley system, whereby the laden trucks descending on one side pulled up the empty ones on the other. Further down the hill the wagons freewheeled under gravity down to the docks, their speed controlled by brakesmen. The railway track ran down the south-west side of the Cavehill Road and the north side of the Limestone Road, thus giv-ing the latter its name. Tunnels were constructed in 1843 to take the line under the Antrim Road, Alexandra Avenue and the Carrickfergus turnpike. Donkeys or horses, again under the guidance of the brakesmen, pulled the empty trucks up the hill for refilling. Who returned the animals to the docks to collect the next set of empty wagons is something of a mystery – perhaps children from the neighbour-hood were given a pittance to do this.

Local residents were not all in favour of such industry on their doorstep. They made reference to the stable boys who tended the livestock and objected to their 'foul oaths' shattering the peace of the countryside. As if that were not bad enough they also complained that the air rang with the 'din and clang of iron being worked' and the 'coarse jests' of those working for the Railway Company.

DADDYSTOWN AND MAMMYSTOWN

As many of these labourers travelled long distances to the Cave Hill each day, the Company built a row of cottages for some of them at the top of the Cavehill Road, called Wallace's Row after the quarry owner. There was also a row called the Donegall Cottages, and two clusters of houses below the quarry known as Daddys-town and Mammystown. Sadly today little remains of these limestone and slate-roofed houses. In 1857 the annual rent for one such house was around £1 10s, payable to Captain Wallace, who had to pay the children's school fees out of the money.

A GRAVE AND A DIAMOND

Somewhere along the Upper Cavehill Lane (more recently referred to as Green Lane, accessible from the entrance at Upper Cavehill Road) was a place known as Norah's Grave. On 12 March 1890 two lovers, George Arthur and Norah Tattersall, met there as was their custom. George had bought a gun a few days earlier, claiming that he wanted to shoot rats. Instead he shot his girlfriend and then turned the gun on himself. The two were buried in a single grave at the City Cemetery. To this day no one knows for certain the reason behind the tragedy, which inspired the words of a ballad:

> 'Tis a tale of love and wild romance
> When Cupid dared to bend
> His mighty bow, and to fan the flame
> Of devouring love, when Norah came
> To her sad and tragic end.

One of the first jobs for Belfast City Council after obtaining the Wallace Estate was

ON THE CAVE HILL RIGHT OF

to clear the Green Lane, which was hidden under several feet of mud and soil that had built up over the years. The road was made passable again, but unfortunately there was no sign of the limestone cairn that had once marked Norah's Grave.

There are other recorded ballads about the Cave Hill, including at least two that mention a Cave Hill Diamond. These were published by J. Nicholson of Belfast around the end of the nineteenth century. As with many legends there are differing versions. One was related in a ballad written by a Robert Hanna and dedicated to Lady Shaftesbury. It is said that the tale of the diamond was at least one hundred years old when he wrote it. The story tells of a young boy who was out on the hill one day and discovered a large stone approximately eleven inches in diameter and weighing about one pound. This stone was purchased by John Erskine who exhibited it under the guise of 'The Cave Hill Diamond'. Some reports tell of it being subsequently sold in 1887 to Madame Tussaud's of London, but there are no official records of this.

There are countless stories about Cave Hill, some true, some manufactured and some based loosely on actual events. Whatever their basis, they contribute to the aura of mystery and fascination that surrounds the hill. Those who walk on the slopes might be fortunate indeed to find a Cave Hill Diamond, or to glimpse the fairies that reputedly live there, but even to discover any signs of the hill's many-faceted history they would have to look closely, for nature has been greening over the quarry faces, the ancient raths and settlements, and the tumbledown estate walls.

Photographer Robert Welch labelled this photograph 'on the Cave Hill Right of Way'.

WITHIN THE LAGAN VALLEY

The Lagan Valley is to the people of south Belfast what the Cave Hill is to those of north Belfast – the nearest piece of countryside and a recreational resource. The origins of the Lagan Valley Regional Park lie in 1963, when the Matthew Stop Line was introduced to limit the spread of urban development around Belfast. The idea of a country park around the river was put forward four years later. It was envisaged as a place where 'town dwellers could enjoy the countryside without travelling too far'. The term regional park, a very different concept to a municipal public park or a country park, was preferred because of the area's size (4,200 acres) and the fact that the land was a mixture of public ownership (e.g. municipal parks) and private ownership (e.g. schools, farmland, housing, factories and golf courses).

The original lines of demarcation of the Lagan Valley Regional Park were determined by what could be seen from the Lagan between the Governor's Bridge in Belfast and the union locks at Lisburn, a total of

Aerial view of part of the Lagan Valley Regional Park, including the Mary Peters Athletics Track, Malone House and Barnett Demesne, and Clement Wilson Park.

BKS SURVEYS LTD

thirteen miles of river. The towpath, once used by horses to pull barges along the Lagan Canal Navigation System, forms a backbone providing a link for walkers, joggers and cyclists. The Regional Park falls within the jurisdiction of three councils – Belfast, Lisburn and Castlereagh. As such it includes a number of Belfast City Council properties, namely Sir Thomas and Lady Dixon Park, Mary Peters Athletic Track, Barnett Demesne, Clement Wilson Park, Lagan Meadows, Sharman Road Open Space and Lagan Lands East.

Since the park's inception all three local authorities have been represented, along with the Department of the Environment, NI, the Rivers Agency (the Department of Agriculture, NI), the National Trust and independent advisers on the Lagan Valley Regional Park Committee. This was set up to conserve and enhance the natural beauty of the river corridor, to advise government departments and local authorities on related matters, to co-ordinate attempts at park improvements, and to oversee the management of the park as an entity. A park officer was first appointed in 1982 and an annual programme of events organised to promote the park and use of the facilities. In 1995 a Lagan Valley Local Plan was adopted, dealing with issues related to landscape preservation, nature conservation, recreation and urban use. A management strategy and a five-year action plan were approved the following year.

Throughout its existence the Lagan Valley Regional Park has achieved many times over that initial goal of providing access to the countryside for town dwellers.

PARKS FOR WILDLIFE

The wildlife value of the public parks within the Lagan Valley Regional Park, the Cave Hill Country Park, and indeed all parks and open spaces within Belfast, has been recognised for many years. Writing in 1935, Professor James Small of Queen's University described an area within Botanic Gardens as having 'dry mounds, and wet corners, little marshy places where local birds are encouraged by means of bird tables and sedgy nesting places'. It is only within the last twenty or thirty years, however, that actual management programmes designed to enhance this wildlife have been introduced, and the need for nature conservation to go hand in hand with municipal horticulture fully acknowledged.

PEREGRINES FLYING

The entire Cave Hill Country Park is a reserve for wildlife, where people and nature exist side by side as they have done for centuries. Each type of habitat in the park contains its own particular species: the rocky outcrops are home to ravens and peregrines, the heath and moors to many delicate orchids and bog plants, the woodlands to a host of songbirds and spring flowers, including the only remaining native Irish site of the town hall clock (*Adoxa moschatellina*), a tiny, insignificant plant, with a flower head consisting of five flowers, four of which face outwards each in a different direction, like the faces of a town hall clock.

These habitats must be sensitively managed to ensure that public use, and possible overuse, does not destroy their intrinsic wildlife value. Sound habitat management is also essential to ensure continuing conservation interest. For example, in the early 1980s Belfast City Council recognised that correct management of the woodlands of Belfast Castle Estate was vital to their long-term survival. A number of problems were apparent. Because all of the trees had been planted around the same time (between 1880 and 1900), there was no variation in woodland structure and little opportunity for natural regeneration. The elms were slowly succumbing to Dutch elm disease. The rhododendrons, a favourite on estates to provide cover for game birds, were spreading vigorously in some areas, and the sycamores were seeding prolifically. Both of these species were threatening to dominate the woodland – undesirable because of their dense shade, which restricts the ground flora. A management programme was initiated, whereby many trees were removed (the elm trees were burned to prevent spread of the disease) and saplings of mixed broadleaf and conifer species planted in their place.

MEADOWLANDS RETURN

From 1984 onwards, Belfast City Council changed its management of nearly one hundred acres of grassland. Areas that were previously mown regularly were left uncut during the spring and summer months to allow the formation of wild flower meadows. These were then cut for hay in August or early September. This regime was tried in areas of Sir Thomas and Lady Dixon, Belmont, Ormeau and Glencairn Parks, Barnett Demesne and other sites, some of which would have been managed as hay meadows on estate lands in the past. During the first season (the summer of 1984) over eighty species of wild flowers and nearly twenty species of grass were identified in the meadows. After several successive seasons with this mowing regime

Many wildflowers and grasses flourish in the meadowlands now maintained in parks such as Barnett Demesne.

ROBERT SCOTT

further species were noted, such as the butterfly orchids (*Platanthera* sp.) and yellow rattle (*Rhinanthus minor*). In addition the meadows attracted animal and invertebrate life. The sound of grasshoppers, and the sight of butterflies (such as the meadow brown and common blue) and kestrels hovering over the grasslands once again became part of the park scene, much as they would have been in times past.

The Parks Department tried an experiment in the grassland at Lagan Meadows. Wild flower seeds were sown in compost blocks at Beechvale nursery using the same method as for bedding plants, and then the young seedlings were planted out in the meadowland using a bulb planter. The results were disappointing. Hot weather meant that many of the blocks dried out, while those that survived the drought were neatly plucked out of their holes by the resident populations of rooks and rabbits.

NEW ISLANDS

In the early 1980s two islands were constructed in the upper pond at the Waterworks. They consisted entirely of inert rubble from demolished houses. Silt and mud were spread around the perimeter of the islands, which were shaped to provide a shallow lagoon in the centre. Reeds and marginal vegetation then established naturally. The neighbourhood birds soon took ownership of the newly formed land. Swans, moorhens and ducks were able to nest relatively undisturbed, and cormorants and herons used the island shores as perches.

SCHOOLCHILDREN

In 1980 a schools education programme was initiated to encourage the use of local parks as a resource for studying natural history, environmental science, geography and other curriculum subjects, and to formalise ad hoc visits to parks that had been taking place for many years. Since then thousands of schoolchildren have enjoyed and benefited from a trip to one of Belfast's many parks. A 'Discovering Trees' programme was initiated in 1984 and was attended by over seven hundred children. Renamed a 'Tree Teach-In', this now attracts up to three thousand schoolchildren from Belfast schools each year.

For a decade schoolchildren used the indoor classroom at Malone House in conjunction with outdoor visits. This facility was replaced in 1993 by a Nature Study Centre at Sir Thomas and Lady Dixon Park. The centre is a converted bungalow, once the home of one of the Department's area managers. The new venue certainly made an impact on one particular child. She was overheard addressing the education officer by the Latin-sounding title of 'Sertimus'. In fact she was saying 'Sir Thomas', obviously thinking it was Sir Thomas Dixon himself who was showing her around the Nature Study Centre!

ON THE WING

In 1987 the open water at Victoria Park, along with an extensive region of Inner Belfast Lough, was declared an Area of Special Scientific Interest (ASSI). Because the water levels within Victoria Park were habitually lowered during winter, many migratory wading birds used the exposed mudflats to feed on invertebrate life, especially when their feeding grounds out in Belfast Lough were covered at high

tide. The North Down Bird Ringing Group monitored the wintering birds for a number of years from the mid-1970s. Birds ringed at Victoria Park were subsequently recorded as far away as Norway and the Baltic Sea, highlighting the importance of the site and of Belfast Lough to migratory waders.

Victoria Park has become a haven for wild birds, especially waterfowl such as swans, geese and ducks.

ROBERT SCOTT

BELFAST'S FOREST

The Forest of Belfast Initiative, launched in 1992 and working closely with local communities and schools, has resulted in thousands of trees being planted around

Belfast, on sites as diverse as public parks, Carnmoney Hill, school grounds, street pavements and cemeteries. Two 'Plantathons' at Ballysillan Playing Fields and Ormeau Park were held in successive years and provided opportunities for volunteers to plant extensive hedgerows. In a campaign to establish yew trees for the third millennium, trees were planted at Roselawn and the City Cemeteries, following the age-old tradition of yew trees in graveyards.

As part of a programme to promote art within parks, the Forest of Belfast officer commissioned local sculptors to make a number of wooden sculptures for Barnett Demesne (around Malone House), Sir Thomas and Lady Dixon Park and Botanic Gardens. The subject matter included a 'frog-on-a-log', an owl perched high on a tree stump, squirrels playing on a fallen tree and a well-fed badger reclining on the grass.

MONITORING

From the early 1980s Belfast City Council began to monitor its parks closely for wildlife. Results showed that the less formal properties around the outskirts attracted a wide range of wild plants and animals, as might have been expected. Several types of orchid were recorded: the early purple orchid (*Orchis mascula*) at Belfast Castle Estate, the heath orchid (*Dactylorhiza maculata*) on Cave Hill, and the helleborine (*Epipactis helleborine*) in a number of shrub borders at Botanic Gardens and Barnett Demesne. Kingfishers were using the sandy banks as nesting sites along the River Lagan in Clement Wilson Park, while red squirrels were spreading from Belvoir Forest into Lagan Meadows, Barnett Demesne and Sir Thomas and Lady Dixon Park. Badgers and foxes were frequently seen in suburban parks as well as some city-bound parks such as Ormeau, and bats were roosting in the eaves of Fernhill House.

Even in the 'unnatural' ornamental plantings and bedding displays of the more central parks, species of birds and butterflies were noted in significant numbers. Wintering redwings fed on berries of shrubs and trees; treecreepers favoured the soft bark of some exotic conifer species such as those in Botanic Gardens; and a dipper, normally a bird of mountain streams and rivers, was recorded as nesting at the Waterworks for several seasons within the stonework of the bridge on the Antrim Road. The bird seemed oblivious of the heavy traffic above it. In damp springs, such as that of 1991, when early grass cutting on lawns proved impossible, extensive fields of lady's smock (*Cardamine pratensis*) developed, attracting countless orange tip butterflies. In a single area at the City of Belfast Playing Fields over two hundred butterflies were recorded within a ten-minute period.

CHANGES WITH TIME

Wildlife populations rarely remain stable, and certainly with the urbanisation of the Belfast region over the years the distribution of many species has changed. At the time when Ormeau Park first opened, for example, corncrakes bred in the marshlands of the Bog Meadows, cuckoos could be heard calling across the fields, buzzards flew over Cave Hill and many waders and wildfowl nested on waste ground that has subsequently vanished under development. But despite the fact that there is a formation on Cave Hill sometimes referred to as Eagle Rock, there are no official records of eagles ever having nested there.

While some species have declined or disappeared completely, others have adapted to live alongside humans. Lapwings and ringed plovers that once nested on the waste ground were discovered nesting at Boucher Road Playing Fields in the 1980s. They had swapped their preferred shingle beaches and rough grassland for the all-weather hockey pitches. Other species have actually increased. The collared doves now numerous in many parks were once unknown in Western Europe; they spread westwards from the Balkans and arrived in Belfast only in the early 1960s.

The story with plant species is similar. Changes in the use of land have doubtless resulted in a reduction in the distribution of some species, although with limited records available this is difficult to quantify. Other species have endured despite the changes: the first specimen of the red broomrape (*Orobanche alba*) in the British Isles was discovered by the naturalist John Templeton on Cave Hill in 1793 – it still grows there today. Still other species have capitalised on human developments. Several plants that were originally imported into gardens and estates during the nineteenth century have established themselves in the wild. Examples include Himalayan balsam (*Impatiens glandulifera*), rosebay willowherb (*Epilobium angustifolium*), giant hogweed (*Heracleum mantegazzianum*) and Japanese knotweed (*Reynoutria japonica*): all four grow in the parks within the Lagan Valley. Rogue seedlings of the oil seed rape varieties (*Brassica* sp.) began to appear in parks a few years after its introduction as an agricultural crop.

URBAN FLORA

In a comprehensive survey of the wild flora in and around Belfast published in 1997, and conducted by local naturalists Stan Beesley and John Wilde, species of interest were recorded within a number of parks. As expected, properties such as Lagan Meadows were rated highly, but unkempt corners at Suffolk Playing Fields, Wedderburn Park and the City Cemetery, the glen in Alexandra Park, the Ballygomartin River at Glencairn Park, and damp areas of Victoria Park and Belmont Park all contained species of note. The survey noted, however, that Musgrave Park and Ballysillan Playing Fields were 'not productive'.

The parks and public spaces of any city represent opportunities for wildlife, and Belfast is no exception. Together with the network of private open spaces and house gardens, they provide hunting grounds, living accommodation, food supplies and shelter to many species, and contribute to the biodiversity within the urban environment. The natural history of parks, having taken its rightful place on the Parks Department's agenda, is an aspect that brings much pleasure to many park users, both those content to feed the pigeons from a park bench or the ducks by the side of the pond, and those who relish a glimpse of some of the rarer inhabitants of Belfast's open spaces.

18

A New Era

On 30 September 1988 Craig Wallace retired as Director of Parks, having served the Parks Department sixteen years to the very day. His Assistant Director, Maurice Parkinson, was appointed as his successor. He had joined the Parks Department on the technical side six years earlier from the Department of Agriculture, having trained at Edinburgh Botanic Gardens and worked for Staffordshire County Council and the Department of the Environment, NI. He was to find circumstances very different from his predecessor: funding would be harder to come by, new structures and concepts for local authorities were just around the corner, and a new era of accountability and public consultation was just beginning.

CHANGE OF HQ

In the early 1990s the Parks Department moved offices yet again, the fifth such move in its lifetime. Fernhill House, which had been extended in 1981–2 to accommodate increasing staff numbers, was finally vacated in 1990. The Department moved to new offices in the Cecil Ward Building in Linenhall Street, a modern atrium block built specifically for the City Council and named after the outgoing Town Clerk. This pressure for space underlined the diversification of the Department's work. By then staff included area managers, superintendents, a training officer, horticultural assistants, recreation staff, an education officer, a countryside officer, a graphic artist, an arboriculturist, landscape architects and engineers, as well as administration personnel. Other members of staff were stationed at satellite points throughout the city, such as Belfast Zoo, Malone House, Belfast Castle and the cemeteries.

CHANGE OF TITLE

One of the most drastic and far-reaching changes to Belfast City Council and its public parks took place during the early 1990s. A major upheaval saw the end of the Parks Department by name, transformed the way in which the city's parks and gardens were maintained, produced new mechanisms by which public open space came into being, and allowed park users a greater input into parks' management.

With the introduction of compulsory competitive tendering (CCT), Belfast City Council underwent a change management process to prepare itself to meet central government demands. The manual workforce was organised into a direct labour organisation, which tendered for and eventually won a five-year grounds maintenance contract that started on 1 April 1996. The technical and administrative staff were fashioned into a Parks and Amenities Section headed up by Maurice Parkinson. The new section reported to a Client Services Committee via a Parks and Amenities Subcommittee.

NEW OPEN SPACES

These changes in local government structures and procedures were accompanied by new methods through which public open space could be established. Although bodies such as the NI Housing Executive and the Department of the Environment, NI had in the past transferred or sold land for public use to Belfast City Council, or drawn up agency agreements for the Parks Department to maintain their land, there was now much more emphasis placed on partnerships between different types of organisations.

Laganside Corporation was established in 1989 to promote the regeneration of the many vacant areas around the River Lagan and the docklands. It set up partnerships with Belfast City Council, the Belfast Harbour Commissioners, Making Belfast Work Initiative and other bodies, and attracted international funding alongside significant private sector investment. As a result extensive regeneration projects were undertaken to provide office accommodation, residential homes and apartments, business opportunities and open space – all planned with considerable community involvement. The open spaces cannot be viewed as public parks in the traditional form, but rather as civic spaces incorporated into development schemes. The areas are more closely aligned with the seventeenth-century walks than with the nineteenth- and twentieth-century parks. They include open space at

Clarendon Dock, walkways alongside the river (perhaps along the lines that George Macartney had envisaged three hundred years earlier – chapter 1), Lanyon Place beside the Waterfront Hall, riverside landscaping near the Lagan Weir, open areas at Ravenhill Reach and May's Meadow, and 'green' areas and water features within the former Gasworks site on the Ormeau Road. This last site has strong historical links with Belfast Corporation and the development of the city.

GASWORKS

Work began on a gas-making industry in 1822 on a site near Cromac, on ground owned by the Marquis of Donegall. During the nineteenth century the industry supplied gas for street lighting, for lighting in the Palm House and for balloon ascents in Botanic Gardens, as well as for domestic and industrial use. The Corporation Gas Department's profits were sufficiently high to pay for the building of the City Hall, opened in 1906. By the end of the Second World War the industry was supplying gas to some 120,000 consumers. Production began to decline during the 1960s and the site formally closed on 30 November 1988. Laganside Corporation, with its partner bodies, was given responsibility for the renovation and development of the site, which includes open space in the form of walkways and attractive water features designed by staff of the Parks and Amenities Section's landscape, planning and development unit.

THE NEW-LOOK CITY HALL GROUNDS

The same unit, in partnership with the Department of the Environment, Roads Service, was responsible for redesigning the grounds of the City Hall in the mid-1990s. These had been originally laid out by Charles McKimm, General Superintendent of Parks (chapter 6), but over the years the number of bedding displays had been greatly reduced until most of the grounds comprised either grass or tarmac. New pathways, lamps, railings, gates, disabled access and planting areas were included in the scheme, designed to complement the statues and memorials, trees and, of course, the City Hall itself. The work was finished in time for the visit to Belfast by President Clinton in November 1995.

CYCLING

The pathways alongside the river provided ideal links for the National Cycle Route through Belfast, a scheme co-ordinated by an organisation called Sustrans (short for sustainable transport) in conjunction with government bodies, local authorities and voluntary groups. The cycle route runs from Hazelbank Park at Newtownabbey, along a specially created path between the M2 motorway and the North Foreshore landfill site, through Duncrue Estate, and along the riverside paths to the River Lagan towpath where it leads on to Lisburn. The route, although aimed primarily for cyclists, can also accommodate wheelchair users and walkers. It is an example of how open space can take a specialised form to meet a specific purpose.

BELFAST 2000 — A CITY WITH A LANDSCAPE

In 1995 an application was made to the Millennium Commission to fund a project entitled 'Belfast 2000 – A City with a Landscape'. This major proposal included ideas for the expansion of initiatives such as the Forest of Belfast, redevelopment of existing buildings including the Floral Hall and Wilmont House, reintroduction of Victorian aspects to Ormeau Park and Botanic Gardens, new developments at the North Foreshore landfill and the Gasworks sites, as well as the improvement of several areas of derelict land and the refurbishment of some local parks that had fallen into decline over recent years. The aim of these improvements throughout the city was to enhance the overall urban environment for residents and tourists alike. In the event only the last two items listed were accepted by the Commission for funding. This allowed for the development of areas at Clara Park, Springhill, Ardoyne, Lenadoon, an open space at Dover Street and redevelopment of the Alderman Tommy Patton Memorial Park (formerly Inverary Playing Fields).

These areas were to be completed by the year 2000. Due to difficulties with land ownership and co-ordination of partnership funding, delays were encountered. Clara Park opened as Clarawood Park in November 1998 and Springhill Park followed in 1999. Millennium parks at Lenadoon, Dover Street, and Alderman Tommy Patton Memorial Park were opened during the year 2000.

The playground at Sir Thomas and Lady Dixon Park remains one of the most popular in Belfast.
ROBERT SCOTT

FRIENDS OF PARKS

The terms of the funding from the Millennium Commission stated that there should be extensive consultation with local residents about what they wanted to see in their area. This interaction was indicative of modern thinking, steered by the policies of successive governments, whereby local authorities were encouraged to take public desires and feelings into account when planning and developing open space. Parks staff had devoted time and effort into developing local partnerships in connection with the design and implementation of new projects; this foundation was then built upon. The Parks and Amenities Section began to conduct annual surveys of park users in 1994. Results illustrated that while most residents were content with their local park, they were concerned about security and toilet facilities. By far the most common suggestion for improvement was for additional children's play equipment to be provided.

The establishment of a number of Friends' Groups marked the way forward for consultation. By the start of the third millennium there were Friends' Groups associated with a number of properties including Belfast Zoo, Botanic Gardens, Dunville and Falls Parks and the City Cemetery, allowing residents direct contact with councillors and staff, and the opportunity to input into the development of these areas.

BEST VALUE

The concept of 'Best Value' was introduced by the Labour government when it came to power in 1997, with the aim of ensuring that local authorities were giving the best value for money and most efficient service to residents. It was not necessarily a criticism of what had gone before but an assurance that services provided by councils would be of the highest possible standard. In the light of this, Belfast Zoo, Belfast Castle and Malone House applied for and achieved Charter Mark Awards, a measure of high public service.

SELLING OFF

Due to the changing requirements of the Section, the Parks and Amenities Sub-committee decided to sell property that was surplus to requirements. This included gate lodges at Barnett Demesne and Sir Thomas and Lady Dixon Park, the superintendent's house in Ormeau Park, and ground at Musgrave Playing Fields. Leasing arrangements with sports clubs were set up to manage some pitches, and a partnership with the Amateur Athletics Association established to manage the Mary Peters Athletics Track.

Neither leasing nor selling, at times contentious, was totally new to Belfast City Council. In 1980 the lock-keeper's house at Sir Thomas and Lady Dixon Park was leased to the HEARTH organisation along with a small amount of land. The same organisation, which refurbished properties for selling, later gave a new lease of life to the Dunmurry Lane workers' cottages, formerly part of Sir Thomas and Lady Dixon Park, and the gate lodge at Alexandra Park. With Belfast's very first park, Ormeau, part of the land was sold for housing to pay for the development of the rest as a public park. Throughout the lifetime of the Parks Department, sections of parks have been sold, vested and exchanged: for example, several portions of land at Botanic Gardens have been swallowed up by Queen's University and the Ulster Museum, and new road developments have cut swathes through Barnett Demesne, Belmont Park and other sites.

INTO THE THIRD MILLENNIUM

Many of the themes touched on in this book are still prevalent today: high priority on the provision of playgrounds, diversification of recreational facilities, maintenance of high horticultural standards, to name but a few. Sadly vandalism also remains a problem, with playgrounds and buildings particularly vulnerable. The bowling pavilion at Botanic Gardens was burned down in the summer of 1987, the wooden pavilion at Musgrave in 1995 (the third time that a building on that site had been destroyed), and the pavilion at Wedderburn in 1999 – highlighting that this problem has not gone away. The monthly cost of malicious damage remains a thorn in the flesh of those working to keep facilities open.

INTERNATIONAL FLAVOUR

Of course the majority of those visiting the parks thankfully remain unaware of this wilful damage. Tourists to the city are usually very complimentary about Belfast's parks, many of which have, or have had at times, a global or international dimension. For example, Belfast Castle and Malone House draw conferences and delegates from Great Britain and beyond, and the rose trials receive new varieties of roses each year from as far away as New Zealand, the USA and many European countries. The World Rose Convention was held in Sir Thomas and Lady Dixon Park in 1991 and international trials are held there annually for roses, camellias and daffodils. Many of the top horticultural sites in Belfast have featured in a number of European gardening magazines, and in 1997 a web site for the parks was established on the Internet.

The City of Belfast Zoological Gardens is high on the province's visitor attraction list, and many foreign tourists come through its turnstiles each year. The zoo is also in contact with other zoos throughout the world with regard to breeding programmes, animal loans and exchange of information. The story of 'Nasibu', the baby gorilla born at Bellevue, epitomises this international liaison. Because the survival rate of 'naturally reared' infants was low, a decision was taken to hand-rear Nasibu from birth. For six months the primate keeper, Kate Harkness, acted as his mother, which meant feeding him every two hours, changing his nappy and taking him home with her every night. She even asked her own mother to 'babysit' while she did her shopping. As gorillas are sociable animals, arrangements were made for Kate to take Nasibu to join other gorillas at Stuttgart Zoo in Germany. Subsequent reports from there stated that Nasibu was doing well, and had even performed his first chest-thumping display in front of an infant female.

SPORT AND SONG

There have also been international connections on the sporting and music scenes. Major athletics meetings have taken place at the Mary Peters Athletics Track and international cross-country runs were held at the City of Belfast Playing Fields

The Mary Peters Athletics Track is used for casual jogging, school sports days and major international athletics meetings as seen here.

MAURICE PARKINSON

from the late 1970s and at Barnett Demesne in the late 1990s. The culmination of this particular sport was the staging of the 27th IAAF World Cross-Country Championships through Barnett Demesne and the neighbouring Queen's University Playing Fields in 1999. Athletes from more than seventy countries took part, and the event was televised live to over thirty different countries. Soccer teams from abroad, visiting the province for matches against Northern Ireland, have used the facilities at Blanchflower Park and the City of Belfast Playing Fields for training and preparation.

Major folk festivals and outdoor concerts have been held at Botanic Gardens – top international artists U2 performed a gig on the lower ground (the former swamp!) in 1997, on a stage that took nearly two weeks to construct.

LOCAL EMPHASIS

This international aspect may be desirable, and even necessary, but the day-to-day use of neighbourhood and community parks by the local residents remains their very lifeblood. Parks are still favourite places to walk, to exercise the dog, to enjoy the flowers, to relax or to participate in sport. With the growing awareness of environmental concerns, they have taken on a role of maintaining local biodiversity and encouraging wildlife in a manner unforeseen by our Victorian ancestors. Even the number of main properties now within Belfast, almost sixty excluding playgrounds and open spaces, would have been beyond their imagination.

No doubt the members of the Victorian Reformist Movement would have been pleased to see such a wide range of public open space in Belfast, so lacking when they voiced their concerns. Of course they would see in today's parks lifestyles and trends worlds apart from their experience: the days of the signs reading 'Keep off the Grass' and 'The Public are Requested to Keep on the Walks' have passed; the Victorian style of horticulture with standard tree planting in neat rows and count-less flower beds is no longer fashionable; the average family tends to travel further for a day out than the local playground or park; and there are simply very few, if any, large tracts of land left within the city to be acquired for public use.

Despite this shift in management and public thinking the parks remain a vital resource and integral part of our everyday lives, whether we use them for play, sport, casual recreation, health, wildlife or horticultural reasons. They play an important 'greening' role in the urban environment, they are part of our social his-tory, and will form an indispensable and integrated part of planning for Belfast's future as a sustainable city. They will continue to be put to good use, and perhaps to new uses, as the twenty-first century gets under way.

Appendix

BELFAST CORPORATION COMMITTEES

established 1866	Cemetery Committee
established 1869	Public Parks Committee
1900–24	Cemeteries and Public Parks Committee
1924–42	Public Parks and Playgrounds Committee (Cemetery Subcommittee)
1942–73	Parks and Cemeteries Committee
1973–76	Parks and Recreation Committee
1976–92	Parks Committee
1992–	Parks and Amenities Subcommittee

SUPERINTENDENTS/DIRECTORS

GENERAL SUPERINTENDENT OF PARKS

1903–7	Charles McKimm

SUPERINTENDENT OF PARKS

1908–28	James Davis
1928–48	George Horscroft

DIRECTOR OF PARKS

1948–56	George Horscroft
1956–72	Reginald Wesley
1972–88	Craig Wallace
1988–92	Maurice Parkinson

HEAD OF SECTION, PARKS AND AMENITIES SECTION

1992–	Maurice Parkinson

PARKS HEADQUARTERS

up to 1933	City Hall
1933–51	Botanic Gardens (front gate lodge)
1951–64	Botanic Gardens (curator's house)
1964–75	Glencairn House
1975–90	Fernhill House
1990–	Cecil Ward Building

Select Bibliography

BARDON, Jonathan. *Belfast: An Illustrated History*, Blackstaff Press, 1982

BECKETT, J.C. et al. *Belfast, the Making of the City*, Appletree Press, 1983

The Belfast Book, Belfast Corporation, 1929

Beesley, S. and J. Urban. *Flora of Belfast*, Institute of Irish Studies, Queen's University Belfast 1997

BENN, George. *A History of the Town of Belfast*, Mackay, 1823

—— *A History of the Town of Belfast from the Earliest Times to the Close of the Eighteenth Century*, Marcus Ward, 1877

BENTLEY, R. *A Walking Tour Round Ireland in 1865 by an Englishman*, Richard Bentley, 1867

BLACK, Eileen. *The People's Park: The Queen's Island, Belfast, 1849–1879*, Linen Hall Library, 1988

Botanic Gardens, Belfast City Council, 1983

CAMBLIN, Gilbert. *The Town in Ulster*, W. Mullan & Son, 1951

The Chapel of the Resurrection, W. & G. Baird, 1891

CLARKE, R.S.J. (ed.). *Gravestone Inscriptions, Belfast*, vols 1 and 3, Ulster Historical Foundation, 1982 and 1986

CORCORAN, Doreen. *A Tour of East Antrim*, Friar's Bush Press, 1990

DEAN, J.A.K. *The Gate Lodges of Ulster*, Ulster Architectural Society, 1994

DOYLE, J. *Tours in Ulster*, Hodges and Smyth, 1854

KILLEN, John. *A History of the Linen Hall Library*, Linen Hall Library, 1990

LARMOUR, Paul. *Belfast: An Illustrated Architectural Guide*, Friar's Bush Press, 1987

LEYDEN, M. *Belfast – City of Song*, Brandon, 1989

LIVINGSTONE, Robin. *The Road: Memories of the Falls*, Blackstaff Press, 1998

LOUDAN, J. *In Search of Water*, W. Mullan & Son, 1940

MCCRACKEN, Eileen. *The Palm House and Botanic Garden, Belfast*, Ulster Architectural Heritage Society, 1971

MCNEILL, Mary. *The Life and Times of Mary Ann McCracken, 1770–1866: A Belfast Panorama*, Allen Figgis, 1960; reissued by Blackstaff Press, 1988

MAGUIRE, W. A. 'Ormeau House', *Ulster Journal of Archaeology*, vol. 42 (1979)

Malone House, Ulster Architectural Heritage Society, 1983

MEYER, Sir Robert. *Public Parks, Recreation Grounds, Open Spaces and Municipal Burial Grounds*, Belfast Corporation, 1922

OWEN, D.J. *History of Belfast*, W. & G. Baird, 1921

Quail, Susan. 'A Vital Urban Open Space', M.Sc. thesis (Queen's University Library), 1984

THOMSON, James. *On Public Parks*, Belfast Social Inquiry Society, Henry Greer, 1852

Acknowledgements

I would like to take this opportunity to thank the many people who have helped to make this book possible. The members of Belfast City Council Parks and Amenities Subcommittee for their support and encouragement. The current Head of the Parks and Amenities Section, Maurice Parkinson, and his staff for their assistance; in particular Paul Barr, Alice Blennerhassett, Lisa Copeland, John Fisher, Fiona Holdsworth, Rosie Joyce, Reg Maxwell, Diana Oxlade, Ben Simon, Evelyn Stainer, John Stronge, Eugene Trainor, and Alan Wilson. Also past members of the Parks Department: Cecil Baxter, Billy Harbinson, Peter Glen and Jean Wallace, and former Director of Parks, Craig Wallace, whose guidance, knowledge and enthusiasm proved invaluable. The various institutions that assisted with archive material and photographic research, and that have kindly given permission for photographs to be reproduced: Belfast Central Library, Belfast Harbour Commissioners, *Belfast Telegraph*, Linen Hall Library, National Library of Ireland, National Museums and Galleries of Northern Ireland: Ulster Museum and Ulster Folk and Transport Museum, Northern Ireland Tourist Board, and the Public Record Office of Northern Ireland. The many individuals, who have given freely of their time during the research, preparation, writing and editing, and to whom I am indebted: in particular Eileen Black, Sir Josias Cunningham, Linda Greenwood, Paul Hackney, Robert Heslip, Eoin Magennis, Bill Maguire, Pat McLean, Stewart McFetridge, Alex McKee, Richard McKimm, Desmond McNeil, Anne McVeigh, Frank O'Hagan, James O'Hagan, Edwin Oxlade, Trevor Parkhill, Vivienne Pollock, Major Robin and Kate Reade, Ken Robinson, Jeanette Scott. The staff at Blackstaff Press for their dedication and professionalism.

Index

NOTE: page numbers in bold refer to illustrations

Abercorn, Duke of, 61
air raid shelters, 99–100, 104
Alderman Tommy Patton
    Memorial Park, **145**, 152, 203
Alexander, Councillor R.B.,104
Alexandra Park, **21**, 21–2, **22**, 50, 54–5, 56, 141,
    168, 199, 204
    during Second World War, 97, 100, 101
    fancy dress cycle parade in, **57**
    playground, 69
    pond, **21**, 71, 180
    vandalism to, 22
Allotment Bill (NI) (1932), 97
allotments, 58–9, 77, **181**, 182
    during the Second World War, 97, 99
Anderson, Sir Robert, 45
angling, 129
Annadale allotments, 182
Archdale, Rear Admiral, CBE, 86
Area of Special Scientific Interest, 196–7
Armagh common ground, 2
Arnold, Dr, 118
arson attacks, 140
Ashley, Lord, 93
Avoniel House, 77, 131
Avoniel Leisure Centre, 131, 143–4
Avoniel Playcentre, 157
Avoniel Playing Fields, 74, 77, 102, 132

Baird, Lady, 95
Baird, Sir Robert, 45
balloon ascents in parks, 36–7
Ballyaghagan Nature Reserve, 186
Ballymacarrett Walkway, 150
Ballysillan allotments, 182
Ballysillan Playcentre, 158
Ballysillan Playing Fields, 74, 75–6, 105, 142,
    158, 198, 199
Balmoral Castle, 92
Balmoral Cemetery, 117–8
Balmoral Industrial School, 64, 69
bands, 5, 35, 40, 50, 53, 69, 71, 79, 83, 102–3,
    138, 138
    performances in parks, 40, 55–6, 139
bandstands, 52, 56, 83, 88
Bannister, Mrs. Grace, JP, 147, 160

Barnett, William, 110–11
Barnett Demesne, 105, 106, 111, 125, 132, 142,
    146, **177**, 181, 183, 185, **192**, 194, **195**,
    200, 204, 205; *see also* Malone House
    arboretum at, 176–7
    improvements to, 111
    sculptures, 198
    wildlife, 198
Barry, Miss Pauline, 133, 135, 136
bathing, 50, 130; *see also* swimming pools
Batt, William, 118
Beck, Fred, 95
bedding displays in parks, 171–2, 180–1
Beechfield Street Playcentre, 157
Beechvale Farm Nursery, 176, 196
Belfast, Earl of, 37, 94
Belfast Allotment Association, 97
Belfast and County Down Railway Co., 49, 50
Belfast Botanic and Horticultural Society, 7, 28,
    30
    financial matters of, 8
Belfast Castle, **91**, 91–3, **92**, 94, 104, 131, 201,
    204, 205
    given to public, 95
    restoration of, 160, 162–4, **163**
    weddings and, 134
Belfast Castle Chapel, 94, **94**
Belfast Castle Estate, 95–6, 136, 142, 175
Belfast Cemetery, 18, 43; *see also* City Cemetery
Belfast Cemetery, Malone, 117
Belfast Charitable Society, 37, 120–1, 122, 123–4
Belfast Corporation Act (1845), 42
Belfast Corporation Act (1899), 45, 56
Belfast Corporation Act (NI) (1930), 70
Belfast Corporation Act (NI) (1943), 45
Belfast County Borough Interim Development
    Order (1934), 75
Belfast Directory (1877), 16
Belfast Dock Act (1854), 48
Belfast Education and Library Board, 128, 152
Belfast Evening Telegraph, 56
Belfast Harbour Act (1870), 48
Belfast Lido, 129–30
Belfast Natural History and Philosophical
    Society, 7, 41
Belfast Naturalists' Field Club, 52, 189

Belfast News-Letter, 15, 17, 22, 63, 86
Belfast Post, 90
Belfast Reservoir Anglers' Association, 129
Belfast Social Enquiry Society, 9
'Belfast 2000 – A City with a Landscape', 203
Belfast Urban Area Plan, 149, 158
Belfast Water Act (1840), 37
Belfast Zoo, 78, **84**, 86–8, **87**, 135, 136, 137,
      141, 142, 201
   colour guide to, 161
   modern zoo, 160–2, 204, 205
Bellevue
   amusements, 102–3, **103**, **135**
   during Second World War, 102, 104
   grand staircase, **82**
   nursery, 175
   Pleasure Gardens, 63–4, 81–4, 103–4, 133, 136
   zoo *see* Belfast Zoo
Belmont allotments, 182
Belmont Park, 100, 132, **145**, 146, 183, 195, 199,
      205
Belvoir Forest Park, 158, 185–6, 198
Benn, George, 3, 120
'Best Value' concept, 204
'Big R.H.', 113, **124**
Bigger, Francis J., 189
birds, 198–9
Bishop, David, 29
'Black Man', 94, 118
Blakiston-Houston Estate, 74, 75
Blanchflower, Danny, 147
Blanchflower Park, **145**, 147, 206
Blanchflower Stadium, 147
Blondin, Mr, 35
Bloomfield Walkway, 153
boating, 17, 41, 71, 130, **136**
Bog Meadows, 77, 157, 198
Boodles Dam, 151
Botanic Gardens, 6–9, **9**, 28–37, **28**, **30**, **33**, 50,
      54, **63**, 63, 67, 71, 78, 125, 127–8, 132–3,
      139, 143, 158, **171**, 175, 176, 206
   additions to, 77
   admission costs, 7–8
   annual visitor figures, 8
   balloon ascents in, 36–7
   bands, 56, 139
   changes to, 51–3
   conservatory of, 29–30
   dancing saloon for, 36
   during Second World War, 97, 99, 100, 104,
      105
   events at, 34–5
   features of garden, **32**, 32–3

   garden party (1945), 104
   grand fête (1918), 59–60
   horticultural apprentices, 173
   hospital, 59
   lily pond, **52**
   Palm House *see* Palm House
   ponds, 71
   professional botanists and, 29
   public meetings in, 35–6
   and Queen's University, 54, 132
   royal visitors to, 53, 104
   sculptures, 198
   Sunday opening, 137
   Tropical Ravine *see* Tropical Ravine
botanists, 29
Boucher Road Playing Fields, 152, 199
Boundary Street Playcentre, 69, 156
bowling greens, 70, 140
bowling pavilions, 168, 170
boxing tournament, **79**, 142–3
Boyce, Tom, 41, 62
Bretland, J.C., 22
Bright Brothers, 49
Bristow, James, 112
Bristow, Rev. William, 120
Brock, Mr, of Crystal Palace, 90
Brown, Councillor John, 16
Bruce-Joy, Albert, 54
Bullaun stone, 120
burial grounds *see* cemeteries
'Burma Road', 148
Butlin's Holiday Campers' Pavilion, 131
bye-laws, 69, 73
   Falls Park, 137
   Ormeau Park, 15, 18, 61
Bythefield Park, 158

Cairns, Councillor Andy, 168
Calcutt, Mr, 43
Campbell, John, 29
carpet bedding, **130**, 180–1
Carr's Glen, 38, 150–1, **151**, 187
Carr's Glen Linear Park, 150, **151**
Carson, James, 73
Carson, Samuel, 44, 45
Castleton Playground and Playcentre, 69, 157
Cathedral Gardens, 153
Cave Hill, 3, **4**, 77, 84, 100, 101, 102, 162,
      187–91, **191**, 198, 199
   early settlers at, 187–91
   history surrounding, 189
   legends surrounding, 190–1
   mining and, 189–90

nature reserve, 187
Cave Hill Country Park, 187, 194–5
Cave Hill Heritage Centre, 164, 187
cemeteries, 19
    Balmoral, 117–18
    City, 18, **42**, 42–3, **44**, 62, 99, 116, 117, 119,
        137, 141, 198, 199
        burials in, 43–4
        extensions to, 45–6
        Glenalina estate and, 46
        ground allocation for, 43
        monuments and mortuary
            chapel, **44**, 44–5
        numbers buried in 1922, 47
        nursery, 176
        prominent graves in, 45
    Clifton Street, 27, 120, **121**
        prominent people buried in, 122–3
    Donegall Road, 124, 158
    Dundonald, 45–6, 63
    Friar's Bush, 43, 122, 124
    Friends', 124
    Knock, 46–7
    Milltown, 43
    paupers' graves, 120–1, 122, 124, 157–8
    pet, 124
    Roselawn, 116, 117, **117**, 141, 176, 198
    Shankill (Rest Garden), **118**, 118–20, **119**,
        139, 141
    stories associated with, 120
Cherryvale House, 132, 133
Cherryvale Playing Fields, 132, 133, 142, 146,
    168, 170
Chichester, Sir Arthur, 11, 106
Christie, Sir William, Lord Mayor, 132
circuses, 142–3
City Cemetery, 18, **42**, 42–3, **44**, 62, 99, 116,
    117, 119, 137, 141, 198, 199
    burials in, 43–4, 59
    extensions to, 45–6
    Friends of, 204
    Glenalina estate and, 46
    ground allocation for, 43
    monuments and mortuary chapel, **44**, 44–5
    numbers buried in 1922, 47
    nursery, 176
    prominent graves in, 45
City Hall grounds, **50**, 69, 99, 104, **130**, 130,
    139, 154–5, 181, 202
City of Belfast Crematorium, 116, **117**
City of Belfast Playing Fields, 132, 138, 142,
    153, 198, 205–6
City of Belfast Zoological Gardens

    see Belfast Zoo
city squares, 1–2
Clanwilliam, Earl of, 131
Clara Street Playcentre, 69, 99, 104, 151, 157
Clarawood Park, 203
Clarence Dock, 202
Clarendon Park Playing Fields, 152
Clement Wilson, Robert, 148
Clement Wilson Park, 148–9, **149**, 181, 194, 198
Clifton Street Graveyard, 27, 120, **121**
    prominent people buried in, 122–3
Cliftonville Playing Fields, 152
Clonard Swimming Club, 72
Coates, Sir W.F., Lord Mayor, 83
Colin Glen Forest Park, 158
Collins, General, 103, 114
common ground, 1–2
competitions, 16, 139, 158, 175
compulsory competitive tendering, 76, 201
Connolly, Gordon, 135
Connolly, Ricky, 141
Connop, J.H., 5, 49, 145
Conservation Volunteers, Northern Ireland
    branch, 170
Cooke, Rev. Henry, 117, 118
Coronation Fête (1838), **7**, 8
coronations, 79, 90
Corry, Councillor William, 146, 149
Coswell, Mr, 36
Craig, Sir James, Bart., MP, 56
Craig Band Fund, 56
Cranfield Park, 152
Cranmore Park, 65; *see also* Drumglass
    Playcentre
Crawford, Mr, 54
crematorium *see* City of Belfast Crematorium
Crichton, Lady, 35
Crystal Palace, Queen's Island, 5–6, 9
Cunningham family, 45, 126–7
cycling in parks, 17, 18, **57**, 202
    tracks, 131

Daddystown and Mammystown, 190
daffodil planting, **177**, 177–8
dancing, 36, 83, 89–90, 93, 102–3, 134–5
Dargan, William, 4–5, 38
Dargan's Island *see* Queen's Island Crystal Palace
Davies, James, 54, 64, 65, 69, 78, 85
Deerpark Estate, 18, 91, 93–4, 95–6
demolition of buildings, 75, 168–9, 170
Deramore Country Park, 184
Deramore Estate (Belvoir), 186
Devonshire, Duke of, 31

Dickson, Pat, 174–5
Dickson, Thomas, 51
Dig-for-Victory campaign, 97, 99
Ditty, Councillor Herbert, 143
Dixon, Lady Edith Stewart (of Wilmont), 64, 114, 138
Dixon, Rt Hon. Herbert, 75
Dixon, Sir Daniel, 45
Dixon, Sir Thomas, 75, 113, 114
    and Wilmont House, 113–14
Dixon Playing Fields, 74–5, 132
Dr John Pitt Memorial Park, 151
dog toilets, 146
Donall's Fortress, 45
Donegall, Earl of, 111
Donegall, second Marquis of, 7, 10, 12, 13, 29, 120, 202
Donegall, third Marquis of, 10, 13, 91–3, 92, 94
Donegall Road Graveyard, 124, 158
Donegall Road Playground, 68–9, 157–8
Dover Street Millennium Park, 203
Doyle, J., 3, 13, 14
Drennan, Dr William, 122
drinking fountains, 139, **139**
drive-in cinema, 136
Drumglass House, 64–5
Drumglass Playcentre, 64–5, 69, 71, 99, 157, 158, 181
Drummond, Dr James L., 7
Drummond, Thomas, 29
Dublin Penny Journal (1834), 47
Duff, William, 71
Dufferin, Marquis and Marchioness of, 34
Dufferin and Ava, Marquis of, 26
Duke of York Flute Band, 53
Dundonald Cemetery, 45–6, 47, 63, 77, 116, 137, 176
Dunville, John, 25
Dunville, Robert Grimshaw, 25
Dunville, William, 25
Dunville family, 123
Dunville Park, **24**, 25–7, 69, 80, 99, 139, 181
    fountain, **26**, 169–70
    Friends of, 204
Durham, Earl of, 35

Eagle Rock, 198–9
Easter activities, 3–4, 62
Easter Recreation Schemes (1947), 158
Edward VII, 17
Edward VIII, 79
Elizabeth II, 104
Ellison McCartney, Rt Hon. Sir W.G., 64

employment schemes, 64, 146
Enterprise Ulster, 146, 150
European Conservation Year, 142
European Regional Development Fund, 164
Ewart, Councillor, 16
Ewart, G. Herbert, 66
Ewart, Lavens Matthew, JP, 66
Ewart, William, Mayor of Belfast, 66
Ewart family of Glenbank, 66, 101

'Fairy Hill', 62
Falls Park, **19**, 22, 55, 56, 60, 69, 70, 80, 132, 137, 139, 178, 181
    allotments, 58, 97
    bands, 139
    during Second World War, 97, 99, 100, 104
    Friends of, 204
    hunting in, 18–19
    new legislation for, 18–19
    outdoor swimming pool, **72**, 138, 143
    playground, 69
    visitor figures for, 20
    water features in, 20
famine years, Belfast during, 8, 122
Farnham, Lord, 53
Fee Farm Grants, 14, 21, 23, 54, 112
Ferguson, Daniel, 29, 30, 31
Ferguson, William Hooker, 31
Fernhill House, 59, **60**, 100, **126**, 126–7, 140, 198, 201
Finlay Park, 145–6, 154
fireworks displays, 35, 40, **41**, 79, 90
First World War, 51, 58–60, 83
    and allotments in public parks, 58–9, 77
    and City Cemetery, 59
    festivities in parks at end of, 59–60
    and temporary hospitals, 59
Flora Street Walkway, 131
floral clock, **130**, 130–1
floral displays, 78, 79
Floral Hall, **81**, **89**, 89–90, 101, 102, 134, 135, **136**, 140, 142, 160
    redevelopment plans for, 169
Flowers of Summer Festival, 133
folk festivals, **143**, 205–6
football, 50, 73–4, **76**
    played on Sunday, 137
Forest of Belfast Initiative, 197–8, 203
Forsyth Johnston, Joseph, 31, 33
Forth River House, 150
Forth River Linear Park, 150
Foster, Dick, 102
Fred Hanna Band, 134

French, Lord, 59–60
Friar's Bush Graveyard, 43, 122, 124
Friends' Burial Ground, 124
Friendship Sundays, 141
friends of parks, 204

Gallaher, Thomas, 45
Gallaher Playcentre, 99, 157
gardening apprentices, 172–3
garden parties, 59–60, 63
Garden Plots Association, 58
gasworks, 202
George v, 17
George vi, 80, 90, 104
giant water lily, 31, **52**, 168
gifts to Belfast's parks, 16, 24, 52, 61, 95
Gilbert Ash Ltd, 176
Glen Road Playing Fields, 148
Glenalina *see* City Cemetery
Glenbank House, **65**, 66
Glenbank Park, 65–6, 69, 155
Glencairn House, 100, 126–7, 199
Glencairn Park, 125, 126–8, 139, 195
Glendivis House, 126–7
Gloucester, Duke of, 114
Glover, Rev. Octavius, 23
golf courses, 60, 71, 111, 153, 158–9, 185
Goodall, Dr Jane, 162
Gordon, Mr, 89
Grand Parade Playing Fields, 75
grant-aid, 150, 154, 164, 169
Graphic, The, 36
grave robbers, 121–2
Great Conservative and Orange meeting, **35**
Great International Fruit and Flower Show
        (1874), 35
Greenville Park, 149–50, 154
Grosvenor Hall Military Band, **138**
Grove House, 73, **74**
Grove Playing Fields, 73–4, 131, 139, 140, 142,
        158
    during Second World War, 99, 100, 103, 104
    pavilion, 168
Grovelands Training Centre, **172**, 172–3

Hammer, The, 69, 157
hanging baskets, 179–80
Harberton, Viscount, 109
Harberton family, 109, 110, 166
Harkness, Kate, 205
Harland, Sir Edward, 45
Hazelwood Estate, 71, **81**, **84**, 85–6, 87, 102
    café, **85**, 136, 160, 187

lake, 137
    nature reserve, 186
    new zoo on, 160-2
Heavey, Timothy, 16, 61
Hemsworth Street Playcentre, 69, 99, 156
Henry, Prince, Duke of Gloucester, 114
Henry Street Playcentre, 69
Herdman Memorial, 45
Higgin family, 110, 166
Hodsman, William, 36, 40
Holidays-at-Home programme, 104, 128
Hopkins, Thelma, 133
Hopkinson, Joseph, 44
Horscroft, George, 78, 125, 172
horses, 62–3
horticultural apprentices, 172–3
horticultural medals, 180
Hughes, Alderman Bernard, 20
Hunter, Richard (Dicky), 78
hunting grounds, 2, 13, 19
Hyndman, George C., 123

ice skating, 20, 25
indoor leisure centres, 143–4
International Camellia Trials, 177, 205
International Rose Garden, 173–5, **174**, **175**
International Rose Trials, 174–5, 205
Inverary Playing Fields, 152, 203
Irish Rose and Floral Society, 63

Jackson, Thomas, 112
Jaffé, Daniel Joseph, 45, 77
Jaffé, Sir Otto, 77
Jaffé memorial fountain, 77, **105**
James i, 11
Japanese Garden, **178**, 178–9
Johnston, Councillor Philip, 15, 54
Johnston, William 'Pipewater', 184
Jones, Valentine, 122–3
Joy, Robert and Henry, 123
Jubilee Garden, 154

Kamiya, Harry, 88–9
Keenan, Mr, 143
Kelvin, Lord, 9, 54
Kemp, Edward, 14
Kertland, Edmund, 109
Kew Gardens, London, 6, 7, 30, 168
King George National Memorial Fund, 76
King George v Playing Fields, 74, 76–7, 132
King William Park, **67**, 67–8, 154
Knock Graveyard, 46–7
Knocknagoney Linear Park, 25, **145**, 150

Knox, Rt Rev. Robert, 94

Lagan Lands East, 186, 194
Lagan Meadows, 37, **183**, 183, 184–6, 194, 198, 199
Lagan Valley Local Plan (1995), 194
Lagan Valley Regional Park, 169, 192–4, 199
Lagan Weir, 202
Laganside Corporation, 201
Lanyon, John, 44, 91–2, 92
Lanyon, Sir Charles, 29, 30, 38
Lanyon Place, Belfast, 202
Leeburn, Thomas, 44
Legge, Florence Wallace, 109
Legge, William Wallace, 108–9, 166
Lenadoon Millennium Park, 203
Lester's Dam, 37, 184
Ligoniel Park, 150–1
linear parks, 150
Lisburn parks, 148
local government restructuring, 147–8, 201
Londonderry, Lord and Lady, 63
London's public parks, 1–2, 4, 6, 7, 168
'Looney Park', 27
Loop River Playcentre, 157
Loughside Park, 150, 154
Loughside Playing Fields, 143, 150
Luftwaffe map of Belfast, **98**
Lynn, W.H., 45, 94

McAlevey, Councillor, 72
Macartney, George, 3, 202
McArt's Fort, 82, 189
McCann, D., 44, 78
McCann, George, 19, 44, 46, 51, 137
McComb, C.R., 31
McCormick, Alderman John, 50
McCracken, Henry Joy, 123
McCracken, Mary Anne, 123
McCullagh, Sir Crawford, Lord Mayor, 89–90, 95
McCullough, Councillor Charles, JP, 131
McDowell monument, 94
McGredy, Sam, 173, 175
McGugan, J.M.K., 110
Mackenzie, Rev., 117, 118
McKimm, Charles, 33–4, 50, 51–2, 53–4, 78, 168, 171
McLachlan, James, 44
McLaughlin and Harvey Ltd, 69
Macrory, A.J., 122
Malone House, 103–4, 106, 108–9, **110**, 125,

147, 170, **177**, **192**, 201, 204, 205; *see also* Barnett Demesne
daffodil planting at, 177–8
fire at, 140
former house, **106**, 106–7, **107**, 108
restoration of, 160, 164–6, **165**
tenants of, 109–11
weddings, 134
Mammystown and Daddystown, 190
Manderson Street Gardens, 154, **154**
maps, **1**, 32, **98**, **106**
Marie Curie Foundation, 178
Marlborough Park, 65
'Martlett Towers', 95, 96
Mary Peters Athletics Track, 152–3, **153**, **192**, 194, 205–6, **206**
Matthew Stop Line, 192–3
meadowlands, 195–6
Meyer, Sir Robert, 84
'Micky Taylor's' lock-keeper's house, **185**, 185–6
Midgley Park, 157
Milewater Stream, 54–5, **55**
military activities in parks, 35, 61, 99–100
Millennium Commission, 203, 204
Milltown Cemetery, 43, 124
miniature railways, **88**, 88–9, 101, 128, 130
mining and quarrying at Cave Hill, 189–90
miscellaneous squads, 155
Mr Crowe's Orchestral Band, 56
Mitchell, David, MP, 168
model traffic area, 131
Montgomery, Thomas, 109
Moran, J.W., 44
Moravian Church, 67–8
Morelands Meadow, 185–6
morgues during Second World War, 102
motor events in parks, 142
Mount Panther House, 165
municipal golf course *see* golf courses
municipal parks *see* public parks
Murney, Paddy, 55
Musgrave, Henry, DL, 64
Musgrave Park, 64–5, 70, 71, 80, 132, 140, 142, 199
allotments, 97
bowling pavilion, **169**, 205
during Second World War, 97, 99, 105
Grovelands Training Centre, **172**, 172–3
Musgrave Playing Fields, 147, 204
music in parks, 55–6, 83; *see also* bands

Nance, Andrew, 82, 83
Napoleon's Nose, 189

National Botanic Gardens, Glasnevin, Dublin, 6,
    168
National Cycling Route, 202
National Playing Fields Association, 73, 131, 156
National Trust, 164, 170
    'Ulster Garden' scheme, 173
nature conservation, 194–9
nature reserves, 186–7
Nature Study Centre, 196
Newforge, 149
Nissen huts, **102**, 102–4
Norah's grave, 190–1
North Down Bird Ringing Group, 197
North Queen Street Playcentre, 69, 105, 157
Northcote, Sir Stafford, 35, 36
Northern Cycling Club, **17**, 18
Northern Ireland Bands Association, 139
Northern Whig, 32, 54, 90
nurseries in parks, 175–6

O'Hare, Councillor John, 136
Oldpark Playcentre, 157
Oldpark Playing Fields, 131, 132
Olympia Playcentre, 157
O'Neill, Mrs Terence, 114
open-air theatre, 96
Open Space Grant Scheme, 154
open spaces, 67–9, 128, 153, 206–7
    as civic spaces, 201–2
    maintenance of, 155
Orangefield Playing Fields, 74–5, 102, 105, 131,
    139, 143, 150, 158
Ormeau cottage, 12
Ormeau Demesne, **11**, 13
    conversion to suburban villas and gardens,
        13–14
Ormeau House, **12**
    crenellated battery of, 12–13
Ormeau Park, 54, 61–2, 71, 97, 125, 142, 143,
    158, 175–6, 178, 181, 195, 198
    allotments, 58, 97
    athletics track, 131
    bands, 55, 56
    bowling green, 70
    burial grounds in, 18
    bye-laws, 15, 18, 61
    centenary, 133–4
    cricket, **134**
    cycling in, 18
    design and layout of, 16
    developments to, 16–17
    during Second World War, 97, 99, 100, 104,
        105

    events in, 142–3
    football at, **76**
    golf course, 60, 105
    marbles and Easter eggs, 62
    medical experiment in, 57
    Middlesex Camp, **62**
    opening of (1870), 10
    opening procession for, 14–15
    park rangers, 15–16
    playground, 69, 157
    royal visitors to, 17
    staffing of, 15–16, 18
    visitor figures for, 20
Ormeau Playing Fields, 152

Palm House (Botanic Gardens), 6, **29**, 30, 33–4,
    52, 60, 78, 133, **171**
    restoration, 160, 166–8
park rangers, 15–16, 140
Parkinson, Maurice, 200, 201
parks *see* public parks
Parks Department
    offices, 125–6, 200–1
    staff transport, 127–8
Patton, Alderman Tommy, 152
paupers' graves, 120–1, 122, 124, 157, 158
pavilions, 168
Paxton, Joseph, 2, 5
People's Park, 6
Peoplestown, 111
personal attacks in parks, 140
pet cemetery, 124
Peters, Mary, 152
pets in parks, 61
photographers, 71, 73
Pirrie, Viscount, Lord Mayor, 17, 45, 53
playcentres, 79, 155–7
playgrounds, 61, 68–9, 88
    equipment for, 66, 155
    offers of land for, 70
playing fields, 73, 132
    charges for use of, 142
    new sites for, 73, 146–7
    Sunday opening for, 138
    supervisor for, 128
pollution levels, 155
Pomeroy, James Spencer, 109
ponds, 20, 38, 50, 71, **89**, 104–5
pony track, 131
Presbyterian Orphan Society, 118
preservation orders, 166–7
promenades, 3, 32
Provisional Order Confirmation Act (1873), 18

public awareness and nature conservation, 198
public common ground, 1–2
Public Health Act (1848), 9
public parks
    annual surveys of users, 204
    Belfast acreage compared to other UK cities,
        158 9
    buildings demolished in, 168–9
    charges for use of facilities, 142
    development of municipal, 2
    diversions in, 57
    earliest reference to parks in Belfast, 2–3
    educational awareness for, 141
    entertainment in, 142–3
    gifts to, 16, 61
    habitats and, 198
    international and local considerations for,
        205–7
    land transfers for, 152
    legal issues and, 75–6
    and local government restructuring, 147–8
    municipal references to, 9
    music in, 55–6
    new post-war styles of, 105
    origins of, 1–3
    rejected sites for, 77–8
    selling and leasing matters, 204–5
    semi-formal, 183–4
    and social gatherings in, 3
    staffing of, 59, 78–9, 181–2
    summer scheme for children and, 158
    and Sunday opening, 137–8
    vegetables grown in, 99, 100
Public Parks (Ireland) Act (1869), 18
public toilet facilities, 24, 53, 170

Queen Mary's Gardens, 70, 99, 128, 130, 139
Queen Mary's Playcentre, 157
Queen's Island Crystal Palace, 4, **5**, 6, 9, 48–9, 55
Queen's University Playing Fields, 108

railings in cemeteries and parks, 99
Ravenhill Reach, 202
Reade, Robert Henry Sturrock, 112, 113, **124**
Reade family, 112–3, **124**
recreational and entertainment officers, 158
recreational facilities in parks, 70, 76
regeneration projects, 201–2
Reid, Ebenezer, 85
reservoirs, 38, **39**, 40, **129**, 129
resurrectionists, 121–2
Richard, Frederick, Earl of Belfast, 94
Ritchie, Francis, 73

Ritchie, William, 123
Robb, John, 14
Rose Society of Northern Ireland, 173–4
rose trials *see* International Rose Trials
Rose Week, 174
Roselawn Cemetery, 116, **117**, 117, 141, 176,
        198
Royal Belfast Botanic and Horticultural Co. Ltd,
        30–1, 51, 122
    financial concerns of, 31
    and selling of botanical garden, 37
Royal Belfast Botanic Garden *see* Botanic
        Gardens
Royal Ulster Constabulary Band, 71
Royal Victoria Hospital, **26**
royal visitors to Belfast parks, 17, 53, 104
running tracks, 131, 152–3, **153**, **192**, 194,
        205–6, **206**

St Anne's Cathedral grounds, 153
St Anne's Market, 68
St Leonard's Street Playcentre, 157
St Patrick's Industrial School, 43
Sam Glover's Dance Orchestra, 134
Schomberg House, 146, 182
school grounds supervisor, 128
schools education programmes, 196
Scotch Row Playcentre, 69, **156**
Scott, Capt. Robert, 114
Seaview allotments, 182
Second World War, 75
    air raids during, 100
    allotments in parks during, 97, 99
    arrival of American GIs, 103–4
    and Bellevue Zoo, 102
    dances during, 102–3
    Easter Monday 1941 attack, 100–1
    and holidays, 104
    and temporary morgues, 102
    uses for parks during, 99–100
    water shortages during, 101–2
semi-formal public parks, 183–4
Shachter, Rabbi, 45
Shaftesbury, Lady, 191
Shaftesbury, eighth Earl and Countess of, 93
Shaftesbury, ninth Earl of, 59, 95
Shankill Graveyard (Rest Garden), **118**, 118–20,
        119, 139, 141
    stories associated with, 120, 121
Sharman Road Open Space, 154, 194
Shaw, Alexander Mackenzie, 112
Shaw's Bridge, **149**, **193**
shelters in parks, **24**, 56, 71, 139, 170

Shore Road Playing Fields, 152
'Show Team', 180
Sinclair, Thomas, 19, 43
Sinclair family, 19, 123
Sir Thomas and Lady Dixon Park, 75, 103, 105,
    111, 114–15, **115**, **138**, 139, 140, 142, 175,
    177, 179, 183, 194
  gate lodges, 204
  International Rose Garden at, 173–5, **174**,
    175
  Japanese garden, **178**, 178–9
  Nissen huts in, **102**, 103
  pet cemetery in, 124
  playground, **203**
  sculptures, 198
  Sunday opening for, 138
  walled garden, 171, **174**
Smith, George, 42, 45
Smith, William, 22
Smyth, Mr, 142
soccer pitches, 131
social gatherings in parks, 3
Sorella trust, 25–6
sports and parks, 17, 20, 25, 50, 70, 76, **79**, **134**,
    205–6
Springhill Park, 203
Stanhope Street Playcentre, 157
Steele Dickson, Rev. William, 122
Stewart, James, 112
Stewart family, 111, 112
Stokes, Colonel G.B., 40–1
Stormont grounds, 159
Strangford Avenue Playing Fields, 152
street names, 12, 92, 93
street play, 70
street trees, 51
Stuart, William, 19
Sufferin, Councillor John, 15
Suffolk Playing Fields, 148, 168, 199
summer schemes for children, 158
Sunday opening and public parks, 137
superintendents, 44, 51, 64, 69, 85, 125, 181–2
swimming pools, 50, 68, 71–3
  closure of, 143–4, 138
Sydenham Playing Fields, 146–7; *see also*
    Blanchflower Park

Teddy Palmer and the Rumble Band, 135
Teetotal Society, 4
Templeton, John, 6, 123, 199
terrorist attacks, 140–1, 160
Thomson, James, 9
toast-rack buses, **88**, 135

Torrens, James, 10, 109
tourism and parks, 205–6
trams, 81–3, 87
tree planting, 51, 176–7, 185, 197–8
  at Wilmont House, 112
Trobridge, George, 109
Tropical Ravine, 32, 33–4, **34**, 51–2, **63**, 99
  restoration, 160, **167**, 167–8
  vandalism to, 31–2
Turner, Richard, 29, 30
Turner, Sir William, Lord Mayor, 72

Ulidia Playing Fields, 152
Ulster Defence Regiment, 141
Ulster Institution for the Deaf, Dumb and
    Blind, 53
Ulster Museum, Belfast, 165
Ulster '71 exhibition, 133
Ulster Unionists Convention (1892), 36
Ulster Volunteer Force, 59, **60**, 127
Ulster Wildlife Trust, 170, 186
unemployment schemes, 64, 146
urban flora, 199
urbanisation, effects of, 3, 8, 198

Valentine, James William, 173
vandalism, 22, 31, 56, 68, 88, 99, 140, 141, 157,
    170, 179, 182
  in cemeteries, 123–4
Vauxhall Gardens, 4
Verner, Thomas, 13
Victoria, Queen, 2, 5, 35
  royal charter, 25
  visits to Belfast, 6
Victoria Fêtes, 5–6
Victoria Park, 2, **48**, 48–9, 71, 140, 142, **145**,
    158, 168, 170, 181, 199
  Duff's shop, 71
  during Second World War, 99, 100, 101
  official opening, 50
  outdoor theatre, 139, 142
  playground, 69
  staffing and tree planting for, 51
  surveyor's report for, 49–50
  swimming pool, 71, 144
  wildlife, 196–7, **197**
Victorian Reformist Movement, 9

Wallace, Capt. W.F.A., 187, 190
Wallace, Craig, 127, 133, 144, 145, 172, 173, 200
Wallace Estate, 190–1
Ward, William, 38
water features, 20, 26

water sources, 184–5
water sports in public parks, 71
water supply during Second World War, 101–2
water supply issues, 38–41
Waterworks, the, 37, **38**, **39**, 70, 128–30, **129**, 137, 140, 146
  bathing at, 72–3, **73**
  birdlife, 198
  brass bands and, 40–1, 55
  during Second World War, **98**, 100–1, 104
  fishing at, 129
  keyholders, 128–9
  new islands in, 196
Wedderburn, Councillor A.M., 148
Wedderburn Park, 138, 148, 199
weddings and dances, 134–5
Wesley, Reginald, 125, 127, 130, 144, 156, 172, 174
Westlink, 154
Whins, The, 132
White, Sir George, 61
Whiterock Playcentre, 157
Whitla, Sir William, 45
wildflowers, 195–6

wildlife, monitoring of, 198
wildlife, parks for, 194–9
William Christie Playing Fields, 132
Willowbank Playcentre, 99, 157
Wilmont Estate, 111
Wilmont House, 112–14, **113**, 169, 179
Woodlands House and Playing Fields, 152
Woodvale Park, **23**, 60, 71, 97, 139, 146
  bands, 56
  boxing, **79**, 140
  during Second World War, 97, 99, 100, **101**, 104, 105
  opening ceremony, 23–4
  pavilions, 168
  pond, **101**
Workman, Councillor Frank, 61
World Rose Convention, 175, 205

York, Duke and Duchess of, 17, 53
York Street hanging baskets, **179**

zoo *see* Belfast Zoo
Zoo Baby Week (1937), 88